Praise for *The California N*

"Everyone interested in creating a sustainable society should have a copy of *The California Naturalist Handbook*."

—Paul R. Ehrlich, coauthor of *The Dominant Animal*

"As the stewards of our planet, now more than ever, we need to be aware of our own effects upon the natural world. I applaud this book for leading Californians in a resurgence of natural history for the twenty-first century."

—Todd Keeler-Wolf, coauthor of *The Manual of California Vegetation*

"*The California Naturalist Handbook* helps build essential naturalist skills. Whether you are a student preparing yourself for a professional career in natural science or a self-taught nature enthusiast, this book will help you look deeper, see more, understand what you find, and ask more profound questions as you explore California."

—John Muir Laws, author of *The Laws Guide to the Sierra Nevada*

"As an instructor, I think this handbook is a wonderful reference tool to use in class or in the field. My students and I really appreciated the tips at the end of each chapter that give you opportunities to explore nature. To be honest, I used these sections to help plan field trips! This book reminds students of what makes California a brilliant place to explore and experience nature."

—Ann Wasser, Pacific Grove Natural History Museum

"*The California Naturalist Handbook* is the new, go-to reference for any question about the nature of the state, its energy resources, land management, and environmental concerns. Not only should a copy ride in the backpack of every naturalist, science teacher, and student, but the crucial information within must be consumed and passed along!"

—Rich Stallcup, author of California Travelers Guidebook *Birds of California*

"This is a dangerous book. If you start reading it, you may find yourself having the uncontrollable desire to study the insects in your backyard, examine the rocks in a local roadcut, or look for frogs along a mountain stream. This book tells you how to do such things in a clear, no-nonsense fashion. It will enable you to explain what you see to your friends and family, even if they are at first reluctant to hear you."

—Peter Moyle, author of *Fishes: An Enthusiast's Guide*

"This handbook celebrates the state's natural heritage and will guide the budding naturalist to develop valuable skills—seeing what is really there, documenting those observations, and understanding nature's interconnectedness. As the reader becomes tethered more intimately to the natural world, his or her increased ecological literacy will broaden nature's constituency, providing a critical link to our future well-being."

—Jules Evens, author of *Introduction to California Birdlife*

"This handbook provides any prospective natural history interpreter with an excellent summary of the unique natural diversity of the state. It's designed to foster life-long learning, sharing of information, and taking action to protect the environment. I highly recommend this handbook to any organization developing a natural resources interpretive program or to anyone desiring a good summary of California's natural history."

—Stephen Barnhart, Academic Director, Pepperwood Preserve

The California Naturalist Handbook

The California
Naturalist Handbook

Greg de Nevers
Deborah Stanger Edelman
Adina M. Merenlender

UNIVERSITY OF CALIFORNIA PRESS
Berkeley · Los Angeles · London

University of California Press, one of the most
distinguished university presses in the United
States, enriches lives around the world by advancing
scholarship in the humanities, social sciences,
and natural sciences. Its activities are supported
by the UC Press Foundation and by philanthropic
contributions from individuals and institutions.
For more information, visit www.ucpress.edu.

University of California Press
Berkeley and Los Angeles, California

University of California Press, Ltd.
London, England

Excerpt from Lucy Smith, page 10, from *The Way We
Lived: California Indian Stories, Songs & Reminis-
cences*, Malcolm Margolin, ed. Berkeley, CA: Heyday
Books and the California Historical Society, 1993.

Cataloging-in-Publication Data for this title is on file
with the Library of Congress.

ISBN 978-0-520-27480-8

Manufactured in China

22 21 20 19 18
10 9 8 7 6 5 4

The paper used in this publication meets the minimum
requirements of ANSI/NISO Z39.48-1992 (R 2002)
(*Permanence of Paper*). ♾

*For all those who have looked at
a bird, a bug, or a seed and wondered—
may the tradition continue.*

Contents

Acknowledgments

The initial development of this handbook and the UC California Naturalist Program was funded in part by the Wildlife Conservation Board and the University of California's Renewable Resources Extension Program. We extend heartfelt thanks to Steve Barnhart, Michael (Shawn) Brumbaugh, Rebecca Perlroth, and others from the Pepperwood Preserve and Santa Rosa Junior College for their collaboration in piloting the program and providing essential feedback about this handbook.

The authors would like to thank the following people for their contributions: Doug McCreary for contributing to the forest chapter, Matt Deitch for contributing to the water chapter, Rebecca Perlroth for additional text on geology, Carol Blaney for adding to the interpretation chapter, M. Kat Anderson for text about Native Americans, Greg Giusti for text on the Redwood Forest Foundation, Mary Ellen Hannibal for the sea otter sidebar, and David Grantz for contributing the air quality section. Thanks also to Rob Blair and Amy Rager of the Minnesota Master Naturalist program, who were so generous in sharing their time, materials, and lessons learned. In addition, we would like to thank the following people for their help in reviewing and contributing to the draft document: Heidi Ballard, Jamie Bartolome, Steve Cardimona, Katie Hardy, Steve Lautze, Brianna McGonagle, Prahlada Papper, Mari Rodin, and Bill Tieje. Thank you to Kerry Heise and Greg Damron for sharing your beautiful photos and to Shane Feirer,

Bill Heise, Geri Hulse-Stephens, and Susan Stanger for help with illustrations. We appreciate Jim Nosera and JT Williams for their good-natured willingness to help with so many aspects of getting this book to press.

Thanks to Louise Doucette, whose edits vastly improved the readability of the text, and to David Peattie of BookMatters for his guidance on production, as well as the entire UC Press team for working so hard with us on this project: Stacy Eisenstark, Hannah Love, Francisco Reinking, and Kim Robinson. Special thanks to Chuck Crumly for his early support of this book.

The work that went into this book spanned several years and we could not have found our way without the support of our families. Greg de Nevers thanks Maggie and David Cavagnaro for teaching him the power and joy of a dissecting microscope, for answering his questions with more questions, and for showing him a vision of how wild and free life can be. Susan, Orion, and Sequoya you are the joy of my life. Deborah Stanger Edelman would like to thank Reid, Eli, and Noah for their unwavering love and encouragement. Adina Merenlender thanks her beloved husband Kerry Heise, favorite son Noah Douglas, and favorite daughter Ariella Rachel for their steadfast support and love.

Finally, a special thank you to Julie Fetherston for her work in the early development of the UC California Naturalist Program.

Preface

California is a naturalist's paradise filled with beauty, from the granite spires of Yosemite, to the wildflowers of the Anza-Borrego Desert, from the rolling oak woodlands of the inland valleys, to the tide pools of the Pacific Coast. This diversity of landscapes combined with a mild Mediterranean climate is part of what makes California so appealing to visitors and residents alike.

California is a global biodiversity hot spot and has a distinct cultural history. It is also a place that has changed dramatically over the past 200 years. Where grizzly bears and herds of elk once roamed through the wetlands of San Francisco Bay, we now see landfills, salt ponds, and skyscrapers. Los Angeles's freeways, shopping malls, and neighborhoods once supported 14,000 acres of wetlands. Central Valley wetlands and woodlands have been converted into the world's most productive farmland.

How do we support California's growing population without destroying the natural landscapes that we love and on which we depend? This is the challenge for Californians today: meeting the demands of a growing human population without irreversibly damaging the ecological communities we live in is a task that is urgent, complicated, and exciting. It will take the participation and involvement of every Californian.

To address this challenge, Californians not only must have an understanding of our natural communities and how they function but also must have ways to communicate about nature to diverse interest groups, as well as experience collecting data and nurturing wild places. This understanding will inform our decision-making processes, from making wise choices about how much water to use in our households to implementing smart growth initiatives.

The California Naturalist Handbook provides science-based information about California's natural history and lays the basis for skills that naturalists use to address today's environmental issues. It also serves as the primary text for the California Naturalist certification program developed by the University of California Cooperative Extension. The UC California Naturalist training program promotes environmental literacy and stewardship through discovery and action. The program provides hands-on instruction and exposure to real-world environmental projects designed to inspire adults to become active citizen scientists and enhance their personal connection with the natural world, as well as tools for collaborative conservation, problem solving, and communication.

The goal of the program is to develop a stronger constituency for nature by working with institutions that provide science-based environmental education to engage a corps of committed volunteer naturalists and citizen scientists. This engaged community of naturalists is essential to natural resource conservation, education, and restoration throughout California. In addition, we hope that by strengthening our constituency for nature we will also raise awareness of the importance of California's institutions for higher education and its museums, field stations, and teaching programs—all of which advance our understanding of botany, zoology, geology, and other natural sciences to the benefit of all. A constituency for nature is important for all living creatures, including the next generation of Californians.

We believe that part of the strength of this book comes from the different perspectives that each of us brings. Greg has 20 years of experience working as a naturalist in California and as a scientist in the New World tropics. He has a talent for pointing out significant details and a flair for storytelling. Greg's broad understanding of plant and animal communities provides the basis for the perspective this book offers California naturalists. Adina is an active researcher in conservation biology and works to deliver applied science to multiple user groups, which requires translating technical information into forms lay audiences grasp. Her ability to see the big picture and draw on work by experts enhanced the book throughout. Deborah has worked on the ground restoring sensitive habitats, as well as with community groups, government agencies, and businesses developing a wide range of environmental programs. She brought a passion for environmental policy and advocacy to the book, and her attention to detail and organizational skills kept us on track. We contributed different levels of effort to each chapter, depending on our expertise. However, through the process of consolidating sections and multiple reviews, we each had substantial input to all chapters and tried to merge our voices to make it enjoyable for the reader. The power of our collaboration and dedication to the California Naturalist Program is what made this book possible.

With this *Handbook* we invite you to deepen your understanding of the natural world around you. To enhance your learning, take a hike in your regional park, participate in a local creek cleanup, and become a citizen scientist. Observe seasonal changes and how they affect your local open space, woodland, or stream. As your understanding of natural communities grows, share your observations with friends and neighbors. Invite them to discover the animals and plants in the area and participate in stewardship and conservation. By observing and communicating with others about California's precious natural heritage, you join a long line of California naturalists and become part of the solution to the complex challenges we face.

We encourage you to delve more deeply into each topic. There are readings and other resources available, as well as information on classes, on the UC California Naturalist Program website, http://ucanr .org/sites/UCCNP/.

1

California Natural History and the Role of Naturalists

California is an incredible place to be a naturalist. For people who like to spend time outside, exploring unique places and sharing their favorite trail or rare species with others, the opportunities in California abound. The variety of landscapes provides diverse and unique living laboratories for aspiring naturalists. We have our nation's oldest lake, the lowest point, and the tallest trees, and seemingly endless opportunities for discovery, action, and stewardship. From discoveries in your own backyard to exploring the far corners of the state, California is an enticing mix of the commonplace and the unusual, where the ordinary is truly extraordinary.

CALIFORNIA'S BIODIVERSITY

California is one of the most diverse places on Earth. There are approximately 30,000 species of insects, 63 of freshwater fish, 46 amphibians, 96 reptiles, 563 birds, 190 mammals, and more than 8,000 plants, many of which are found only in California. Within the state lines, California has huge variations in topography and climate, with dramatic mountain ranges, valleys, and deserts where distinct natural communities have evolved. These variations result in 10 different bioregions, each with its characteristic drainages, topography, climate, and habitat types. California harbors such a wide variety of habitats and species that it is recognized as a global biodiversity hot spot.

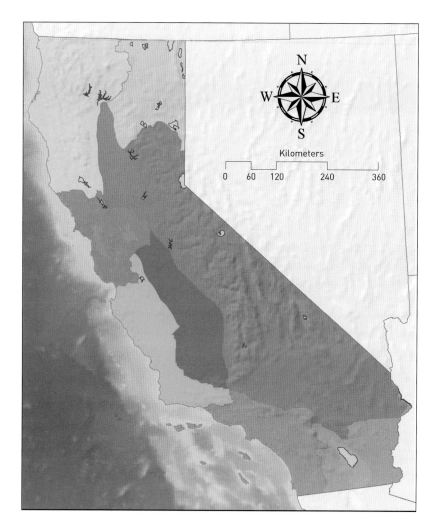

Bioregions

Bay / Delta	Mojave
Central Coast	Sacramento Valley
Colorado Desert	San Joaquin Valley
Klamath / North Coast	Sierrra
Modoc	South Coast

The bioregions of California are distinguished from one another by their geology, climate, topography, and associated plant and animal communities.The boundaries are similar to those of the 10 major regions defined in the *Jepson Manual: Vascular Plants of California* (UC Press, 2012). Modified from Fire and Resource Assessment Program (FRAP) map of California bioregions, California Department of Forestry and Fire Protection (CAL FIRE)

Biodiversity is the diversity of life found at all hierarchical levels, from genes, species, and communities to entire ecosystems. In California, high levels of biodiversity are in evidence everywhere, from tiny mosses to giant redwoods to all the different genetic stocks of salmon runs that depend on coastal watershed communities. California has the largest number of endemic species of any state. *Endemic* is a term that indicates a species is uniquely found within a specific geographic range. A species can be endemic to Solano County, like the delta green ground beetle, which lives in Solano County and nowhere else on Earth. Another can be endemic to California, like the blue oak, which is widespread in California but grows in none of the other 49 states or on other continents. A species can be endemic to the New World, like the puma and the jaguar. On the other hand, some taxa are cosmopolitan. For example, the bracken fern (*Pteridium aquilinum*) can be found on all continents except Antarctica. In sum, *endemic* is usually used to refer to species that have limited geographic ranges.

California contains a variety of topographical and physical features that result in wide variation in temperature, rainfall, and soil type that has led to the evolution of species found nowhere else. These factors, coupled with its large size, result in the 10 distinct bioregions. Most other states are far more homogeneous and hence encompass fewer bioregions. Minnesota, for example, has only 3 bioregions. With so many unique species and different ecosystems, human-induced disturbance has broad implications for the flora and fauna of California. For example, when valley oak woodland is converted to a housing development, it can be difficult to find similar habitat nearby to substitute for what was lost. If the soils, slope, topography, temperature, and water availability are outside of the range tolerated by valley oak trees, then a valley oak woodland cannot be newly established. With valley oak woodlands occupying only a portion of their historical range, continued loss of these woodlands puts this natural community at risk.

THE BIODIVERSITY CRISIS

The global rate of species extinction is orders of magnitude higher today than it was before modern times. If the current rate of biodiversity loss continues, we will experience the most extreme extinction event of the past 65 million years.

Land-use change is the primary driver of habitat loss and ecosystem degradation, and it greatly exacerbates most of the other threats to the

Unique California: Largest, Oldest, Hottest...

California is unusual in so many ways that it is difficult to enumerate them all. Here are a few fun facts.

OLDEST, LARGEST, TALLEST

- Clear Lake is the largest lake entirely within California and probably the oldest in North America.
- Methuselah, a great basin bristlecone pine (*Pinus longaeva*) in the White Mountains is the oldest living tree in the Western Hemisphere at nearly 5,000 years old.
- The General Sherman tree, a giant sequoia (*Sequoiadendron giganteum*) over 370 feet tall in Sequoia National Park, is the largest (by volume) tree in the world.
- The tallest trees in the world are coast redwoods (*Sequoia sempervirens*), along California's north coast.
- San Francisco Bay and Delta together make up the West Coast's largest estuary, the second largest in the nation.

NATURAL EXTREMES

- The lowest point in North America, at 282 feet below sea level in Death Valley, is located less than 100 miles from 14,505-foot Mt. Whitney, the highest peak in the contiguous United States.
- Death Valley also has the hottest and the driest points in North America.
- California is unusual in that all three kinds of tectonic plate movements (divergent, convergent, and transform) occur in and have shaped the state.
- California has hot dry summers and cool wet winters and is one of only five regions in the world with this Mediterranean type climate.

(continued)

environment. Accelerated rates of land-use change are due to the fact that the world's human population has increased sevenfold since the 1800s, and the Earth has been transformed to accommodate our rising consumption of natural resources. The Wildlife Conservation Society calculated that the human footprint is detectable across 83 percent of the land area in the world, excluding Antarctica. A good example of what can result from extensive land-use change is Southern California,

(continued)

BIODIVERSITY

- The California Floristic Province is one of 25 global biodiversity hot spots. All hot spots have lost at least 70 percent of their original habitat and contain at least 1,500 species of endemic vascular plants.
- More than half (63%) of California's native freshwater fishes are endemic.

PEOPLE AND ECONOMY

- California is the most populous state in the United States, with over 38 million people in 2010—one out of every eight Americans lives in California.
- Three of the 10 largest US cities are in the state of California: Los Angeles, San Diego, and San Jose.
- California grows nearly half of the fruits, nuts, and vegetables for the entire country. Almost all almonds, artichokes, dates, figs, kiwifruit, olives, persimmons, pistachios, prunes, raisins, wine grapes, and walnuts bought in the United States are grown in California.
- California has the largest economy of any state in the country and in 2010 was the eighth largest economy in the world.

where as much as 90 percent of the historic riparian habitat has been lost to agriculture, urban development, flood control, and other alterations.

Synergistic effects between habitat loss, habitat fragmentation, and global warming can compound the effects of habitat loss on biodiversity and it is unclear whether or not species will be able to shift their geographical range or evolve new adaptations fast enough to survive climate change. The expected loss of species due to continued land-use change and global climate change will impact humans because we depend on the goods and services that natural ecosystems provide. Many of our medicines, food, and fiber—indeed, the basis for our economies and survival—come from plants and animals. Biodiversity and natural processes are responsible for what we need to live on Earth, such as maintaining air quality, soil productivity, and nutrient cycling; moderating climate; providing fresh water, food, and pollination services; breaking down pollutants and waste; and controlling parasites and diseases. These ecosystem services are divided into three different types by

**Establishing Local Ecological Literacy:
Where Are You Now?**

- What watershed do you live in?
- What stream is closest to your house?
- Does it have water in it all year long or just seasonally? If seasonally, when does it go dry?
- What is the name of the nearest mountain range?
- What kind of trees are on your property? Plants? Insects?
- Describe where you live, in terms of both natural resources and the built environment.
- What was where you live 100 years ago?

scientists. Products obtained from species and ecosystems, such as food, fiber, energy, and freshwater, are referred to as *provisioning services*; benefits obtained from ecosystem processes, such as the regulation of climate, water, and diseases, are referred to as *regulating services*; and last but equally important are *cultural services*, or the nonmaterial benefits people obtain from nature, such as spiritual enrichment, cognitive development, enjoyment, and aesthetic experiences.

Some scientists quantify these types of ecosystem services in financial terms. One study estimated that the Earth's biosphere provides 16 to 54 trillion US dollars worth of services per year that we currently do not pay for. While quantifying these ecosystem services does enlighten people to the importance of natural systems in their daily life, it is difficult to quantify the entire value to humans of each of the 10 to 30 million species inhabiting the Earth and all natural processes and ecosystem functions. The ecology of most species is unknown to us. Others are minute but play key roles in the functioning of natural communities and our own survival. For example, if it were not for a few kinds of microorganisms that can digest chitin, the shed exoskeletons of arthropods would bury the surface of the Earth.

While the interdependency of humans on other species and the ecosystem services that they provide people are important to recognize and provide strong justification for conservation, the intrinsic value of nature is equally important in motivating people to conserve resources and protect natural ecosystems. Habitat loss and extinction result in lost opportunities for personal inspiration and cultural enrichment,

The California condor, the largest land bird in North America, is a scavenger left over from the days of the megafauna. Photo by Ram Vasudev

whether by bird-watching, catching and releasing wild salmon, or simply enjoying a natural scenic view. To really improve as stewards of the Earth, we need to acknowledge our interdependence with nature and our ethical and moral responsibility to prevent damage to the Earth's systems.

California, Hawaii, and Florida lead the nation in number of endangered species. Typically one of five of the species you will come to know in California has been declared endangered, threatened, or "of special concern" by agencies of the state and federal governments. Some of these species are protected under the federal and state Endangered Species Acts, which list species known to be in serious danger of becom-

The Endangered Species Act

The Endangered Species Act (ESA) was passed in 1973 to prevent species extinctions by protecting threatened and endangered species and their habitats. The ESA defines an endangered species as one "in danger of extinction throughout all or a significant portion of its range."

Here are some better-known recipients of ESA protection:

- The American peregrine falcon, which increased from 324 pairs in 1975 to 1,700 pairs in 2000, was delisted in 1999. Population estimates currently range from 2,000 to 3,000 breeding pairs.
- The gray wolf, which was nearly gone from the continental United States in 1974, was delisted in some western states, due in part to its recovery.
- The bald eagle was delisted in 2007. Thanks to reductions in DDT use, we have nearly 10,000 nesting pairs today.
- The California condor declined to only 22 individuals! The condor is currently under intensive management, including captive breeding, in an attempt to rescue it.

The state of California has 289 federally listed species, the greatest number per state, along with Florida and Hawaii. This means naturalists are more important than ever to our future. There is also a California Endangered Species Act (CESA) that includes an additional 104 animals and 95 plants not listed under the federal ESA. However, there are limitations to both these laws, in terms of what protections they actually provide:

- Species are not listed until numbers are dangerously low. Many biologists would like to see protections in place before numbers get perilously small.
- Low levels of funding and political maneuvering can affect how these laws are enforced.
- Since species and their habitats are protected on both public and private land, some landowners are hostile toward endangered species regulations because they view restrictions generated by them as an intrusion on property rights.
- Focus on protection of a single species may no longer be possible in parts of California where so many species are listed, so attempts are being made to protect entire natural communities through habitat and natural community conservation plans.

ing extinct and make it illegal to take or harm these species through habitat loss or degradation.

Humans have the intelligence to understand the impacts of our actions and change or modify our actions accordingly. The question is, can people continue to prosper while simultaneously minimizing our impact on other species on which we depend? Can we learn to conserve the ecological communities that we value? It is imperative that we do so, and soon.

A BRIEF HISTORY OF NATURAL HISTORY AND NATURALISTS

What is a naturalist? Today we define naturalists as people who observe, study, and interpret the natural world. Humans have always been scientists and natural historians by necessity. Just to survive we have had to observe, measure, speculate about, and communicate about the world. Indigenous people lived, and in some areas still live, deeply aware of their surrounding ecosystems, relying on observing, knowing, harvesting, and teaching about nature for survival. Hence they are the quintessential naturalists. The recorded history of the human enterprise is full of questioning, argument, and assertion about how the world operates. Every indigenous culture on Earth has explored the geography and ecology of its local environment. The knowledge of indigenous peoples is often astonishing in its breadth, detail, and accuracy. The drive to explore, understand, and utilize natural resources is a basic human trait. From the most seemingly depauperate oceanic atolls to the most diverse tropical rainforests, people around the world have discovered foods, medicines, poisons, and aesthetic appeals in the ecosystems they inhabit. That is the crux of being a naturalist: to observe the world, to report back to your fellow humans, and to protect the environment.

Traditional Ecological Knowledge

We had many relatives and we all had to live together, so we'd better learn how to get along with each other. She (my mother) said it wasn't too hard to do. It was just like taking care of your younger brother or sister. You got to know them, find out what they like and what made them cry, so you'd know what to do. If you took good care of them, you didn't have to work as hard. Sounds like it is not true but it is. When that baby gets to be a man or woman, they are going to help you out.

You know, I thought she was talking about us Indians and

how we are supposed to get along. I found out later by my older sister that mother wasn't just talking about Indians, but the plants, animals, birds—everything on this earth. They are our relatives and we better know how to act around them or they'll get after us.

—Lucy Smith, Dry Creek Pomo

There are many ways of learning about the world, many ways of talking about the world, and many ways of thinking about the world. The Western scientific approach, where possible explanations for observations are proposed and then tested against evidence, is one way of increasing knowledge. Native peoples who have extensive experience of a place may use very different ways of gaining and passing on knowledge.

Native peoples all over the globe are expert naturalists with remarkable observations and insight into the natural processes, habitats, and organisms with whom they share a long history. The same is true of California native peoples, who have 10,000 or more years of experience observing, talking about, and depending on California's flora and fauna.

In Western tradition, knowledge is passed from generation to generation using the written word, often supplemented with images (drawings, paintings, photographs). Native Americans traditionally passed knowledge from generation to generation experientially and orally. A mother would take her daughter out to dig roots for basket making. The daughter would be in the habitat, feel the sand, sweat in the heat of the day, and struggle to pull the roots up. The mother might also talk about the activity, give verbal instruction about technique, or pass on customary knowledge associated with the experience. The words the daughter heard might be in the form of literal information or in a metaphoric form: a story, a song, a recollection, or a myth. The Pomo, for example, say that designs for baskets and other instructions are often transmitted through shared dreams.

The experiences and observations contained in what is called traditional ecological knowledge represent a wealth of information. Native Americans accumulated information about what plants and animals could be eaten, when they were available for harvest, and how they varied from season to season, as well as how to collect and process them. Native Americans passed along detailed ideas for habitat management, especially regarding the use of fire as a management tool to promote habitat diversity and to encourage the production of useful animals and plants. The legacy of traditional ecological knowledge

A Pomo woman in California is picking wild grapes (*Vitis californica*) prior to 1924. Photo by Edward S. Curtis, NAA INV 03299400, Photo Lot 59, National Anthropological Archives, Smithsonian Institution, published as plate no. 480 in Volume 17 of the *North American Indian*

includes observations and ideas that correspond neatly with Western knowledge, and may contain ideas or observations outside the realm of Western thought.

Traditional cultures often emphasize the interconnected relationships between humans and the natural world. In part this is because traditional foods and cultural practices rely on natural products that often can be harvested only from intact natural communities. Practices that tie people to the land form the basis for a strong sense of place and responsibility for the world around us. Plants, animals, and physical factors such as water and mountains are not seen as mere commodities for human use, but as sacred. Since nature has spirit, using natural resources is more of an exchange, so their philosophy is to take only what is needed and to honor what is taken. Many tribes have ceremonies, dances, and songs dedicated to the Earth's spirit that provides a bounty of acorns, strawberries, and salmon.

The way that native people obtain goods and use services provided by ecosystems is often more sustainable than the way Western cultures tend to exploit natural resources. There are many examples of native Californians managing nature to be more productive. Examples are distributing bulbs while harvesting, and plucking grasses rather than uprooting them. This demonstrates another important lesson from native people, which is that managing natural resources can help preserve them for future generations. Ancient practices have proven to be beneficial today for native plant restoration and regeneration efforts to enhance biodiversity across many habitat types. After all, California Indians have been nurturing native plants for thousands of years. The long history of native people in California had an important role in shaping the natural communities we see today.

The use of fire is one area where Native Americans in California had a highly developed and nuanced understanding. Native Californians used fire to drive and concentrate game, to open paths for travel, to alter habitat mosaics, to protect against enemies, and to safeguard villages from fire, as well as to promote the growth of desirable plants and to stimulate the production of specific plant parts. The Pomo burned certain chaparral stands to stimulate coppice growth (resprouting) of redbud (*Cercis occidentalis*). This resulted in the new growth of long redbud stems which were valued for design elements in Pomo coiled baskets.

It is important to keep in mind that native Californians represent a huge variety of culture and language stemming from 500 relatively small tribal groups. Once again California trumps many other places with its diversity—in this case, historical cultural diversity. Even groups with the same name often varied widely. For example, the Pomo spoke at least seven distinct languages that are thought to share a common origin. In addition to this incredible diversity, California supported the highest density of native people north of Mexico in pre-Columbian times. The rapid and devastating loss of the 300,000 or more California Indians started in 1769 with the first Spanish colonists and accelerated as the missions were established and Westerners arrived seeking timber, gold, and fertile farmland, and at the same time bringing new diseases to the region. The existing scholarship, artifacts, and overall body of work that we have to draw on cannot possibly capture all we would like to know about this rich history. Thanks to the efforts of many California tribes, today many important traditions and practices survive within native communities.

Though this book takes a Western scientific approach to looking at California natural history, we draw inspiration from traditional ecological knowledge and the reverence for natural processes that are embodied in that tradition.

WHY BE A NATURALIST?

Naturalists are generalists in the best sense—cross-disciplinary, with knowledge of a system as a whole, not just the pieces. In the eighteenth and nineteenth centuries, before the formal fields of ecology, entomology, geology, zoology, and others emerged, it was naturalists who undertook these sciences. They collected specimens, recorded their observations, and became experts in certain habitats or species. Their work and collections were central to the origins of natural history museums and to the development of the theoretical underpinnings of current scientific thought. This connection is still vital today; naturalists form a key link between common and scientific understanding. By becoming a naturalist, you are taking a place in an important tradition of knowledge keepers. Naturalists make the world accessible to all and bring out our interest in and wonder at nature.

One of the most notable naturalists, Charles Darwin, changed the field of science. Using data from his own observations and experiments, as well as information garnered from his voracious reading, Darwin described the process of evolution by natural selection which remains the greatest explanatory tool of the biological sciences. Others, such as John Muir and Rachel Carson, wrote essays that changed our views of nature and inspired their readership to protect the environment. John Muir is the quintessential California naturalist. Muir possessed the two key qualities vital to any naturalist: the power of careful observation and the ability to communicate and inspire others. From his extensive time in wilderness he had a full appreciation for the interconnectedness of nature and noted, "When we try to pick out anything by itself, we find it hitched to everything else in the universe." Muir is best known for his fight to prevent the damming of Hetch Hetchy Valley; his efforts to protect Yosemite Valley, Sequoia and Kings Canyon, the

Thinking in Geologic Time

We tend to think of the world as always looking about the way it looks today, but one of the first conceptual abilities a naturalist must develop is the facility to imagine huge expanses of time. When we drive across the Golden Gate Bridge today, we see it crossing the mouth of a huge bay. On a clear day we look 25 miles west to see the granite spires of the Farallon Islands. Ten thousand years ago there would have been no bridge for us to cross, but we would have been able to walk on dry land to the Farallons! If we had taken that walk 35 million years ago, we would have passed through a forest with avocado trees! These lower sea levels also meant people from northeastern Asia could have walked to Alaska with relative ease when the Beringia land bridge was above sea level.

Grand Canyon, and Mt. Rainier as national parks; and the founding of the Sierra Club. However, those activities were only a part of his life-work. Muir loved to roam the mountains, drawing and making notes as he went. He authored several books about the geology and natural history of the Sierra Nevada, turning his observations into writings that stirred people to visit and protect wild areas. Though he only had a few college classes in geology and botany, he was among the first people to recognize that Yosemite Valley was formed by glacial action, a conclusion he arrived at through his intimate acquaintance with the area.

Rachel Carson was a biologist and natural history writer. She was one of the first women to be hired by the US Bureau of Fisheries as a professional biologist. During and after her fisheries career, Carson wrote numerous award-winning books and articles about the natural world. Her book *Silent Spring* brought attention to the damage caused by pesticide use, awakened the public to the severe consequences of environmental contamination, and ultimately influenced public policy.

FIELD NOTEBOOK: AN ESSENTIAL RECORD FOR EVERY NATURALIST

While indigenous people and early explorers created the foundation of what we know today, there is still a lot to explore and discover about the natural world. Describing what you observe is an important part of discovery, and keeping a field notebook and a naturalist journal is one

A naturalist at play—observing and recording observations and thoughts in a journal. Photo by Kerry Heise

of the best ways to learn. A journal is a place to note your experiences, frame your questions, and check your facts. Some naturalists prefer to keep only a small field notebook with them while out in nature and to enter this information and additional facts and experiences in a more complete journal at a later time. The best naturalists, like Darwin and Lewis and Clark, all kept journals that we value highly today for the insights that they provide into the thoughts and experiences of our ancestors. If Columbus hadn't written it down, we would have no way of knowing which island he actually landed on, what the people living there were like, or how long he lingered. Meriwether Lewis is famous for the maps he included in his journal which make it possible for us today to accurately retrace the progress of the first transcontinental expedition, and even pinpoint many of the camp sites and the places where significant events occurred. A simple thing like noting the first lilac bloom in your yard allows you to check next year when your friend mentions that the lilacs are blooming early (or late) this year. Thoreau's journal entries on blooming times of flowers around Walden Pond are proving to be useful to climate scientists today. Journaling is a way of setting aside time to put your thoughts in order, to frame your experience, to help you share with others, and to prompt you to be exact in your observations.

One reason for keeping a naturalist journal is that it emphasizes and explicitly values your own experience. It is a place to say "today I saw the first eastern kingbird of my life!" Every time you venture out into the natural world, you will have many experiences, at least some of which may be interesting or new to you. If so, write them down. It is critical that you value your own experience. It doesn't matter how many people before you have seen an eastern kingbird. In fact, it is not only the first time you see something that it is special. Every time you see a hummingbird visit a paintbrush flower is special, if you imbue it with value. Many people like to draw in their journals. Try taking a few colored pencils along to draw a particularly appealing moss or the pattern of facial stripes on a bird. Drawing can be a wonderful way to encourage yourself to slow down, to take the time to observe nature more closely. So, let your journal be your own. Interact with your journal in whatever way appeals to you and expresses who you are. Share it with whomever you think is appropriate, or with no one if that is your preference. But do try using this tool to sharpen your skills of observation and interpretation.

We recommend using a variation of the Grinnell method that emphasizes the collection and organization of field observations for scientific investigation. This method was developed by Joseph Grinnell (1877–1939), a noted field biologist and the first director of UC Berkeley's Museum of Vertebrate Zoology. For over a century, field biology and natural history students at UC Berkeley have been trained in this method, and it is probably the method most used by professional naturalists. While we recommend this general format because it provides a good framework for making and recording observations, don't lose sight of the fact that this is your journal—over time you may modify or develop new techniques that work best for you. The important point is to record detailed observations. Below are guidelines on how to keep a field notebook and a journal based on the Grinnell method.

Field Notebook

This is actually what you will need in the field for recording your observations. The notebook can be spiral or hardbound; the format is flexible. It often helps to have an "observation checklist" in your notebook (on either the first or last page) that you can reference for your notes. This information will often make up the first part of the written description in your field journal:

- Time and date (use 24-hour clock format—"1330" for 1:30 PM)
- Location (with arrival and departure time)
- Route traveled
- Weather (include temperature, wind, precipitation type, cloud cover, other)
- Habitat/vegetation type (woodland, grassland, wetland, etc.)
- Species, rocks, or other natural objects seen
- General observations and comments
- Drawings, maps, photos (with digital photo number)

Field Journal

Some naturalists choose to also keep a journal where they rewrite their field observations from the field notebook in a format that is easy for you and others to read. Each field day should have a separate journal entry that should have a written description of the day's observations (including a species list, maps, drawings, etc.). A species account (if any) and a catalog of collected specimens (if any) will also be included with the day's entry.

General Journaling Practices. Here are some specific points that can help format a journal:

- Duration—each journal should cover one calendar year.
- Margins—leave 3 centimeters from the left side and from the top of the sheet.
- Date each entry in the space to the left of the page margin.
- Put your name and the year in the upper left corner of each page.
- Number all pages—this often goes in the upper right on the page.
- Avoid abbreviations, as it is easy to forget these, or other readers may not be able to interpret them.
- Use a pencil or pen with water-resistant ink.
- Use a bound journal with acid-free paper whenever possible.

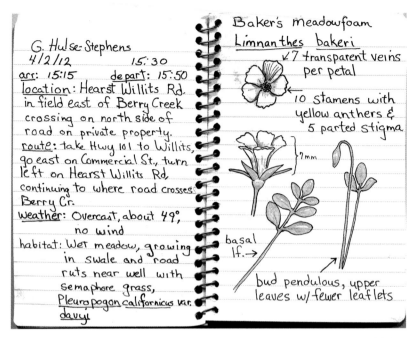

G. Hulse-Stephens
4/2/12   15:30
arr: 15:15   depart: 15:50
location: Hearst Willits Rd.
in field east of Berry Creek
crossing on north side of
road on private property.
route: take Hwy 101 to Willits,
go east on Commercial St., turn
left on Hearst Willits Rd.
continuing to where road crosses
Berry Cr.
weather: Overcast, about 49°,
        no wind
habitat: Wet meadow, growing
        in swale and road
        ruts near well with
        Semaphore grass,
        Pleuropogon californicus var.
davyi

Baker's meadowfoam
Limnanthes bakeri
        ∠7 transparent veins
        per petal
        10 stamens with
        yellow anthers &
        5 parted stigma
        7mm
basal
lf.→
bud pendulous, upper
leaves w/ fewer leaflets

Format for a field notebook. These observations will later be recopied into a field journal. Courtesy of Geri Hulse-Stephens

Written Description. This is a general account of the day's events including where you went, the conditions, what you saw, and any additional thoughts or comments.

- Begin each entry with the location of that day's observation. This should be underlined with a wavy line.

- Write in full sentences and narrate what you observed.

- Only write on one side of a sheet. Use the opposing page for sketches, maps, or photos (taped onto the page).

- Underline species names. Use straight lines for scientific names (*Genus species*) and wavy lines for common names (this helps in scanning your journal for observations).

- Compile a species list at the end of the written description of the day's events. It is helpful to have different categories (e.g., birds, plants in flower, rocks).

- Include maps (pasted into your journal, or drawn) that show locations of your route and/or activities.

Tools of the Trade

Certain items are indispensable when you are are observing nature: a map, binoculars, camera, magnifying lens, pocket knife, waterproof notebook and pencil (pen won't write on wet paper and ink runs), a small first aid kit, sunscreen, hat, water, snack food, layers of clothing, and a watch.

These additional items may also be helpful, especially if you are leading a group: field guides, GPS (global positioning system), cell phone, star charts, flashlight, pocket mirror, clear vials for specimens, tape measure, flagging tape, an old toothbrush for cleaning fossils or rocks, small shovel, watercolors and paper for artwork, duct tape, name tags, butcher paper and charcoal for rubbings of trees or signs, a magnet, and matches or a lighter.

Species Account. This is a record of *specific* nature observations of interest, usually in a single place and pertaining to the ecology or behavior of a specific species, although this could really apply to any natural phenomena (e.g., weather, rock formations, wave action). Each account starts with the name of the species.

Catalog. This is a record of any specimens that you collect. Make sure to label or tag each specimen you collect with the following information: catalog number, date collected, collection location, collector's name, and identification.

THE LANGUAGE OF NATURALISTS

The scientific community has developed a language all its own to clearly and accurately identify organisms. With 250,000 kinds of plants on Earth we can't simply refer to the one we want to discuss as "that tree." The problem is even more overwhelming with insects, where the numbers are truly phenomenal. The number of insects that have been described by scientists is around 750,000, and these are just the ones we have identified. The actual number of insects on Earth is estimated to be between 5 and 10 million! In order for us to communicate clearly about this number of organisms, a special set of terms was developed. Using a unique scientific name for each species allows people from all over the world to refer to the same species by the same name. This is not the case for common names that are often employed. With all the variations in native California languages, there were many words applied to the same animal, for example. The raccoon (*Procyon lotor*) was referred to as *kahdoos* by some Pomo people and *hoo-ma-ka* by the Coast Miwok. Likewise, we use *cat* in English and *gato* in Spanish, but Spanish and English speakers can be sure they are referring to the same animal when they use *Felis catus*.

Linnaeus's Classification System

The system scientists have devised is elegant in its simplicity and formality. It is based on the classification system created by Carl Linnaeus (1707–1778). Linnaeus was one of the first people to attempt to list all the plants and animals known at the time, to give each a unique name, and to classify them in a coherent manner. At the time of Linnaeus, Latin was the language that scientists used to communicate with one another across the globe, so Linnaeus and his contemporaries used Latin when classifying species. This tradition carries through today as scientists continue to use Greek or Latin for genus and species names.

Each species is assigned a two-part name, a binomial. The first word of the binomial designates the genus to which the organism has been assigned, while the second designates the species. People are familiar with binomials, whether they realize it or not. *Tyrannosaurus rex* is a binomial designating a large, extinct carnivore. *Tyrannosaurus* is the genus name and the first half of a binomial, and the second half is *rex*— the species name. Many of the scientific names designating organisms have made it into popular usage, although the majority have not. One of the useful aspects of this naming system is that each organism has been assigned a *unique* binomial. Thus we are *Homo sapiens*, which translates to "knowing man," the black rat is *Rattus rattus*, and the house cat is *Felis catus*. Each has a unique binomial. One of the great advantages of this scientific naming system is it reflects relationship among species. *Felis catus* is not the only member of the genus *Felis*. In fact, the genus *Felis* is global in distribution and contains about 28 species. The fact that all have been assigned to the genus *Felis* indicates that the people who have studied the relationships of the mammals think that all 28 species of *Felis* share a recent common ancestor and thus can be considered closely related. The same is true for their prey the rats, which total to 64 extant species, with the best known being the black rat and the brown rat (*Rattus norvegicus*). The most recent addition to the list is the largest of the rats. In 2009, scientists discovered what may be the largest rat species in a remote rainforest in Papua New Guinea.

The scientific system of naming, starting with the binomial designating each species, is a hierarchical system. The system is designed to indicate nested levels of relationship. Just as we recognize close family relationships among people with certain terms (brother, sister) and less closely related people with other terms (uncle, cousin, friend), the scientific system of naming uses nested, hierarchical levels to indicate degrees of relationship. For example, you may recognize that rats and mice are more closely related to each other than to cats. Thus, at the next higher level above genus, cats are assigned to the family Felidae, whereas rats, mice, and hamsters are placed together in the family Muridae. Placing all these familiar rodents together in the family Muridae indicates that they are more closely related to each other than any is to the cats. The hierarchical scientific naming system consists of seven nested levels, like seven progressively smaller mixing bowls. Each bigger bowl is more inclusive; it embraces more diverse types of organisms. The whole system looks like this for the brown rat:

Kingdom: Animalia
Phylum: Chordata
Class: Mammalia
Order: Rodentia
Family: Muridae
Genus: *Rattus*
Species: *norvegicus*

The highest taxonomic level, the kingdom Animalia, includes all "animals" but not plants, bacteria, or viruses. The phylum Chordata includes all animals with backbones but excludes invertebrates like insects, spiders, and clams. The class Mammalia includes all animals with backbones that have hair, feed young with milk, and are warm-blooded but excludes other chordates (animals with backbones) like birds and amphibians. The order Rodentia includes mice, rats, squirrels, porcupines, beavers, guinea pigs, and hamsters—all have continuously growing front teeth in the upper and lower jaws that are kept short by use. The family Muridae includes all the Old World rats and mice. The genus *Rattus* contains the closely related rat species. Finally, the binomial *Rattus norvegicus* designates uniquely one species of brown rat, sometimes referred to as the Norwegian sewer rat, and excludes its close relative the black rat.

Some species have been further divided into multiple subspecies to allow scientists to distinguish differences between similar groups of individuals within one species. Subspecies can usually interbreed and produce viable offspring. Examples of two you know are *Canis lupus familiaris*, the domestic dog, and the Australian dingo *Canis lupus dingo*. These two types of dogs readily breed with one another but have distinct physical characteristics that scientists deduced warranted subspecies designations. The gray wolf is also *Canis lupus*, which tells us how closely related domestic dogs and wolves are—no surprise they can successfully interbreed. So, when referring to a particular subspecies, it is important to refer to the genus and species names followed by the subspecies name.

Using this system, you may begin to develop a mental map of the relationships of organisms. This is an incredibly useful exercise for thinking about how evolution shapes the species and their relationships to one another. For example, at the family level you can see that peaches, apples, and pears are all closely related and that pine trees and oaks are very different from them! Classifying species is just one of the tools that naturalists and scientists use to conceptualize and communicate about the natural world.

Geographic Range

Each species has tolerance limits beyond which they are not able to live. These tolerances are dynamic and can change with time and conditions. The terms below describe environmental conditions that influence the distribution of species and habitats. They may be familiar, but for naturalists they have specialized meanings.

Geographic range is the area within which a given species can be found. However, geographic ranges are not static. Plant and animal species shift their ranges over time. They are constantly probing the boundaries of their ranges to see if they can be expanded. Geographic ranges also change as climate and topography change. The determining factors that dictate where a species of plant can grow are things like soil, aspect, topography, position on the slope, elevation, rainfall, wind, temperature, distance from the coast, and the size of the surrounding plants. The same is true for many animal species, whose distributions are limited by environmental conditions as well.

Topography, wind, and distance from the coast all play roles in whether a plant is able to grow in a certain place or not. Think of the

Naturalists of all ages are characterized by close observation and questioning.
Photo by Kerry Heise

Coast Ranges of California as a wall blocking the flow of air from the Pacific Ocean toward the Central Valley. The lowest gap in the wall is the Golden Gate, and that is the first place air (wind) pushes through the Coast Ranges to reach the Central Valley. This gap allows cool, moist Pacific air to move inland daily, bringing moisture and lowering temperature everywhere it penetrates. Contrast this with the imposing wall of hills along the Big Sur coast, extending from Monterey to Morro Bay. This range of hills (the Santa Lucia Range) effectively stops the flow of cool, moist Pacific air from reaching inland. As a result, at Vallejo, 30 miles inland from the gap between San Francisco and Marin, the temperature at 6 PM in July might be 55 degrees and the relative humidity 80 percent, while 30 miles inland from the Big Sur coast the temperature might be 82 degrees and the relative humidity hovering at 17 percent. These are very different conditions for plants and animals to cope with.

Aspect generally refers to orientation, or the direction that a slope faces. Imagine a big isolated hill, Mt. Diablo for instance, which has four sides that face north, east, south, and west. Each side of the hill will be exposed to the sun for different portions of the day and different parts of the year. Here in the Northern Hemisphere, the sun shines from the south, so south-facing slopes are hotter and dryer than north-facing slopes. It is typical in coastal California for cool, moist north-facing slopes to support more conifer trees (e.g., redwood, Douglas-fir), while hot, dry south-facing slopes are often covered in oaks or chaparral. A similar though less intense distinction can be drawn between east- and west-facing slopes.

Closely related to aspect is slope. *Slope* is a measure of steepness, with vertical (90 degrees) being one extreme and flat (0 degrees) being the other. Most hills vary between 15 percent and 30 percent slope. The flats at the bases of hills collect soils washed off of the hills by landslides and streams, so soils on slopes tend to be shallower and rockier than soils on flats. Plant communities will differ depending on where on the slope the community is located, from the flats at the base, to the steep mid-slope, to the gently rounded top of a hill. Airflow up and down hills varies with the topography and also shapes natural communities.

In general, warm air rises, while cold air sinks. Thus, during the day, especially in the afternoon, wind tends to blow up canyons, while cool air tends to flow down canyons at night. This can be quite pronounced, and temperatures at the base of a hill can be very different from those at mid-slope or at the summit. Cool air tends to pool at the base of hills, causing valleys to be covered in frost while the hills around the valley may be frost-free.

Temperature and rainfall, as well as the seasonal distribution of these factors, are huge influences in determining plant and animal distributions on biogeography. It is not the averages but the extremes that generally determine geographic ranges. Imagine a plant that can tolerate 35°F or 2°C but is killed when the temperature dips below freezing. It doesn't matter if the weather is balmy and warm most of the time. If the mercury dips below freezing one day per year in a specific valley, that plant will be excluded from the site. The same can be imagined on a multiyear scale. Suppose you have a run of 20 "good" years, where the temperature never dips below freezing, but every twentieth year the temperature drops to 17 degrees. Our hypothetical plant will still be excluded. We are all familiar with this phenomenon because we hear news reports every 7 or 8 years of the citrus crop in Florida or California being wiped out by a cold snap. Occasional cold snaps interrupt fruit production in oranges and grapefruits. Even more extreme, every 20 to 50 years we hear about the citrus trees themselves being killed. Citrus growers push the limits of the temperature tolerance of the trees they cultivate, and periodically they pay the price.

Topography also plays a determining role in temperature and rainfall. As a cloud is pushed up a slope, its temperature drops. As the temperature in the cloud drops, its ability to carry water is diminished. The reduced capacity is noticed on the ground as rainfall. When clouds are pushed off of the Pacific and up the slope of coastal mountains, they tend to drop moisture. An extreme example of this is that clouds passing over the low topography of San Francisco are not pushed upward and so are not wrung of moisture, and the annual rainfall in San Francisco is about 20 inches. A few miles to the north, the same clouds intersect Mt. Tamalpais, are driven up 2,000 or more feet, and dump their moisture in such a dramatic way that Kentfield has 60 inches of annual rainfall, three times that of nearby San Francisco! As you can imagine, the plant communities that grow in the two areas are quite different.

Soils have different chemical compositions and physical structures, depending on their parent materials and how and where they were formed. Granite, of which most of the Sierra Nevada is composed, forms very different soils than the volcanic soils around the base of Mt. Shasta. Both of these soil types are chemically and physically distinct from the serpentine soils of the Klamath Range. Plants respond to these differences, and soil chemistry is a primary determinant of plant community composition. The leather oak (*Quercus durata*) is a reasonably good indicator of serpentine soils. Leather oak grows only on serpentine soils, though certainly not on all serpentine soils. Thus, geologists looking for serpentine soils can drive along looking for leather oaks as a first indication.

GETTING OUT AND ABOUT

Learning about the world never ends. Every year, new plants (including huge trees!), insects, birds, and mammals are "discovered." These species are "new to science." But an equally interesting category is "new to you." Take time to notice something around you, birdsong, trees planted in your neighborhood park, and native bees visiting your sunflowers. These experiences offer opportunities close at hand for enriching your life, and deepening your understanding of the natural world.

While outside observing nature, pay special attention to current

Explore!

THE TEN-MINUTE NATURALIST:
GETTING TO KNOW YOUR OWN BACKYARD

Spend 10 minutes every day or a half hour once a week outside at the same spot just observing. Change the time that you go, if possible, to observe differences between morning and evening. Write down what you see: birds, plants, insects, flowers, and the condition of trees or a creek. Begin the first session by simply walking the spot's perimeter and noting its contours and boundaries, and making a simple map of the landscape and important features within it (large trees, structures, streams, fences, etc.). Over time you will deepen your understanding of how nature works. It's best to choose a safe place that's easy to get to, so you can visit it often.

START YOUR OWN NATURE JOURNAL

Nature journals are a time-honored tradition among naturalists and explorers. They can be simple, like a small spiral notebook with quick notes in it, or elaborate affairs with drawings and specimens pressed into them. Whatever kind you choose, remember to include the date, time, location, and weather with each entry.

NATURALIST ASPIRATIONS

So many amazing naturalists have preceded us, and they can provide inspiration for our own endeavors. Think of naturalists you admire. Research them and read some of their journal entries. Then write down some of the qualities and skills you admire about those people in your journal (e.g., "can distinguish metamorphic rocks from sedimentary and is comfortable tramping around outside in the snow"). Which of these qualities and skills do you already possess? Which would you like to acquire? Make a list and check it in six months. Which qualities and skills have you gained?

weather conditions, regional climate patterns, topography, and soil, as these factors may explain in part which species you see and the composition of surrounding plant and animal communities. Conversely, the plants and animals that you observe can tell you a lot about physical conditions such as the climate and soils. Sight, sound, smell, and touch, when safe and appropriate, can all provide valuable clues about the nature of a species. Sometimes even *taste* can be included in your exploration.

2

Geology, Climate, and Soils

As a first approximation, the topographic shape of California can be thought of as a bathtub with a ring-shaped set of mountain ranges enclosing a flat, central valley. The next layer of complexity is that the Coast Ranges are far smaller in height than the Sierra Nevada (2,000 to 4,000 feet vs 8,000 to 14,000 feet), so one wall of the tub is shorter than the other. There is one low gap at San Francisco Bay, where the rivers that flow down off of the west slope of the Sierra, and that are gathered in the Central Valley, cut down to sea level through the Coast Ranges to reach the sea.

North of San Francisco Bay, the Coast Ranges form an unbroken wall all the way to Oregon, and south of San Francisco Bay, the Coast Ranges form a mostly unbroken wall all the way to Ventura. The spine of the Sierra Nevada bends west at its southern end, and mountains then essentially continue south unbroken all the way through Baja California in Mexico. These north-south mountain ranges actually continue much farther than just California, linking up with the Cascades through Oregon and Washington, and on north to Alaska, as well as south into Mexico.

At the northern end of the Central Valley, also called the Great Valley, the Coast Ranges are linked to the Sierra-Cascade axis by the Klamath and Siskiyou Mountains. At the southern end of the Central Valley, the Coast Ranges are linked to the Sierra by the Trans-

Relief map of California. A ring of mountains (pinkish brown) surrounds the Central Valley (green). Water appears deep blue. Fault lines appear as prominent straight features. Courtesy of the National Aeronautics and Space Administration

verse Ranges. The mountain ranges south of the Transverse Ranges are called the Peninsular Ranges. So the backbone of California is formed by one tall range of mountains, the Sierra-Cascade axis, which joins the east-west trending Transverse Ranges, and then the north-south trending Peninsular Ranges.

This mountain wall running north-south, dividing eastern California from the west, is very important climatically and biologically. To the west of the Sierra-Cascade axis the land is called cismontane Cali-

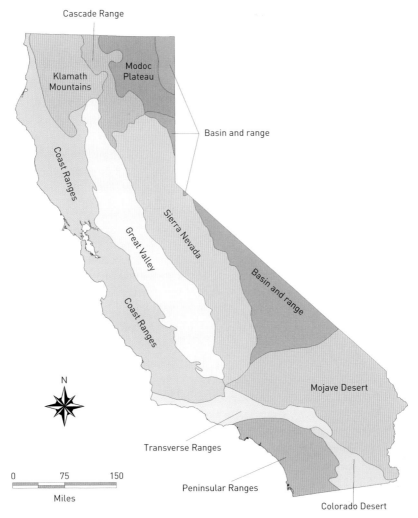

California geomorphic provinces. The mapped geological and topographic features correspond closely to regions distinguished by organisms. Courtesy of the California Geological Survey

fornia, and east of the mountains it is called transmontane California. East of the Sierra-Cascade axis are more north-south trending mountain ranges. These additional ranges include such long and important features as the Inyo-White Mountains, the Panamint Range (which is the west wall of Death Valley), the Warner Mountains of northeastern

California, and a number of smaller ranges scattered across the desert east of the Sierra-Cascade axis.

The final features to plug into a mental map of California are the one bump in the otherwise flat Central Valley (the Sutter Buttes), and the California islands. The Sutter Buttes are the eroded remnants of a volcano that arose on the floor of the flat Central Valley about 1.5 million years ago and are perhaps best thought of as the southernmost outlier of the volcanic Cascade Range. The California islands are a series of offshore lands west of Los Angeles, Ventura, and San Francisco. The southern California islands are called the Channel Islands, while the miniscule dots west of San Francisco are called the Farallons.

EARTH'S FORMATION AND PLATE TECTONICS

One of the biggest challenges to studying geology is grasping the temporal scale usually involved in geologic processes. For example, the western edge of North America, where California sits, started to take shape approximately 350 million years ago. This is when the North American continent collided with the ocean floor, scraping off and crushing the oceanic sediments to form mountains that defined the western edge of North America. The evidence of this edge can now be seen as the eastern edge of the Sierra Nevada with the more recent western part of the state forming from slower sediment accumulation. Ever since this event, more collisions, trenches, and breaks along fault lines have created the landscape we see today.

The topographic structure of Earth's surface is a result of global, regional, and local geological processes that occur over long periods of time. The Earth has a layered structure with a solid inner core, a molten outer core, and a solid but ductile mantle. The upper mantle exists under such extreme pressure and at such high temperature (near the melting point) that although it is solid, it can move like an extremely viscous fluid. On the surface of the mantle is the crust, far thinner than the skin of an apple in comparison, a relatively cool, solid skin for the Earth. It is here that we live our lives. The uppermost part of the mantle together with the crust are called the lithosphere.

The lithosphere is composed of a series of relatively separate pieces, called plates, like pieces of a jigsaw puzzle, which are pushed about by the motion of the mantle. The plates come into contact with each other, in which case they bump and grind, slide one over the other, rub along-

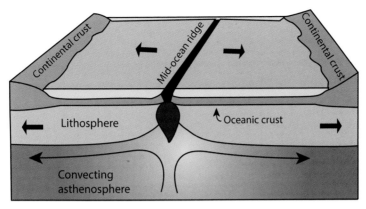

Divergent plate boundary showing relative directions of movement.
Courtesy of Rebecca Perlroth, Santa Rosa Junior College

side each other, or crash head-on and crumple at the margins. We call these plate motions and interactions tectonics. The idea that the Earth is made of a series of moving plates is barely 100 years old. Plate tectonics is the unifying concept that allows geologists to coherently explain earthquakes, volcanoes, mountain building, and all of the other geological phenomena we observe. Geology is perhaps the most blessed of the natural sciences, in that it has one, central, coherent theory that links all the disparate phenomena we observe around the globe, to the envy of biologists.

There are fundamentally three different types of plate boundaries: divergent, convergent, and transform. Divergent plate boundaries are locations where plates split apart or separate from one another and allow molten mantle material to rise up. The resulting elevated area is called a mid-ocean ridge or spreading center, as it is usually located in the middle of an ocean basin and is a topographically tall feature.

Because convection is a process that continually repeats itself, ocean basins get progressively wider as time passes. If plates were all diverging from one another, and new crust were continually being formed, think about what would happen to the Earth. More and more crust on Earth's surface would unavoidably increase the size of the planet! We know that this is not happening, and therefore, if crust is being created at one location, it must be destroyed or consumed at another. Both oceanic and continental lithosphere (plates) can bump into one another. We call this a convergent plate boundary. Because oceanic lithosphere

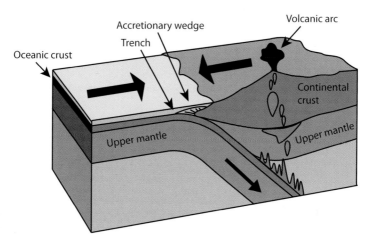

Convergent plate boundary. Oceanic crust always is subducted beneath continental crust because oceanic crust is more dense. Courtesy of Rebecca Perlroth, Santa Rosa Junior College

is denser than continental lithosphere, any time oceanic lithosphere bumps into continental lithosphere at a convergent plate boundary, a structure called a subduction zone is formed. The heavier oceanic plate sinks (is subducted) into the mantle, where it is eventually reabsorbed into the lower mantle or rises as magma.

When two continental plates collide at a convergent plate boundary, the result is somewhat different. Because continental crust is so buoyant, it will not subduct into the mantle. This would be like expecting an ice cube to sink into a glass of water. Instead, the two continental plates simply push into each other, like pushing two blobs of Play-Doh together, creating a huge thickening of the crust. The material cannot go sideways, so it gets pushed up and down. The Himalayas in Asia are a fantastic example of two continental plates colliding. India is moving north and colliding with Asia, causing the Himalayas to rise about 1 centimeter per year or 10 kilometers per million years.

The third type of plate boundary occurs when two plates slide horizontally past one another in opposite directions. This is called a transform plate boundary. The San Andreas Fault is perhaps the best known and best studied transform fault on Earth because it slices through over a thousand miles of continental real estate. The land west of the San Andreas Fault is part of the Pacific Plate, and the rest of North America

Surface rupture caused by movement along the San Andreas Fault in 1906. Fault trace 2 miles north of the Skinner Ranch at Olema, near Point Reyes (Marin County). Tomales Bay in the distance. Courtesy of the US Geological Survey

is on the North American Plate. These plates slide past one another horizontally, with the Pacific Plate moving relatively to the northwest and the North American Plate moving relatively to the southeast.

SHAPING CALIFORNIA

California is unusual geologically in that all three types of plate boundaries are responsible for the formation of the state and all three are *currently active* within the state. Divergence is occurring in Southern California, in an area called the Salton Trough, where the state is being stretched out. The Salton Trough area will eventually thin enough to connect with the Gulf of California, and will eventually be underwater.

Convergence is occurring north of Shelter Cove, where the Juan de Fuca Plate is subducting beneath the North America Plate. Convergence along the western margin of the North American continent ended around 30 million years ago and became lateral slippage to create the San Andreas Fault transform boundary that we are familiar with today. Transform plate motion is the primary cause of California's earthquakes. In 1906 an earthquake along the San Andreas Fault caused 21 feet of horizontal displacement and started a devastating fire that destroyed San Francisco. Major parts of the state are west of the San Andreas Fault and thus are not, geologically speaking, part of North America. They are riding the Pacific Plate as it glides north. The Farallon Islands off of San Francisco actually originated on the Big Sur coast and have rafted north from there! Stick around a few million years and Los Angeles will be just west of San Francisco.

One result of all this plate movement is the creation of mountains. The volcanoes of California were formed by the melting and upwelling of subducting plates. The Coast Ranges were formed when the Pacific Plate subducted below the North American Plate and the sea floor crumpled and folded. These mountains are an accretionary wedge, that is, sea floor sediments scraped off the top of the Pacific Plate. The resulting mix of rocks is called the Franciscan complex. Most of the landforms we see in California are only a few million years old, young in geologic time, and mountain building is still in an active phase.

We think of mountain building as a slow, long-term process, and on a human scale it is. But it is important to put actual numbers on some of the geologic phenomena we talk about, because geology can happen on surprisingly short time scales. Mt. Shasta is the second highest peak in California and is a classic, cone-shaped volcano (stratovolcano). But how old is Mt. Shasta? Shasta has erupted intermittently for the last 100,000 years. Three of the four major cones that form the current mountain are 12,000 years old or less, with much of the mountain being rebuilt in the last 2,000 years! On a geologic scale, that is surprisingly young. Another important ongoing geological phenomenon is erosion. Shasta, and every other mountain in the world, is constantly being eroded. Landslides, glacial action, wind, rain, snow, freezing, and thawing constantly gnaw away at mountains in an apparent attempt to make the whole world completely flat. If it

The vertical, glacially carved walls of Half Dome (right) and El Capitan (left), Yosemite Valley. The valley floor is covered in a dense forest of white firs and visitors! Photo by Deborah Stanger Edelman

weren't for continuing growth, mountains would (relatively) quickly disappear.

When a mountain like Mt. Shasta falls and is ripped apart by erosion, the resulting debris ends up somewhere below. It piles up, and it often forms sedimentary rocks. The flatness of the Central Valley is the result of this process, where sediments were deposited as rivers ran off of the Sierra into the Pacific Ocean 10 or more million years ago. The sediments in the current Central Valley may be as much as 40,000 feet deep!

Another important geological force that has shaped the landscape of California is the action of glaciers. As global climate has vacillated over the last 3 million years, the Earth has experienced a series of much colder and then warmer phases. During the colder eras, glaciers formed in the higher altitudes of the state and pushed down mountain slopes, carving rock and pushing sediment in front of them. The Yosemite and Hetch Hetchy Valleys are perhaps the most famous glacially carved valleys in the state. The vertical walls of these striking valleys resulted from glaciers cutting through very hard, stable stone, which then stood as huge walls when the glaciers retreated (melted).

ROCKS IN CALIFORNIA

The movement of plates influences the kinds of rocks found throughout the state. As the Juan de Fuca Plate is subducted beneath the North American Plate, there are two possible outcomes for the rocks that end up underneath. They can melt and become magma and return to the Earth's surface as igneous rocks (volcanoes or granite). Or they may not melt but change under the extreme pressures and high temperatures deep in the Earth, becoming metamorphic rocks.

When a plate is subducted and the leading edge is melted, the magma may work its way up through the overlying continental rock. Magma that reaches the surface hot and semifluid forms what we call extrusive igneous rock. In general, extrusive igneous rocks are volcanic. If the rising magma cools to form rock before reaching the surface, it forms intrusive igneous rocks. Granite is the most widespread and familiar intrusive igneous rock in California. The important point is that both intrusive igneous rocks (like granite) and extrusive igneous rocks (like volcanic Mt. Shasta) have similar origins; they come from magma at a plate boundary where subduction is active. In California, Mt. Lassen is a convenient place marker for the dividing line between volcanic rocks to the north and granitic rocks to the south, though there are exceptions.

If sedimentary limestone is subducted at a plate boundary and then later is uplifted and reaches the surface again, it may return changed, or metamorphosed. The atoms of the rock rearrange themselves into the smallest, tightest form they can under the influence of extreme pressure and temperature deep in the Earth. When the limestone returns, it may be changed to what we call marble, a metamorphic rock. Sedimentary sandstone may be changed into metamorphic quartzite, a harder, finer-grained version of the original sandstone. Sedimentary shale can be metamorphosed into slate or schist.

We call the transformation of one rock type into another by geological processes the rock cycle. On a long time scale, rocks are continuously recycled: Oceanic crust is subducted, melts, and rises through continental crust to become a volcano. The volcano is worn down by erosion and becomes a sedimentary rock. The sedimentary rock is subjected to heat and pressure and metamorphosed. The changes of the rock cycle are continuous and slow and behave a bit like the life cycle of a living organism, or a geochemical cycle.

Alternating layers of sandstone and shale in the Gualala watershed, coastal Northern California. Photo by Kerry Heise

All three of these rock types (igneous, sedimentary, and metamorphic) occur widely in California. Depending on where you are in the Golden State, you may not need to travel far to see all three. Great examples of sedimentary rocks can be found all along the lower slopes of the Sierra. Around Lake Shasta is where the largest sedimentary limestone caves in California occur. The spine of the Sierra, as well as the Transverse and Peninsular Ranges, are granitic. The Coast Range between Monterey and Ventura is also granitic.

Common igneous rocks in California are

- *Granite*: coarse-grained, light-colored intrusive igneous rock. It forms the high peaks in the Sierra Nevada and is prominent in the Transverse and Peninsular Ranges, as well as in parts of the Coast Ranges.

- *Basalt*: fine-grained, black to rust-colored extrusive igneous rock. Basalt is common in many of the volcanic areas in California, including the Modoc Plateau, Mt. Lassen, and the Mojave Desert. One can view dramatic columnar basalt at Devil's Postpile National Monument near Mammoth Lakes.

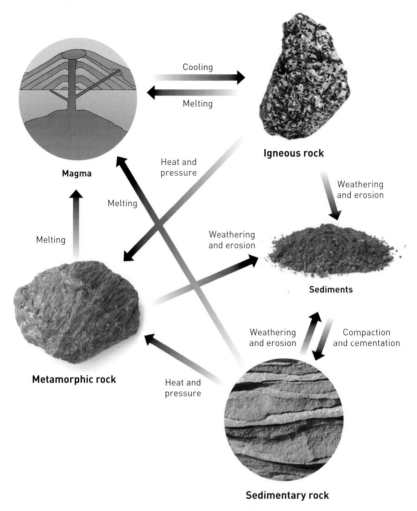

The rock cycle. Multiple pathways of change as rocks are subjected to erosion, deposition, heat, and pressure. Used with permission from the National Energy Education Development Project, www.need.org

- *Other volcanic rocks:* rhyolite and andesite form from lavas that have more silica and are stickier than basalt. Tuff is a light-colored, often low-density rock formed when lava is ejected into the atmosphere. Pumice has a frothy texture and is filled with holes making it lightweight. Obsidian is typically a black and glassy rock formed when lava cools quickly. These materials are volcanic in origin and are common in many locations with ongoing or past volcanic activity, including the Cascades Range volcanoes and the eastern Sierra near the towns of Mammoth Lakes and Bishop.

Common sedimentary rocks in California are

- *Shale*: extremely fine-grained detrital sedimentary rock (formed from lithified mud). This forms in calm environments such as deep marine and lacustrine (lake) settings and is common in the Coast Ranges and the foothills of the Sierra Nevada.
- *Sandstone*: medium-grained detrital sedimentary rock (formed from lithified sand). This forms in continental and nearshore marine environments and is common in the Central Valley and desert provinces but can be found in all provinces of California.
- *Chert*: organic sedimentary rock composed of layers of microscopic silica-rich shells deposited on the deep marine floor. Chert is generally rust red in California but can be deep green, yellow, orange, or gray to black. It is common in the Coast Ranges and in the foothills of the Sierra Nevada.
- *Limestone*: a sedimentary rock composed of layers of carbonate-rich shells deposited in generally shallow marine waters, such as reefs.

Common metamorphic rocks in California are

- *Serpentinite*: the state rock of California! This rock is green to black, waxy, and extremely soft. It is the result of tectonic compression and hydrothermal alteration of dark igneous rock (like peridotite and basalt) at an ocean-continent convergent boundary. Serpentinite is common in the Coast Ranges and the foothills of the Sierra Nevada.
- *Slate*: fine-grained foliated metamorphic rock produced from alteration of shale or mudstone. This rock is common in the foothills of the Sierra Nevada.
- *Schist*: medium-grained, sparkling, foliated metamorphic rock produced from alteration of sedimentary or volcanic rocks. Schist is common in the Coast Ranges, the foothills of the Sierra Nevada, and the Transverse Ranges. It is common to see a particular variety of schist, called blueschist, in the Coast Ranges.

CALIFORNIA'S CLIMATE

The climate of California west of the Sierra-Cascade axis is entirely different from the climate found across the rest of the North American continent. It is so different from the continental climate east of the Sierra-Cascade axis, it might as well be on a separate continent, or its own island. Elna Bakker titled her wonderful introduction to California biodiversity *An Island Called California,* in homage to this contrast. In California, continental climate is turned completely on its head. Instead of having the wet season and the warm season at the same time, they are mostly nonoverlapping. The warm season (May to October) in California is characterized by unrelenting drought. It virtually never rains in most of California during the warm season (an exception is summer thunderstorms over the Sierra Nevada). On the other hand, during the "cold season" we get most of our rain. However, it seldom freezes at lower elevations in California. Rain falls here during the cool season, from November to April. This reversal of conjunctions, warm with dry and cool with wet, and extreme (freezing) cold basically lacking, are the prime characteristics of a strange, globally rare climate type.

This climate type is called Mediterranean, and globally we share this climate type with four other areas, all on the western edges of continents roughly between 30 and 40 degrees latitude: the Mediterranean basin, Chile, southwestern Australia, and the Cape region of South Africa. These five areas have more in common with each other than any do with the geographically adjacent areas of their own continents. Climatically and biologically, California is more like Greece or Chile than it is like Nevada. To the extent that climate determines the direction of evolution, these five areas have been subject to evolutionary pressures of a very similar type. One of the outcomes of hot, dry summers and mild, rainy "winters" is that the normal vocabulary we use to describe climate is strangely at odds with California organisms. If "spring" is the time of year when seeds sprout and perennial herbs initiate growth, then spring in continental climate is in April, but in California it is in November! Spring in November? Yes! If "winter" is when mammals hibernate, that would be November to March in Siberia but would be June to October in California. We even have a separate word for going dormant in the hot, dry season. We say that animals estivate rather than saying that they hibernate. If "summer" is the prime growing season for plants, when grass grows, summer is May to September in New York. But in California, by this definition, summer is November to March! California is so strange climatically, so reversed and mixed up, that most of the trees and shrubs fail to lose their leaves at all. In fact, all of the Mediterranean climate areas of the world are characterized by a very high proportion of evergreen trees and shrubs, compared with plants in continental climate areas.

DIVERSITY OF CALIFORNIA MICROCLIMATES

The five Mediterranean climate areas of the globe are all on the western edges of continents. This is because the Earth spins in one direction on its axis. Global winds form as a result of air in the tropics heating and rising, flowing toward the poles, then descending as it cools. The spinning of the earth causes these global air movements to bend (the Coriolis effect). The result in California is that the large-scale winds usually blow from west to east, from the ocean onto the continent.

In California, this means that the wind generally blows off of the Pacific Ocean, blows east across the state and over the Sierra, and continues east across the continent. The wind blowing off of the Pacific is full of moisture from passing over open ocean. When this moist wind hits the continent, it rises, cools, and loses some of its ability to carry water. As the wind cools, it drops its moisture, which hits the earth as rain. As clouds rise to pass over the north-south mountain ranges of California, they are thus wrung of moisture. For each thousand feet of elevation gain that a cloud experiences, its temperature drops about 3.5°F. To pass over the 2,000-to-4,000-foot wall of the Coast Ranges, a cloud will drop 7 to 14 degrees. This drop in temperature causes the cloud to drop moisture on the Coast Ranges.

After passing over the Coast Ranges, the clouds descend into the basin of the Central Valley, increasing in temperature as they descend. The increase in temperature causes the clouds to have additional ability to carry moisture. For this reason the Central Valley tends to be drier, with lower rainfall than the Coast Ranges. The same relationship exists east and west of the Peninsular Ranges. As the clouds rise to ascend the Sierra, they cool once again. The mid-elevation forests of the Sierra get abundant moisture as the clouds rise through elevations they have not previously seen in the Coast Ranges. By the time the clouds reach the highest elevations of the Sierra, most of the moisture has been left behind at mid-elevation, and the highest elevations of California mountains are dry, very cold deserts. After passing over the 4,000-to-8,000-foot wall of the Sierra, the clouds again descend to the 5,000-foot elevation of the transmontane basins, where there is little chance of dropping rain. Consequently, the basins east of the Sierra are largely desert country.

In sum, the west slopes of mountains in California are hit with clouds first, and the east sides are rain shadow areas. The west sides get more rain, the east sides receive less. The entire Central Valley is in the rain shadow of the Coast Ranges, and the desert lands east of the Sierra and Peninsular Ranges are dry because the rain has been squeezed out of the clouds as they pass over the mountains.

Another pattern prevails as you travel from south to north through the state. Broadly, rainfall increases as you proceed north. In the Coast Ranges rainfall is greater in the Santa Cruz Mountains (north of Monterey) than it is in the Gabilan Range (south of Monterey). Continuing north, rainfall is greater around Mendocino than in Santa Cruz, and still greater in Arcata than in Mendocino, given similar elevations. The same pattern prevails in the Sierra: the farther north, the more moisture is delivered as rain or snow at the same elevation.

The result of this complex interplay of wind, cloud, rain, and topography is a wide range of microclimates. Microclimates are small zones where climatic factors differ from the surrounding area due to localized influences such as slope, aspect, and elevation. These microclimates play a strong role in limiting or allowing the growth of plants and animals on the landscape, since plant and animal distributions are strongly constrained by temperature and moisture.

SOIL STRUCTURE AND NUTRIENTS

Plants depend on the sun for their energy but must get water and the mineral nutrients necessary for growth from the soil. Soil is formed from the weathering of bedrock and contains both inorganic and organic components. Differing amounts of mineral material, organic matter, water, and air can be found in local soil. Animals and plants that live in the soil affect soil properties, such as the amount of organic matter and water content, and vice versa—vital minerals in soil are absorbed by plants and ingested by animals. Soil scientists classify lay-

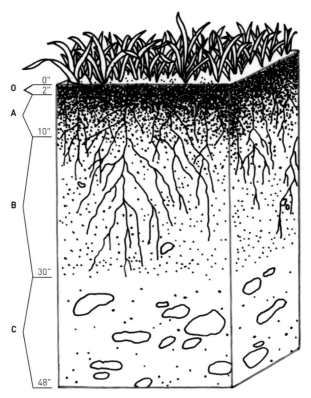

An idealized soil profile. The deeper one digs, the less organic matter and the coarser the rocks and stones. Adapted by Math/Science Nucleus (www.msnucleus.org) from a US Department of Agriculture bulletin

ers of soil into different horizons according to their characteristics, which are related to depth:

O horizon—surface: organic material, dead plants, animal material

A horizon—topsoil: plant roots, bacteria, fungi, small animals

B horizon—subsoil: fewer organisms, less topsoil; plants don't grow well

C horizon—altered parent material: weathered, less living matter; layers above were formed from it

Different rock types have different chemical compositions, and as rocks break down to form soils, the parent rock determines the chemistry of the soil formed upon it. Plants are sensitive to different soil chemistries, and some soils generally promote the growth of all plants, while other soils are inhibiting or even toxic to some or all plants. A dramatic example is the presence of salt in a soil. When rocks are eroded by moving water, salts will be moved by rivers to the sea. But if the rivers or streams flow into an enclosed basin with no outlet to the sea, like Mono Lake and Owens Lake, the salt accumulates in the basin and a salt lake or alkali lake results. Soils impregnated with high concentrations of salt are toxic to most plants and thus exclude them. Dozens of these dry salt pans exist in the California desert and produce remarkable landscapes, such as those in Death Valley.

Another unusual type of soil that supports a large number of endemic plants is serpentine soil. Serpentine is a rock associated with subduction zones, crumpling, and accretion at plate margins. Serpentine soils are characterized by a striking calcium-magnesium imbalance. Calcium is an essential plant nutrient. Most soils have lots of calcium and little magnesium, so plants generally ignore calcium. It is a common, easily available plant nutrient. However, serpentine soils have very little calcium but are high in magnesium. Calcium and magnesium are chemically very similar and therefore seem alike to plants. In serpentine soils, generalist plants that don't bother to distinguish between calcium and magnesium take up both indiscriminately, and they are poisoned by an overabundance of magnesium before they can get enough calcium to meet their needs. Thus many generalist plants are excluded from serpentine soils, leaving an open niche which some native California plants have taken advantage of as they have become serpentine specialists. One of these serpentine specialists is the leather oak (*Quercus durata*), which grows only on serpentine. The boundary between serpentine and nonserpentine soils can be very sharp, and the vegetation may distinguish the soil boundary visually for observant naturalists.

Another of the essential nutrients plants must acquire to grow is nitrogen. Nitrogen is present in most soils but not in amounts that allow luxuriant growth. Nitrogen and phosphorus are two of the most common "fertilizers" farmers apply to crops to increase growth. Some plants have found a way to acquire nitrogen from the air, thus avoiding dependence on whatever nitrogen may be available in the soil. These plants produce tiny hollow nodules on their roots that are a perfect habitat for specialist bacteria that eat atmospheric nitrogen. As the bacteria complete their life span of a few hours or days and die, they decompose in the nodule and release nitrogen to the plant, which "fertilizes" it. In chaparral, buckbrush (*Ceanothus*) develops nitrogen-harboring nodules. Along streams, alders (*Alnus*) do the same thing, and in grasslands, lupines (*Lupinus*) make root nodules for bacteria. As the alders, buckbrush, and lupines complete their life spans of 1 to 60 years, they decompose and release the nitrogen they have harvested from the atmosphere (via their bacterial symbionts) to the soil, thus fertilizing the soil for other plants.

NUTRIENT CYCLING

Outside of a few infalling meteors and outflying spaceships,
the Earth is a closed chemical system.
—William H. Schlesinger

The Earth is an elegant system. Soil, air, and water characteristics change and adapt according to the flow of chemicals, nutrients, and materials through integrated natural cycles. Materials cycling through the Earth's systems go in and out of biotic and abiotic stages. Living things grow, reproduce, die, decompose, and become part of another living thing. Nonliving things accumulate, break down, are utilized by or stored in a living organism, get excreted and redeposited, reformed, or reused. The movement of matter through Earth's systems is described as biogeochemical cycles. Some parts of these cycles take relatively little time, while others can take place over millennia. Among the best known and most important cycles are the rock cycle, the water cycle, the carbon cycle, the nitrogen cycle, and the phosphorous cycle.

Throughout these cycles, nutrients fluctuate between being available and unavailable for utilization by living organisms. Nutrients are released and become available through decomposition, respiration, excretion, erosion, and combustion. They are taken up by organisms through photosynthesis, ingestion and assimilation, sedimentation, and fossilization. Nutrients remain in these different states, or reservoirs, for different residence times. For example, carbon remains in plants for five years on average. Most carbon on Earth is found in the form of rocks and may remain locked there for millions of years.

Awareness of cycles is critical to understanding Earth processes, as our actions can greatly influence biogeochemical cycles. Like other liv-

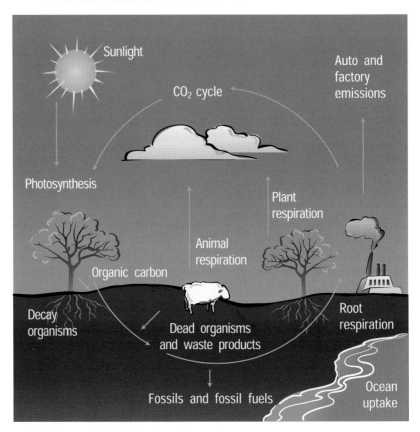

The carbon cycle. Carbon moves via multiple pathways between the atmosphere, the geosphere, living and dead organisms, and the ocean. Copyright, University Corporation for Atmospheric Research

ing things, people are a part of the Earth's systems. We have an impact on their expression, as we regularly introduce materials at a much faster rate than natural cycling processes can absorb them.

The nitrogen cycle provides an excellent illustration of this point. Nitrogen is important for agriculture because it is often a limiting factor for plant growth. For that reason, farmers often apply large amounts of nitrogen in the form of nitrate to increase crop yields. Unfortunately, modern agriculture applies more nitrogen than plants can absorb. Nitrates are highly water soluble. What is not used by plants can move out of soils and become a source of water pollution in streams and lakes. Other land-use activities such as mining, timber

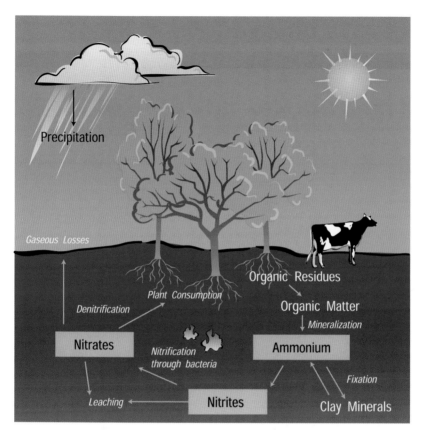

The nitrogen cycle. The nitrogen cycle describes the process by which nitrogen circulates among air, soil, water, and organisms in various chemical forms. Copyright, University Corporation for Atmospheric Research

harvest, and urban development can alter nutrient cycling over long periods of time.

DECOMPOSITION

Every organism on Earth dies. No matter if it is a bacterium that lives a few hours, a turtle that lives 250 years, a bristlecone pine that lives 5,600 years, or a redwood clone that may live many thousands of years, eventually every individual dies. And when each organism dies, its body is recycled. This is one of the bedrock principals of the biosphere: everything can be and is used again. Atoms and simple chemicals are built into more complex chemicals, complex chemicals are molded into cells, cells are aggregated into multicellular organisms, and complexity is increased. But when the organism is no longer capable of absorbing the energy necessary to maintain complexity, entropy takes over and simplification occurs.

There are lots of animals, bacteria, and fungi that make their living breaking down the undefended bodies of dead organisms. Some attack only freshly dead animals; others specialize in slowly extracting the nutrients from long-dead carcasses. We'll follow the decomposition of a raccoon for a moment to highlight some of the stages decomposition goes through. Imagine a raccoon that falls from a tree and dies on impact. Within a few hours, bacteria begin to break into its cells to mine nutrients. Coyotes, foxes, crows, or vultures may rip open and devour the best parts of the carcass (muscles, organs, intestines). Before the scavengers have even finished their meal, flies are on the carcass laying eggs that will hatch into larvae (maggots) that will devour most of the remaining muscle, blood vessels, and tendons. After a few weeks, when the fly maggots have cleaned up all the easily available soft tissues and pupated, there will be a pile of hair, skin, and bones left. Even these are concentrated piles of opportunity, and beetles that specialize in hair or skin arrive to deposit eggs. When at last the bones are clean (three to six months), they will be gnawed on by mice seeking calcium. Any or all of these organisms may pee or poop or die under the tree as they enjoy their meal. In this case the tree may take up the discarded nutrients that were once the raccoon, became the coyote or the fly, and were discarded to the soil realm.

Decomposition is a complex process and varies depending on the organism being simplified, the habitat in which it dies, the time of year it dies, and the available scavengers, insects, and microorganisms. Plants decompose more slowly than animals, but in both cases there is a long line of applicants for the position of simplifier of complex bodies for their own gain. When a leaf falls to the forest floor in the fall, there are specialist insects that eat only the outer layer of the blade, others that rip apart the veins, and still others that lay eggs on the petiole! In the broadest grouping of organisms in an ecosystem, we think of autotrophs and heterotrophs. Autotrophs are the organisms that produce (or capture) their own energy, generally from the sun. In other words autotrophs make their own food. Heterotrophs are those that eat other organisms to acquire energy. Heterotrophs don't make their own food.

Decomposers are simply a variation on the heterotroph theme, specializing on dead organisms for their energy (food) needs. Many people think of decomposers as including only "microorganisms." Other people include microorganisms and fungi in their decomposer conception. It may be more helpful to think of all organisms as either food producers (autotrophs) or food consumers (heterotrophs).

MYCORRHIZAL RELATIONSHIPS

Fungi are strange organisms—some consume only dead leaves or rhinoceros dung (saprophytic fungi). Others are parasites that attack living flies or wheat (parasitic fungi). Some, like the oyster mushroom (*Pleurotus*) commonly seen as white shelves on alder trunks, are active predators, snaring nematodes (tiny invertebrates), anesthetizing and consuming them. Fungi are all heterotrophs, depending on other organisms to gather food the fungus can consume. One of the little-appreciated roles fungi play, and perhaps the most important ecologically, is as symbiotic partners with plants (mycorrhizal fungi). Fungi consist of elongate, tubular, string-like cells called hyphae. It is these hyphae that form the white filamentous mats (mycelia) often attached to mushrooms people dig up in soil or manure. The white netlike structure (mycelium) is the actual body of the organism, while the "mushroom" is the reproductive part (the "fruiting body").

In mycorrhizal fungi, the hyphae wrap around or penetrate the roots of trees. The tree and the fungus then exchange materials. Generally, the tree gives the fungus the products of photosynthesis (carbohydrates, or food). The fungus, in turn, hands the tree water and mineral nutrients like nitrogen, phosphorus, zinc, and copper. Mushroom hyphae are far finer in diameter than tree roots. They form a much more intimate, penetrating relationship with soil particles than tree roots, and thus they are able to find water and nutrients that trees would miss. This type of symbiosis is so important to the health of trees that about 80 percent of the species of trees in the world are involved in these kinds of symbiotic relationships. Because a few species of pine trees in the Northern Hemisphere have so many individuals (think of the acres of boreal forest!), perhaps 99 percent of all individual trees in the world are involved in mycorrhizal relationships. Mycorrhizal fungi are unable to live without their tree partners. Trees stripped of their fungal partners experience decline or poor growth. Many tree-fungus partnerships are very specific. People have tried for years to cultivate truffles, but the symbiotic partnership between truffles and hazelnut trees limits the success of this venture. Madrone trees (*Arbutus menziesii*) are notoriously difficult to grow in nurseries, apparently because culturing the symbiotic partner is difficult. On the other hand, some trees are catholic in their symbiont partners. Douglas-fir trees may have 50 or more species of mycorrhizal fungal partners attached to a single tree!

MINING IN CALIFORNIA

One of the by-products of the geologic diversity of California is deposits of ores that are useful to human society. California's love affair with mining didn't end with the Gold Rush. Many people are surprised to learn that a substantial amount of mining continues to this day. In fact, California is second in the country in nonfuel mineral production, and the mining industry was valued at $3.7 billion in 2005. These products include boron, Portland cement, gold, sand and gravel, bentonite clay, pumice, salt, lime, feldspar, limestone, and kaolin clay, among many others. These are all important industrial materials that modern society depends on. Nonetheless, the impacts of both current and historic mining on the environment can be substantial.

Many historic mines have environmental impacts that continue to be felt today. Mercury is used in gold mining to separate the gold from the ore. Unfortunately, mercury-laden sediments remain from old gold mines and provide a continual source of contamination of fish, wildlife, and water. One example of long-term mining impacts is the Iron Mountain Mine, a Superfund site near Redding. The Iron Mountain Mine was at one time the largest copper mine in California. Though mining there ended in 1963, an EPA case study of the site states, "Nearly 100 years of mining activity at Iron Mountain left numerous waste rock and tailings piles, massive fracturing of the bedrock overlying the extensive underground mine workings and remaining sulfide deposits, sinkholes, seeps, and contaminated sediments in nearby water bodies. The uncontrolled acid mine drainage from Iron Mountain Mine was the largest source of surface water pollution in the U.S." Through cleanup efforts, the site is now 95 percent contained.

Explore!

TAKE AN EARTHQUAKE WALK

Point Reyes National Seashore has a popular trail called the Earthquake Walk that follows the fault line. USGS has an excellent guide titled *Where's the San Andreas Fault? A Guidebook to Tracing the Fault on Public Lands in the San Francisco Bay Area* with information about earthquake touring from the Hollister and San Juan Bautista areas to the Santa Cruz Mountains and the San Mateo coast.

TAKE THE CALIFORNIA GEOTOUR

The California Geological Survey has a great list of geologic field trip guides statewide. See www.consrv.ca.gov/cgs/geotour/Pages/Index .aspx.

GO SPELUNKING

Mercer Caverns, Moaning Cavern, and California Caverns are all worth seeing in Calavaras County.

3

Water

To say that water is important for human survival is an understatement. It is more than the fluid that passes through us; it's in every part of us. Water is not just in our blood; it's in our tissues, our bones, our organs. We're not just more water, by weight, than anything else; we're more water than everything else combined. We need to drink water because it is a critical component of the processes that allow us to live, as it is critical for all living things on Earth.

In addition to being important for life on Earth, water is also important for shaping the earth. The movement of water is driven by gravity. It falls from the sky as precipitation, moves in rivers from higher to lower elevation, and depending on the amount of water and the shape of the channel, moving water can spill over riverbanks. Water moves fine sand and large boulders alike, and washes away trees and anything else that happens to be on the riverbank. Cars and parts of houses are occasionally seen floating downstream, a result of poor planning and not appreciating the power of water in shaping Earth's surface. Yet as destructive as these forces can be, high-flow events, and the renewing processes that occur during the lower-flow conditions that follow, are essential for sustaining aquatic ecosystems that have characterized rivers for millions of years.

SCALING WATER: FROM MOLECULES TO OUR ENVIRONMENT

Two atoms hydrogen, one atom oxygen—on its face, water seems so simple. Yet its molecular shape, and the capacity of hydrogen and oxy-

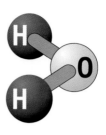

The water molecule. The polarity of the molecule is shown as dark hydrogen atoms (positive) bonded to a light oxygen atom (negative). Used with permission from the National Energy Education Development Project, www.need.org

gen to act independently and together, allows water molecules to interact in ways that other molecules cannot. Water is unique at a molecular scale because it can take a solid particle, break it apart, and hold it in a liquid form. The polarity of water (its nonlinear, asymmetrical shape and charge) allows it to dissolve salts and other compounds like ammonia and urea, as well as larger molecules that need to be exported from the body.

The chemical properties of water have other important implications for life on Earth. One of the most important of these is that hydrogen bonds are regularly formed between adjacent water molecules: Hydrogen bonds are relatively weak forces, compared with bonds that hold atoms together within a molecule, but it's these weak bonds that allow water molecules to form liquid water, water vapor, and solid ice, a unique natural phenomenon. In liquid water, hydrogen bonds form and fall apart quickly and locally (at the molecular level) but provide sufficient structure to give water its surface tension. Surface tension due to hydrogen bonds provides the resistance that allows water striders to skate on the water's surface. In its solid form (ice), hydrogen bonds are more stable and create an organized lattice of molecules that are less tightly packed, compared with water in the liquid form.

One of the most important and rarest properties of water is that ice floats because water is denser than ice. The tendency for solid ice to float is why we can skate, walk, and drive over frozen water bodies even if they are not frozen solid. More important for Earth's ecology, however, is the fact that plants and animals can survive beneath ice that covers lakes, despite freezing outside air temperatures. If ice sank to the bottom of a lake, it would eventually fill the lake and trap organisms living in the lake. Instead, ice formed on the top of lakes, rivers, and oceans remains floating on the top, while the water below and many of the organisms within it generally remain above freezing for the entire winter. Ice fishermen have hydrogen bonds to thank for their recreational activity and may also have hydrogen bonds to blame when pipes burst as a result of freezing. On a larger scale, this is also the reason we have icebergs and Arctic sea ice, which climate scientists have found are important for regulating air and water temperatures across the planet.

THE WATER CYCLE

There is an amazing synchrony between Earth's climate and the properties of water: the planet's temperatures tend to fluctuate between freezing and boiling, so we have water as a liquid in oceans and as it flows and rests on land in rivers and lakes; as solid ice in colder environments; and as gas in the atmosphere. But where is most of our water, and how does it reach us? These questions can be answered as we consider the water cycle.

The location and movement of liquid water is controlled by gravity. Rain falls downward, rivers flow from higher elevation to lower, and lakes and vernal pools seep slowly into the soil, all because liquid water is more dense than air. Despite the fact that most of the water we commonly see is flowing over or sitting on land, freshwater represents a small fraction of all the water on Earth. In fact, it's a very small fraction—only 1 percent of all water on Earth is present as freshwater, including all lakes and rivers, all groundwater, and all the water present in living things. Approximately 2 percent of Earth's water is frozen as glaciers, even with recent climatic warming. In contrast, 97 percent of the water on Earth is found in the ocean as salt water.

If you've ever sat on the banks of a river, it may have crossed your mind that water is constantly moving from the mountains to the sea. The Sacramento River, the Los Angeles River, and all other rivers are on the move. But where does the water in rivers come from? And why don't rivers eventually run dry? Hydrologists call water's journey, from land to oceans and back to land, the water cycle. The key to the cyclical movement of water between land and sea is the repeated transformations between its solid, liquid, and gas forms.

Evaporation of ocean water can be considered the first step of the water cycle. Though we commonly think of the movement of water from liquid to gas as happening through boiling, the ocean doesn't boil (unless it's near volcanic vents like those in Hawaii and Iceland). Evaporation in the ocean occurs as a result of wind and solar radiation

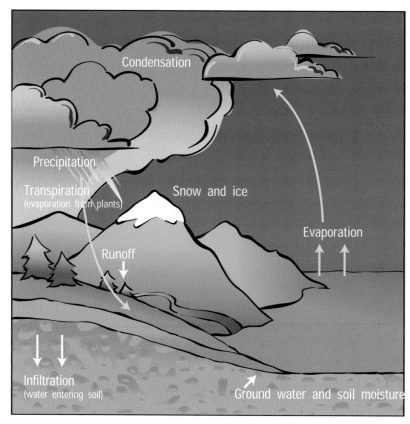

The water cycle is driven by energy from the sun. Copyright, University Corporation for Atmospheric Research

at a microscopic scale, and it occurs over an incredibly large area—recall that over two-thirds of Earth's surface is ocean. Once water is converted to a gas, it may rise, cool, condense into tiny droplets, and join with other tiny droplets, forming clouds. If the droplets continue to combine and get large and heavy enough, they will fall as rain or snow, depending on the air temperature. Most precipitation occurs over the ocean, but if wind blows clouds over land, there's a good chance that some of that water will fall on land as well.

Whether precipitation falls as rain or snow has important implications for the water cycle. In general, most rain that falls on land is absorbed into the ground. Lakes and rivers themselves cover only a

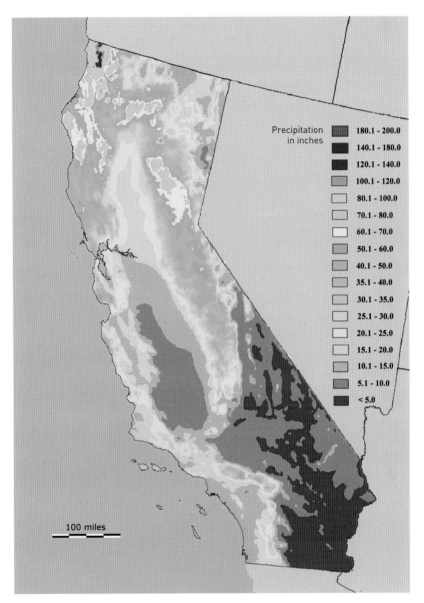

Precipitation in inches	
	180.1 - 200.0
	140.1 - 180.0
	120.1 - 140.0
	100.1 - 120.0
	80.1 - 100.0
	70.1 - 80.0
	60.1 - 70.0
	50.1 - 60.0
	40.1 - 50.0
	35.1 - 40.0
	30.1 - 35.0
	25.1 - 30.0
	20.1 - 25.0
	15.1 - 20.0
	10.1 - 15.0
	5.1 - 10.0
	< 5.0

100 miles

California precipitation. Annual average rainfall generally increases from south to north and decreases on the east side of mountain ranges (rain shadows). Modified from the *National Atlas*, 2005, US Geological Survey, www.nationalatlas.gov.

small fraction of the land surface, and physical processes such as sheet-flow—water physically moving across the surface as a sheet, rather than concentrated in a channel—are rare under natural conditions. Sheetflow is common in urban environments where roads and other impervious surfaces don't let water seep through, producing rapid runoff. Most water that reaches streams does so by traveling underground. When it rains, water soaks into the ground, through the soil and into groundwater-holding areas. However, groundwater bodies may be less permeable than the soil above, so water may accumulate in the soil as it slowly percolates downward. As the amount of water in the soil increases, the level of saturated soils (or the water table) rises. Eventually, the water table can reach the surface, filling low-lying pools and stream channels.

Approximately 60 percent of precipitation ends up in streams in a typical year. Some of the remaining water that does not convert to stream flow reaches deeper groundwater, and some is taken up by plants. The water taken up by plants in California is less, in general, than in other parts of the United States because most precipitation here occurs during the less biologically active season of lower temperatures and fewer hours of sunlight. A very small amount of water is consumed by animals, and some evaporates directly from rivers and lakes.

Most rainfall is converted to runoff relatively quickly, usually in less than a day, so elevated stream flow tends to occur on the same day as a rainfall event. As a result, the highest levels of stream flow occur during the rainy season (November to April), when precipitation is greatest in California.

Some fraction of the water that is not converted to runoff percolates through the subsurface and becomes groundwater. Think of dripping water onto a dry sponge. At first the water is all absorbed. When the sponge's water-holding capacity is full, water begins to drip out of the sponge. In this analogy, the sponge is soil and subsurface. Some water gets stored in bedrock, which includes the range of igneous, sedimentary, and metamorphic rocks below Earth's surface. These different types of bedrock have a wide range of permeability, which is the capacity of material to allow water to pass through. Bedrock with very low permeability acts as an aquiclude (a barrier to groundwater movement), and bedrock with relatively high permeability, such as sandstone and limestone, acts as an aquifer. Aquifers are of particular value because of their capacity to store and provide a water supply at a fast

North fork of the Garcia River, Mendocino County, June photo. Water level is low and will drop through October. In winter, when stream flow is highest, all the rocks in the photo would be submerged. Photo by Kerry Heise

enough rate to be beneficial for human use. Some types of volcanic rock are highly porous and may hold huge amounts of water in underground aquifers.

Snowfall is retained throughout the winter and generally is not converted to stream flow until spring and summer. Snowmelt tends to arrive in streams in late spring and summer when air temperatures are sufficient to melt snow. However, there can be an exception to this pattern when air temperatures are warm enough for precipitation to fall as rain at high elevations where snow is already on the ground. This phenomenon is termed a "rain-on-snow event." Snow covering the land acts as a barrier to absorption. In addition, the rain melts the snow, causing a doubling of effective precipitation; the rapid conversion of rainfall and snowmelt into stream flow tends to cause flooding both locally and in valleys downstream.

Most streams in California eventually run into the ocean, but not all: in some parts of the state, streams drain to low-lying basins, a fea-

Soda Lake, seen from the southwest flank of Little Cowhole Mountain, Mojave National Preserve, San Bernardino County. Photo by Stan Shebs, licensed under Creative Commons (CC-BY-SA-3.0-migrated) (commons.wikimedia.org/wiki/File:Mojave_Preserve_Soda_Dry_Lake_2.jpg)

ture of land-locked areas called internal (or endorheic) basins. This occurs almost exclusively in areas that can be technically defined as desert (areas having less than 10 inches of rain annually). These basins include the Mojave River which feeds the seasonal Soda Lake in San Bernardino County; the Owens River which historically fed Owens Lake in Inyo County; and Walker, Lee Vining, and Rush Creeks which feed Mono Lake.

Lakes in low-lying desert basins such as these are referred to as alkaline because of their high salt content. They have high salt concentrations because rainfall leaches salt from rocks and soil. When streams with any amount of salt, however tiny, run into an undrained basin, the salt accumulates. The alkaline Great Salt Lake in Utah is a result of this natural process. Several southern Central Valley rivers, including the Kern, Kaweah, and Kings, were historically disconnected from the ocean for all but the wettest years, when the entire valley could flood and connect these streams to ocean-going rivers to the north. Before the lower Central Valley was channelized and divided up into cropland, these rivers comprised much of the source of historical Tulare Lake, a low-lying chain of lakes south of the San Joaquin River that historically was only connected to the San Joaquin during the wettest of years. For this reason the south Central Valley is considered an alkaline basin.

Though the topography and geology of California generally does not lend itself to the formation of large natural lakes, there are a few, including Lake Tahoe, Clear Lake in Lake County, and Upper Klamath Lake (just to the north, in Oregon). Water reaching Upper Klamath Lake drains from over 3,800 square miles (an area larger than the entire Eel River watershed). From there the Klamath River continues to flow through Northern California, having drained a total area of over 12,000 square miles by the time it reaches the ocean.

Clear Lake is the largest natural lake located entirely in California, and thought to be the oldest lake in North America. Its outlet is the source of Cache Creek, which drains to the Sacramento Valley. Approximately 10,000 years ago, Clear Lake drained to the Russian River, before a landslide changed its course. Lake Tahoe is the source of the Truckee River, which flows east into a closed basin in western Nevada. Most naturally occurring lakes in California are much smaller than these three. Hundreds of tiny alpine lakes are nestled in mountain cirques across the high Sierra Nevada, Cascade, and Southern California mountains. Cirques (pronounced "serks") are bowl-shaped depressions carved by glaciers. The coastal mountains of California notably have very few natural lakes.

STREAM PROCESSES

Water that reaches a stream channel takes a gravity-driven journey that plays a significant role in shaping the physical and biological landscape. Rivers and creeks, collectively referred to as streams, vary considerably from the smallest rivulets in the mountains to the large, broad waterways that form complex estuaries when they reach the ocean. Whether as small tributary streams in mountain headwaters (the beginnings of streams) or reaches (any other stream segments) farther downstream in a broad river valley, streams have a number of important functions.

The particular characteristics of a stream are heavily influenced by features of its watershed. A watershed includes all of the land from which rain drains through a common stream point. Watersheds are sometimes referred to as catchments or drainage basins, both referring to the idea of water being "caught" as rain or snow and draining to a

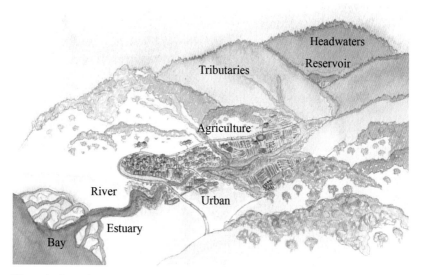

Watershed vocabulary: rain falls in the headwaters, runs from tributary streams into the mainstem river, which meets the estuary just before running through the bay into the ocean. Watercolor by Jenny McIlvaine for the Napa County Resource Conservation District

particular common point. Think of a bathtub with a single outlet; that is a watershed. When your shower water misses the tub and lands on the floor, it has moved into a different watershed! Small streams have small watersheds, but as two small streams join to make a larger one, the stream's watershed becomes larger as well.

Streams are classified based on their location and relative size in a river system. This classification system, termed stream order, designates small headwater streams as order 1 (first order) and the largest rivers as order 10 (tenth order). When two first-order streams meet, they form a second-order stream; when two second-order streams meet, they form a third-order stream, and so on. Stream order only increases when two streams of the *same* order meet; thus, a third-order stream meeting a second-order stream remains a third-order stream. As a result, a large stream increases in order only when an equally large stream joins it. Though it might be expected that large rivers in California would have large stream orders, the Russian River in northern coastal California is only sixth order, and the Sacramento River is only seventh order. The stream order system as applied today in California is based on streams identified by the US Geological Survey in the late nineteenth and early

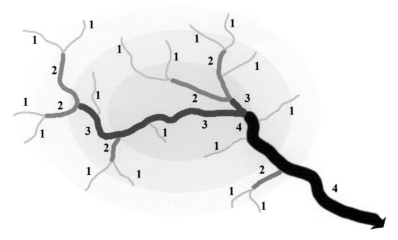

Stream order numeration: 1 = first order, 2 = second order, 3 = third order, and 4 = fourth order. When two first-order streams join, a second-order stream is formed; when two second-order streams meet, a third-order stream is formed, and so on.

twentieth centuries. Nationally rivers range from first order, with no branches, to tenth order, as represented by the Mississippi.

BIOLOGICAL INPUTS

A watershed provides more to its stream than just the water that falls within its boundaries. In addition to water, the watershed provides anything else that can be transported downstream by water. These inputs may be biological, chemical, or physical, and all are relevant to stream ecology.

The insects, fish, mammals, clams, and other animals that live in a stream reach (particular section of a stream) depend on biological inputs such as leaf litter as a food supply. These inputs can come downstream from uplands or from the immediate riparian zone—the transition area between the stream and the terrestrial habitats nearby. The riparian zone is frequently characterized by specialized plants and animals that rely on water from the stream to some extent, but there is a good deal of overlap between these species and those found in the uplands. Biological inputs also come from the ocean to a river! When salmon, lamprey, and other anadromous fish (fish that spend most of their lives in ocean habitats but migrate to freshwater for breeding) swim upstream, they bring energy and nutrients from the ocean to the river.

Invasive Species and Water Systems

Rivers and streams can act as transport systems for aquatic invasive species, allowing them to spread quickly throughout a watershed and into other river systems. The California Department of Fish and Game website neatly summarizes the problem: "State surveys of California's coastal waters have identified at least 312 species of aquatic invaders. These invaders cause major impacts: disrupting agriculture, shipping, water delivery, recreational and commercial fishing; undermining levees, docks and environmental restoration activities; impeding navigation and enjoyment of the state's waterways; and damaging native habitats and the species that depend on them."

A small sampling of aquatic invasive species to watch for, and prevent the spread of, in California include:

Water hyacinth: Introduced as an ornamental plant for water gardens, this plant can double the area it covers every 10 days in hot weather, clog slow-moving rivers, and blanket over 4,000 acres of the Sacramento-San Joaquin Delta in summer.

Hydrilla: Introduced from Asia as an aquarium plant, Hydrilla forms dense mats that clog waterways. It can reproduce from small fragments that are likely spread by recreational watercraft.

Bullfrog: This large aquatic frog is a voracious predator native to eastern North America. Bullfrogs eat many native aquatic species; sometimes this results in extirpation.

Largemouth bass: This fish native to the eastern United States has been introduced into most California rivers for sportfishing. It preys on native fish and amphibians, including endangered salmonids.

Nutria: This semiaquatic rodent was introduced from South America for fur farming. It escaped from the farms and has populated waters throughout North America. It disrupts riparian vegetation, undermines stream banks, and weakens levees.

Asian overbite clam: The clam is hermaphroditic and therefore can reproduce rapidly. It has been found at astonishing densities of up to 48,000 clams per cubic meter. The clam filters small food organisms and is responsible for declines in fish and shrimp populations in San Francisco Bay.

In addition to providing food, biological inputs from the riparian zone support other stream functions. Trees and branches that have died or have been loosened from the soil sufficiently to fall down a hillslope may end up in the stream; this material, called large woody debris, provides several important instream functions. For some organisms (e.g., for insects that pupate), it provides a substrate for growth or for undergoing life cycle changes. Equally important, it provides a source of nutrients as it breaks down and releases nitrogen, phosphorus, and other elements that aquatic organisms need to survive. Large woody debris also plays an important role in shaping the stream channel. As water moves around it, irregularities in the channel bed form. As water flows over the debris materials, the water scours deeper pools below them. The resulting pools and other variations in the channel shape provide places for smaller fish to hide from predators—protection that is necessary during high flows for fish and other animals at various stages of their life cycles. Maintaining and restoring large woody debris is essential for stream restoration because of the critical role it plays in shaping the channel and providing cover, shelter, and feeding opportunities for stream organisms.

CHEMICAL INPUTS

The chemical properties of water make it well suited for transporting ionic compounds (all together referred to as salts) as the stream moves from headwaters to lower reaches. Water can weather rocks both on and below the surface; in doing so, it can dissolve ionic compounds from rock surfaces it comes into contact with and carry the compounds downstream. This is the primary mechanism that makes desert lakes salty: streams that feed those lakes continuously carry ionic compounds to the lake. As the water evaporates each year, the weathered salts remain in the lake beds.

Other chemical inputs from the watershed have effects on stream ecology. Nutrients that are important for plant growth, such as phosphorus, nitrogen, and carbon, can be weathered from soil and bedrock. These nutrient inputs are autochthonous, meaning that they come from within the watershed. They are important for the growth of algae and other periphyton (simple organisms, sometimes referred to as biofilm, that attach to the bed of a stream), which provide the foundation for many aquatic food webs. These small organisms at the base of aquatic

Point Source and Nonpoint Source Water Pollution

A point source of pollution is pollution that originates from a specific spot, such as an oil refinery. Nonpoint source (often abbreviated NPS) pollution is what cumulatively comes from many scattered sources. When rain or snow falls, pollutants flow into natural waterways, ending up in streams, lakes, and rivers, which can affect drinking water, wildlife, fisheries, and recreation. Spilling just 1 quart of oil down a storm drain can contaminate 2 million gallons of freshwater. The EPA lists nonpoint pollutants as:

- Excess fertilizers, herbicides, and insecticides from agricultural lands and residential areas
- Oil, grease, and toxic chemicals from urban runoff and energy production
- Sediment from improperly managed construction sites, crop and forest lands, and eroding stream banks
- Salt from irrigation practices and acid drainage from abandoned mines
- Bacteria and nutrients from livestock, pet wastes, and faulty septic systems
- Atmospheric deposition and the alteration of the hydrologic characteristics of freshwater ecosystems, or hydromodification.

ecosystem food webs are an important food source for larger organisms such as small aquatic insects and other macroinvertebrates (animals that are large enough to see but that don't have vertebrae, or backbones). These primary consumers (plant eaters) serve in turn as food for larger organisms, including other insects, fish, and birds that turn to aquatic ecosystems for a food source.

A watershed may sometimes provide an unhealthy amount of nutrients to a stream or lake. Water bodies containing large amounts of nutrients are described by the word *eutrophic* (meaning "well fed," as opposed to *oligotrophic*, meaning "poorly fed") and are frequently characterized by large amounts of algae, other periphyton, or plants. Humans may contribute to nutrient loading in streams and lakes by applying fertilizer to crops or lawns, which may then be carried to streams and lakes. Eutrophic water bodies pose threats to aquatic ecosystems because periphyton and plants that accumulate in lakes eventually die and are decomposed. The bacteria responsible for their decomposition consume oxygen dissolved in the water, which can cause water bodies to become anoxic (without oxygen), meaning that oxygen levels fall below thresholds of tolerance for aquatic animals. In extreme cases, nutrient runoff can lead to dead zones. The Gulf of Mexico Dead Zone covers over 6,000 square miles and is formed each spring because of nutrients (especially phosphorous and nitrogen from fertilizers, sewage, and animal wastes) that run off from farms in the Mississippi River watershed. For more on dead zones see Chapter 7.

PHYSICAL INPUTS

Physical material inputs to a stream play an important role in creating and changing the shape of a stream channel, and in organizing the size and distribution of stream surfaces that support many ecological processes. Geologists and geomorphologists refer to all loose minerals and rock in the river as sediment (the contrast to sediment is bedrock). Sediment refers to a range of size classes, from large boulders to fine silt. Sediments are delivered to streams through two mechanisms: alluvial forces and colluvial forces. Alluvial sediment (or alluvium) is material that has been moved by water, for example, during high-flow events, when channel bed materials are carried downstream by the force of flowing water. High flows may also erode the banks of the channel, taking material previously not in the stream and moving it downstream as alluvium.

Colluvium is sediment that reaches the streams by gravity but not by water. Most commonly, colluvium enters the stream channel through hillslope failures (also termed shallow landslides), when fine and coarse materials (soil and rocks), along with vegetation attached to them, fall into the stream. Rocky materials, such as large boulders that have been fractured and loosened from the bedrock, can enter the stream by colluvial forces but may be too large to be moved by the stream. These boulders are great for climbing or sitting on during the dry season. Frequently, landslides produce a large amount of material that emerges from the rest and forms a "toe" where the landslide meets the river, just like our toes emerge from the base of our feet. Landslide toes may push the creek to the opposite side of the channel or fill the channel completely, causing the stream to begin a search for the weakest or lowest portion of the filled channel to begin carving a new path.

The power of water is ominous and often underestimated. Most material moved by rivers, actually about 90 percent, is suspended in

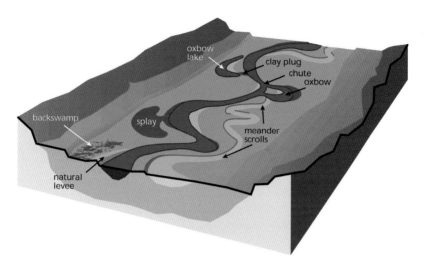

River vocabulary: rivers move in characteristic ways, creating predictable landform patterns, including oxbows and chutes, oxbow lakes, levees, meander scrolls, and backswamps. From *Stream Corridor Restoration: Principles, Processes, and Practices*, Federal Interagency Stream Restoration Working Group (FISRWG), October 1998

the water. This suspended load can be composed of various materials, including fine sediment that gives high-flowing rivers a muddy appearance. The other 10 percent is bedload, the material that bounces along the streambed. Bedload includes coarse cobble (technically material ranging up to 360 millimeters in size), finer gravels, and sand, as well as boulders that roll along the channel bed under very-high-flow conditions. Next time you're near a boulder-strewn river or stream, listen for cobble movement. Especially during high-flow events, you may hear cobbles and boulders bouncing along the streambed as bedload!

Though colluvial processes are considered distinct from alluvial ones, hillslope failures generally result from events in which colluvial and alluvial processes coincide. High-flow events that erode the stream channel may undercut hillslopes, causing them to destabilize. Here again we see the incredible force of water from its ability to undermine the stability of whole hillsides. Additionally, hillslope failures often occur when soil is saturated with water, such as during or following a heavy rainfall; hillslopes become much heavier when saturated with water and may become unstable. An underlying principal of hillslope and stream channel erosion is that erosion is a natural process: without erosion, there would be no sediment. Problems can arise, however, when the rates of erosion increase due to land-use activities and more sediment is produced than can be moved downstream by natural alluvial processes. Too much fine sediment in stream reaches can present problems for aquatic organisms that are dependent on clear water and substrate for habitat. For example, in the Elkhorn Slough watershed, upland agriculture led to increased sediment transport between farms and the marsh, burying native pickleweed (*Salicornia virginica*). Restoration including native vegetation planting, water diversions, construction of water and sediment control basins, and stream channel stabilization resulted in pickleweed marsh recovery.

THE PATH OF A RIVER

The path of a river, from its headwaters as a first-order stream to its outlet, most commonly the ocean, is a complex one. Though most rivers in California run through broad valleys (such as the Sacramento, San Joaquin, Salinas, Los Angeles, and Santa Maria), the majority of a river's drainage network, by length, is found in the headwaters. For example, more than 75 percent of the Russian River drainage network, in northern coastal California, is composed of first- and second-order streams. For perspective, these streams may range from 8 to 15 feet wide. These river headwaters are commonly in mountain canyons or narrow valleys, where rivers have little room to meander and cut a channel through alluvium. The term for streams whose pathways are limited by canyon walls is *confined*. Confined streams are not always small; for example, the lower Klamath River, which drains more than 10,000 square miles, runs mostly as a confined stream as it passes through the Klamath Mountains in northwestern California.

The Klamath River is an exception, however. Most rivers across the globe are oriented with headwaters in mountains and then valleys in their downstream portions. Geologists and geomorphologists, frequently thinking about earth-shaping processes over the long term, often refer to valleys along the lower portions of rivers as alluvial valleys, where most of the material filling the valleys has been generated in the mountains farther upstream. Many of the valleys of California formed as long ago as the Pleistocene epoch (2.6 million to 11,700 years ago).

Rivers that run through alluvial valleys are unconfined by mountain walls. They can cut meandering paths through their valleys by eroding banks in places where water moves swiftly (called erosion zones) and

Mouth of the Klamath River in June. The sandbar nearly
blocking the mouth of the river changes shape continuously.
During winter high flows it would be far less prominent.
Courtesy of the US Army Corps of Engineers

then re-depositing alluvium in slower portions of the river (deposition
zones). Like landslides, erosion of river channels is a natural process, as
you can see when flying over any river valley. By air, it's easy to see old
sections of meandering stream channel that may not have been occupied by the river for thousands of years. Recently abandoned segments
of river channel may still fill with water and have aquatic vegetation.
We call these abandoned channels oxbow lakes. Areas abandoned longer ago may be of lower elevation and be marked by darker land features due to the fact that former river substrate holds more water than
nonriver land nearby.

In addition to meandering stream channels, rivers running through
alluvial valleys commonly have clearly defined floodplains with riparian vegetation. As the name implies, floodplains are areas that are inundated by water during floods; vegetation comprising a river's riparian
zone is generally adapted to the frequency of flooding, which varies
relative to its distance from and height above the channel. Trees such
as willows, alders, and cottonwoods may be able to withstand, and
in some cases require, regular annual flooding to populate the floodplain near the river itself. Other trees with lower tolerance for flooding, including ash, maple, and some types of oak, may be present in
the floodplain at greater distances from and heights above the stream
channel.

The inundation of floodplains has other important implications for river ecosystems. Water spilling onto a floodplain moves much slower than water in a river channel. As a result, very fine sediment (or silt) in the water has the opportunity to settle on the floodplain. This silt contains nutrients that support aquatic plants and animals, so floodplains provide very productive habitat for native fish rearing, and they make productive farmland. The largest trees usually grow in the deep, rich, well-watered soil of floodplains. Today we see the permanent use of floodplains by agriculture throughout California: over 90 percent of floodplain habitat in the Central Valley has been converted to agriculture. There are now attempts to restore floodplains to their original periodic flooding pattern to help recover salmon and other native species.

The large amounts of sediment gathered from confined reaches of a stream are often too great to continue moving downstream once the stream reaches an alluvial valley; as a result, sediment builds up and forms an alluvial fan, so named because it tends to be fan shaped. It is highest near the stream at the base of the mountain slopes and gets lower moving away from the channel and into the valley.

ESTUARIES

An estuary is a semi-enclosed mixing zone where a river meets the ocean. From a chemical perspective, estuaries tend to have a lower concentration of salt water than the ocean, allowing many organisms in estuaries to be either primarily salt-water dwelling or primarily freshwater dwelling but capable of tolerating both. Some organisms in estuaries, such as pickleweed, are specialized to the moderate salinity found in neither freshwater rivers nor the ocean. You can taste the salt in pickleweed if you take a bite. Nutrient inputs from land and constant mixing by tides make estuaries among the most productive of aquatic ecosystems. In an estuary you can see a mix of wildlife from the ocean, the river, and the terrestrial habitat. River otters and mergansers mix with seals and pelicans as osprey circle overhead.

While many lakes and rivers are eutrophic, the ocean is generally considered oligotrophic; in fact, the absence of nutrients in the ocean is a primary reason why the ocean appears to be blue. Alpine lakes, like Lake Tahoe, Donner Lake, and Convict Lake, are blue because they are oligotrophic. Estuaries are generally not blue. The brown and green is as much a result of biological production as it is of the silt and sediment the river carries to the ocean. Although oceans in general are oligotrophic, the nearshore ocean off of California is enriched by upwelling.

Gualala estuary, Mendocino County. The meandering course of the Gualala River estuary is the mixing zone for freshwater from the river and salt water from the ocean. Photo © 2002 P.T. Nunn

Upwelling happens when deep currents rise to the surface and bring up nutrients from the deep that support rich aquatic food chains including fish, birds, and mammals.

The dynamics of salinity in estuaries can vary according to several factors. The tides affect salt concentrations at any given point throughout the day. At high tide, estuaries tend to be more saline because oceans force salt water up the estuary and may even push back freshwater to a location farther inland. During low tide, freshwater can extend farther toward the ocean, providing the nutrients and other matter from the watershed to the estuary. The salinity of estuaries also varies seasonally. During periods of higher river flow, such as the California wet season, estuaries may become dominated by freshwater and silt delivered after storm events. The salinity of a particular location in the estuary may also vary with depth: because salt water is more dense than freshwater, it may settle below freshwater and create a vertical salinity gradient. Therefore, the species that inhabit estuaries must be able to tolerate a wide range of salinity.

Some estuaries are marked by deposition of large amounts of sediment and referred to as deltas. Deltas are formed by processes similar to those that make alluvial fans: large amounts of sediment are carried to a point where they can no longer be transported, resulting in a depositional formation shaped like the Greek letter *delta*, which is a triangle. The amount of material a stream carries depends on its speed and volume. When its speed drops to zero on entering a lake or estuary, its carrying capacity disappears and the sediments are deposited immediately.

INTERTIDAL ZONE

As rivers reach the ocean, whether by passing through an estuary or by falling down from a coastal bluff, the freshwater of the river merges with the salt water of the ocean. All along the California coast, from Mexico to Oregon, the environment nearest the shore is called the intertidal zone. California's is strikingly beautiful, composed of over 3,000 miles of tidal shoreline, including beaches, piers, bluffs, rocky coves, ports, and harbors. California residents have a long history of fighting for public access, so today we can all enjoy much of our coastline. The vast majority of Californians live within 30 miles of the coast, and billions of dollars of economic activity depends on coastal resources, including tourism, recreation, fishing, shipping, and commercial and residential development.

The intertidal zone is characterized by high energy. Anyone who has visited the seashore along California's Pacific coast will be familiar with this idea. Waves constantly break upon the shore, whether on a sandy beach or a rocky headland. Waves pound the shore delivering energy continuously. This pounding is one of the defining features of the intertidal zone, and all organisms living in the intertidal zone must adapt to it, from sea stars to urchins to anemones. Two common adaptations are a hard exoskeleton (also known as a shell) and the ability to adhere to rocks.

High energy has both positive and negative attributes. Waves may carry sand or rocks which erode or crush the shells of even well-protected organisms such as whelks. Waves also bring a fresh supply of highly oxygenated water which may also be high in nutrients. The intertidal environment can be very harsh. The costs (dangers) of life in the intertidal zone are great, but these rich environments are filled with food, making it worthwhile for species to inhabit these areas and adapt to the forces of nature.

The second physical factor that characterizes the intertidal zone is the rise and fall of the tides. The moon orbits the Earth, and the Earth orbits the sun, and the gravitational tug of the moon and sun causes two bulges in the planet's oceans, or its hydrosphere. As the Earth spins through its 24-hour rotational cycle, any point on the Earth passes through these bulges twice each day. The result is the rise and fall of tides. The effect of rising and falling water levels on organisms living in the intertidal zone is intense. They must adapt to life underwater and to life exposed to dry air and full sun! Intertidal organisms must be both aquatic and terrestrial! They may be attacked by aquatic and terrestrial predators, round stingrays and raccoons! The other limit tidal cycles impose on intertidal organisms is that their food source may be missing for half the day! Many intertidal organisms are filter feeders. They stretch a web or net that floats in the water and traps nutrients, or they pump water through their body cavities like the Pacific razor clam and filter out nutrients inside their shells. In either case, when the organisms are exposed to air rather than to water, no feeding is possible.

The shoreline of California is rich in habitat diversity. A couple of factors that help naturalists to see the distinctions in seashore habitat are substrate and position (depth). *Substrate* refers to the physical composition of the shore. It may vary from fine mud in an intertidal estuary, to coarse sand on a sandy beach, to cobbles or boulders, to bedrock on exposed headlands, and it may include combinations of these. The group of organisms that inhabits mudflats in an estuary is almost completely different from the group that lives on rocky cliffs exposed to the tides. *Tidal zone* on the shore, relative to the tide elevation, refers to water depth. *Tidal flux* refers to the difference in water level between high tide and low tide (high tide level minus low tide level, typically measured in feet). If the tidal flux is 1 foot and the tidal cycle takes 12 hours (to go from high tide to low tide to high tide), the point highest on the shore is exposed for about 11 hours and the lowest point may be exposed for only a few minutes. Positions are often described using terms like *spray zone* (*splash zone*), *upper intertidal zone, middle intertidal zone, lower intertidal zone,* and *subtidal zone.*

The intertidal zone is a place of fascination and wonder, with organisms that appear to our terrestrial eyes both bizarre and beautiful. If you spend time in the intertidal zone, you may see a clam spit a jet of water 3 feet in the air; have an anemone grab your finger with mobile, Velcro-like tentacles; or come across the sea clown nudibranch, a white "sea slug" with red bumps and projections that looks ready for use in the *Star Wars* movies. The intertidal zone provides multiple ecosystem functions, including foraging and nesting habitat for birds and mating sites for elephant seals. This zone is also highly vulnerable to damage from oil spills, invasive species, and pollution, and it will be among the most affected by climate change as sea levels rise.

WETLANDS

Wetlands are transitional zones between land and water that are inundated with water periodically. Among the several types of wetlands are marshes, bogs, vernal pools, swamps, baylands, salt marsh, and riparian areas. Keep in mind that not all wetlands are freshwater. Some have high salt concentrations and support an entirely different suite of species, such as shrimp, mollusks, and pickleweed. A large number of native aquatic plants can be observed in wetlands. Pond lilies, cattails, sedges, bulrush, and arrowhead are a few examples. On a rainy day or spring evening it's hard to ignore the loud call of California tree frogs coming from vernal pools and wetlands. In addition to frogs, other amphibians and also reptiles and waterfowl depend on wetlands. Prior to the conversion of most of California's wetlands, there were herds of elk, flocks of birds that darkened the sky, and grizzly bears along the shores, and mussels, oysters, salmon, and sea otters were abundant in the water.

Wetlands provide the following ecosystem functions, processes, and services, as identified by the California Resources Agency:

- *Biological diversity*: Wetlands provide important habitat for diverse communities of plants and animals, including over 50 percent of the federally listed threatened or endangered species in California.
- *Waterfowl habitat*: Wetlands provide the principal habitat for migratory waterfowl (birds associated with water). California wetlands provide critical wintering habitat for millions of waterfowl migrating along the Pacific Flyway, which extends from Canada to Mexico.
- *Fisheries*: Wetlands provide spawning and rearing habitats and food supply that supports both freshwater and marine fisheries.

- *Flood control*: Wetlands detain flood flows, reducing the size and destructiveness of floods.
- *Water quality*: Wetlands absorb and filter pollutants that could otherwise degrade groundwater or the water quality of rivers, lakes, and estuaries.
- *Groundwater recharge*: Some wetlands recharge aquifers that provide urban and agricultural water supplies.
- *Recreation*: Wetlands support a multi-million-dollar fishing, hunting, and outdoor recreation industry nationwide.

Despite these benefits, wetlands in California have been under pressure for many years. Historically, wetlands were viewed as dumping grounds and pest-ridden bogs to be drained, filled, and developed. For example, the San Francisco Estuary, the largest estuary on the West Coast, has lost nearly 97 percent of its historic wetlands and is one of the most invaded estuaries in North America. Like the intertidal zone, estuaries and other wetlands are vulnerable to rising sea levels, invasive species, nonpoint source pollution, and conflicts over water use and development.

CALIFORNIA'S LAKES

Lakes support a myriad of plant and animal species which mostly can be found in the littoral zone. The littoral zone is found at the top of a lake or pond and receives the most sunlight. Thanks to the energy from the sun, this zone can support a diverse biological community, including several species of algae (like diatoms), rooted and floating aquatic plants, grazing snails, clams, insects, crustaceans, fish, and amphibians. Dragonflies and midge eggs and larvae hang out here. Many of these species are important foods for turtles, snakes, and ducks.

California has some of the most unusual lakes in North America. Lake Tahoe, nestled near the crest of the Sierra Nevada, is the tenth deepest lake in the world and the second deepest in the United States. It is famed for its blueness, clarity, and alpine surroundings. Since 1959, Lake Tahoe has lost one-third of its remarkable transparency, and algal growth has increased by about 5 percent per year. Small particles of dust and sediment remain suspended in the water column for years, adding to the gradual but relentless transparency loss. Air pollution is a factor; nitrogen pollution of the lake from atmospheric deposition is

Lake Tahoe, a unique alpine lake, sits at 6,225 feet altitude and is 1,645 feet deep.
Photo by Adina Merenlender

greater than from stream water input! These changes have resulted in fewer native fish and an increase in exotic fish that can tolerate warmer and more polluted waters. Warming of Lake Tahoe due to surrounding land use as well as climate change presents a real threat to this unusual ecosystem. There is, however, growing public understanding of the value of this unique natural resource and a desire to protect the lake from further degradation.

CALIFORNIA'S FRESHWATER FISH

California's large size, complex topography, and geographic variability have given rise to a diverse assemblage of native freshwater fish species, many of which are endemic to (occurring only in) the state. A total of 129 native freshwater fish taxa are recognized in California. California has both anadromous fish, such as salmon and lamprey that migrate long distances between marine and freshwater environments, and resident fish species that thrive in isolated desert springs, intermittent streams, and alkaline lakes. However, in comparison to riv-

Mono Lake: An Important Case Study

Mono Lake is an alkali lake in a closed basin east of the Sierra Nevada. Photo by Kerry Heise.

Mono Lake is a unique natural resource in California and the rest of the world. The lake evolved as a hydrologically closed basin, having no ocean outlet. Estimated to be 1 million years old, it is a remnant of the much larger ice-age Lake Russell. Early in the twentieth century, the City of Los Angeles bought up vast tracts of land with their riparian water rights—which allow use of the stream's water on adjoining land—in the Owens Valley and the Mono Basin, which lies north of the valley. In about 1913 the Los Angeles Department of Water and Power (LADWP) began exporting these waters for urban use via an aqueduct system to Southern California. While this project

(continued)

ers of the eastern United States, rivers in California support a smaller number of fish species. This is a consequence of the harsh environment in which California's fish fauna evolved. The region has been subject to dramatic climate variation, including periods of glaciation and prolonged droughts. On an annual basis, streams in California fluctuate considerably from raging torrents in the wet season to dry or low-flowing trickles in the dry season. The species that have persisted was certainly an engineering marvel and provided Los Angeles with high-quality, inexpensive water, it also led to the demise of agriculture and components of the natural ecosystem in the Owens Valley.

Owens Lake dried down as sections of the Owens River channel were left dry and tributary streams were dammed and diverted. Mono Lake was also altered as the level of Mono Lake dropped from an elevation of 6,417 feet to 6,372 feet—a decrease of approximately 45 feet. The iconic tufa towers of Mono Lake became highly visible only after lake levels dropped. The associated increased salinity threatened the productivity of the brine shrimp population and associated phytoplankton. In addition, the drop in lake levels caused the loss of the hard-bottom habitat that is critical for the alkali fly. Mono Lake's brine shrimp and alkali flies are critical food resources for many migratory and breeding birds such as the California gull and snowy plover.

The environmental community recognized the deterioration in Mono Lake and the surrounding areas and worked together to stop this legal diversion of water by Los Angeles. Prompted in 1976 by student research findings showing severe impacts of water diversions on the Mono Basin ecosystem, students, scientists, and other conservation-minded individuals undertook a massive, grassroots effort, "Save Mono Lake." Litigation ensued in the form of suits filed under the Public Trust Doctrine (in 1979) and the California Fish and Game Code (in 1985).

After many years in court and the establishment of the region as the Mono Lake National Scenic Area under congressional directive, the State Water Resources Control Board in September 1994 issued an order (Decision 1631) to reduce greatly LADWP's diversions of water from the Mono Basin and restore the lake to an elevation of 6,392 feet, a level last seen in 1964. This level was a compromise that would achieve several, but not all, ecosystem health objectives.

Adapted from Deborah Elliot-Fiske, 1995. "Mono Lake Compromise: A Model for Conflict Resolution." *California Agriculture*.

demonstrate a range of local adaptations to thrive under these variable and often stressful conditions. For example, several species of pupfish persist in the few streams and pools found in California's southeastern deserts, despite extreme water temperature and salinity levels. Thus, while relatively low in species *richness* (the total number of species), there is high diversity in morphology, behavior, and life history patterns in California's fish fauna.

The transformation of California's landscape throughout the nineteenth and twentieth centuries from mining, farming, and population growth has led to dramatic declines in freshwater fish populations. About 83 percent of California's native freshwater fish species are extinct or endangered. The decline in native fish fauna has been caused by a wide range of human activities, including dams, water diversion, habitat modification, and introduction of nonnative species. Many of California's rivers have been dammed or diverted. Dams disrupt connectivity within river networks, prevent the migration of salmon, and isolate fish populations above dams. Dams and diversions also alter the natural flow regime of rivers, reducing or eliminating peak flows, artificially enhancing summer flows, and changing cold-water rivers to rivers with warm-water conditions.

The loss and modification of freshwater habitat is another challenge to California fish fauna. The alterations to river corridors by land-use conversion, flood protection infrastructure, and riparian vegetation removal have altered habitats and natural ecosystem processes that native fish depend on. The Sacramento-San Joaquin Delta was once an enormous tule marsh with meandering rivers providing excellent habitat for rearing juvenile salmon and other native fish. It has been largely drained for farmlands protected by levees along dredged river channels. The Los Angeles River now flows for 50 miles within a concrete-lined channel. Virtually all forested watersheds in Northern California have been altered by massive sediment runoff caused by logging and hydraulic mining.

At least 50 nonnative freshwater fish species have been introduced in California and have had widespread negative effects on the state's native fish through hybridization, predation, competition, and disease. Most introductions of nonnative fish were deliberate attempts to improve sportfishing or aquaculture, although accidental introductions of aquarium fish have occurred. The introduction of fish and invertebrates from the ballast water in cargo ships is a growing problem, and many refer to the San Francisco Bay as the "most invaded estuary in the world." The success of introduced aquatic species in California is associated with modifications of aquatic habitats: nonnative species thrive in artificial reservoirs, drainage canals, and regulated rivers. A dramatic example is the Russian River. An interbasin hydroelectric diversion from the Eel River has changed the Russian River from a flashy, cold-water, intermittent stream with renowned steelhead runs to a perennial, warm-water river with abundant introduced warm-water species. The Russian used to dry up every summer! Its slow summer meander now makes it an inner-tuber's paradise, although the fabled steelhead runs are on their last legs.

Based on current trends, much of California's native fish fauna is likely to disappear in the next century. Because many of California's fish are endemic, their extinction would represent a significant loss of global biodiversity. The need for freshwater ecosystem restoration and conservation planning is critical. The multifaceted and complex causes of fish population declines require that freshwater conservation measures be integrated with water management and land-use planning.

RIVERS TODAY

Over the past several thousand years, humans have changed rivers in many important ways. Natural river processes are seen as hurdles to human development; most notably, humans are averse to flooding and drought. To prevent flood damage, people build levees, usually earthen walls along riverbanks to prevent the river from spilling onto the floodplain. Levees disrupt the natural process of flooding and the deposition of sediment and nutrients on the floodplain, and they threaten the survival of organisms that depend on periodic inundation. Levees are not a permanent solution, and over time, levees degrade and break, especially during high-stream-flow events.

Dams provide more reliable protection from flooding than levees do. They have greater impact on natural ecological processes, as well. Rather than keeping water in the channel from spilling onto the floodplain, a dam prevents water from flowing into the channel altogether. In doing so, a dam completely alters the river's natural flow regime, which the organisms living in it have adapted to. Changing a stream's natural flow regime can change its shape, the type and size of sediment accumulating in the riverbed, the type of fish and other aquatic life that can be supported, and the type of plants found along the river. Like levees, dams are not permanent. Many dams in California are filling in with sediment and now store only a small volume of water, relative to their original capacity.

As patterns of floodplain land use have changed over time, dams have become increasingly important for preserving human settlements and infrastructure. An example is Folsom Dam, which regulates flow in the American River and protects the city of Sacramento from flooding. While providing flood protection, these dams alter the *magnitude* of

Shasta Dam. Courtesy of the US Bureau of Reclamation

high-flow events. Water stored behind dams can also be released at different times than would naturally occur, affecting the *timing* of flow. For example, if dams are also managed for agricultural purposes, as many dams in California now are, water may be stored in a reservoir behind the dam throughout the wet season, for release as needed by farmers in the dry season. Some large dams also have large diversion channels operated by irrigation districts to distribute water to farmers, such as the Friant-Kern and Madera Canals, which divert water from the San Joaquin River stored behind Friant Dam. Similar diversions are operated for municipal drinking water, as are the Coyote reservoir in Mendocino County, Hennessey reservoir in Napa County, and Hetch Hetchy reservoir in Yosemite National Park. Other dams function primarily for power generation, such as those on Iron Gate, Copco, and Boyle reservoirs on the Klamath River along the Oregon-California border.

Once a vast tidal marsh, the Sacramento-San Joaquin Bay-Delta is now a key center of water supply linkages, transportation infrastructure, and agricultural productivity in California. Where the Sacramento and San Joaquin Rivers meet, the Bay-Delta begins, establishing the eastern boundary of the San Francisco Estuary, the West Coast's largest estuary. The Bay-Delta provides drinking water for 25 million

Californians, and it supports irrigation supplies for a $27 billion agricultural industry. The Bay-Delta harbors 57 major reclaimed islands, 1,100 miles of levees, and hundreds of thousands of acres of marshes, mudflats, and farmland, making the entire system hydraulically, ecologically, economically, and socially complex. Land subsidence, sea level rise, earthquake risk, development, and ecosystem degradation now threaten the benefits the Delta provides.

More than 700 plant and animal species, some unique to this system, are dependent on the Bay-Delta. For avid bird-watchers this extensive estuary provides ideal viewing of waterfowl species, and many species stop to feed and rest as they pass along the Pacific Flyway. The Delta once supported some of the state's largest fisheries, and many people are working to bring back winter- and spring-run Chinook salmon (*Oncorhynchus tshawytscha*), Central Valley steelhead (*Oncorhynchus mykiss irideus*), delta smelt (*Hypomesus transpacificus*), Sacramento splittail (*Pogonichthys macrolepidotus*), and southern green sturgeon (*Acipenser medirostris*). Invasive species now pose a threat to native populations in the Bay-Delta, however, as the estuary has experienced the arrival of more than 250 alien aquatic and plant species.

Management in the Bay-Delta traditionally addressed a multitude of purposes, including water supply, flood control, irrigation, power production, and navigation. The federal Central Valley Project and State Water Project comprise the two major California water development systems that use dams and canals to store and distribute water, generally from Northern California sources to Southern California cities and San Joaquin Valley farmers. California's 2009 Delta Reform Act requires future water management policy to address newly coequal goals: to improve water supply reliability and to protect, restore, and enhance the Delta ecosystem. Today's efforts to restore Bay-Delta ecology require large multiagency coordinated planning efforts. Some have proposed bold plans for a peripheral canal, which would ship water around the Delta from the Sacramento River to the southern part of the state. If implemented properly (i.e., with no net increase in water diversion), the peripheral canal could increase flow conditions in the Delta, which would benefit some endangered species. Changes in salinity levels in the Bay-Delta resulting from management decisions for a new canal might negatively affect biota and agricultural uses, however, so the peripheral canal proposal is controversial. Still, the peripheral canal debate highlights the need for long-term planning and policy setting for the region and for the state.

Six Ways You Can Prevent Water Pollution

- Never throw anything down storm drains.
- Avoid using chemical herbicides, fertilizers, and insecticides. Use natural alternatives instead.
- Properly dispose of household hazardous wastes, including batteries, paint thinner, motor oil, and drain and oven cleaners. Never pour these products down any drain or toilet or discard them with regular household trash. Contact your local disposal company to find out where to take these products.
- Repair ranch roads using methods that reduce erosion. Your local Resource Conservation District can provide help.
- Keep livestock away from water sources, and clean up after your pet.
- Leave buffer strips of vegetation along waterways to filter pollutants and improve fish habitat, and revegetate where necessary with native vegetation.

In addition to the dozens of large dams in California that store water for irrigation, drinking, and power generation, thousands of small reservoirs speckle the California landscape. Small reservoirs are commonly designed to supply a landowner or property manager with a supply of water for that given property, removing the need for reliance on a water agency or irrigation district. Many such reservoirs are located on small streams, first order or even smaller. In California, these streams generally flow during the wet season and flow very little, if at all, during the dry season. Because they are designed for an individual property, they are generally composed of earthen fill and do not have capacity to release water until they are filled, at which time they overflow into the channel.

Because it stores a small amount of water relative to the overall discharge of a larger drainage network and is on a small stream, a small reservoir on a headwater stream may not have as much adverse impact to stream processes as a dam on a larger channel farther downstream. But several small reservoirs operating together may have substantial cumulative effects, causing a greater impact than a single reservoir could have alone. Together, they may withhold enough water to significantly reduce the discharge in a creek that salmon or steelhead need for spawning and rearing. The abundant small dams on tiny headwater streams also alter habitat by providing water sources in an otherwise summer-dry environment. Invasive species like feral pigs and bullfrogs are aided greatly by these water sources.

CALIFORNIA WATER MANAGEMENT AND LAW

The management of water resources is one of the greatest challenges facing officials in the state of California today: we must meet the demands of a growing population and a sizable agricultural economy while maintaining the sustainability of aquatic ecosystems. Today, efforts are underway to ensure that the means to acquire water to meet human needs preserve both the quality and quantity of stream ecosystems across the state. Adding to the problem are uncertainties surrounding future climate change that may change the timing and amount of water availability as well as result in increased demand.

Since it became a state in 1850, California has granted people the right to take water from streams for beneficial uses. The right to divert water from surface water bodies is overseen by a complex system of rules that combines two basic doctrines of water rights: the riparian doctrine and the doctrine of prior appropriation, which together are called the California doctrine. Under the doctrine of prior appropriation, water users follow a prioritization of diversion according to seniority; under the riparian doctrine, water users divert as needed, in proportion to what is available during times of shortage. The right of people to divert water from streams is overseen by the State Water Resources Control Board (SWRCB). Though the SWRCB has had the power to oversee diversion of stream flow since the 1910s, it does not have the ability to oversee the pumping of groundwater, except in cases where groundwater is in clear and definite connection with surface water. Areas not served by irrigation districts rely more heavily on riparian and appropriative doctrines because, in addition to groundwater resources that may or may not be available, they provide water security for residential and agricultural uses.

The criteria used to determine whether a water right can be granted have changed over the past few decades. Many of these changes came about because the law now includes ecosystem functions as a beneficial use of water equal to other uses, such as for agriculture and cities. For example, water needed to provide habitat for fish is now considered a beneficial use. This means that in some cases water rights can be exercised only if enough water is left in the stream to provide conditions necessary for fish to survive. Some of these cases are further

Water Conservation: More than a Drop in the Bucket

Every person can do a huge amount to conserve water. Watering yards and washing cars often use the lion's share of our household water, so they are good places to start.

- Use trickle irrigation to water your lawn rather than a sprinkler, and water at dawn or dusk. Water deeply and less frequently.
- Replace water-hungry lawns with native grasses, xeriscaping, or vegetable gardens.
- Don't wash your car at home. Use car washes, which have the filtration systems necessary to keep detergent from entering storm drains.
- Fix leaks, take short showers, and wash only full loads of clothes and dishes.
- Use the garbage disposal sparingly, if at all. Compost vegetable food waste instead to save gallons of water.

complicated by federal laws to protect endangered species, which provide additional protections of specific instream flow conditions. In the 1980s, the California Supreme Court also decided that the State Water Resources Control Board had to consider the public interest in preserving natural resources when granting water rights permits. The legal recognition of public trust resources was the foundation for restoring water to Mono Lake (see Mono Lake: An Important Case Study).

CHALLENGES FOR THE FUTURE: POPULATION GROWTH AND CLIMATE CHANGE

One of the largest questions regarding California water is how the dynamics of stream processes will change as Earth's climate changes and as population grows. As our population grows, our need for water will increase. California's population is estimated to grow from 37 million to more than 50 million by 2050, leading to increased demand for urban and agricultural water supply. Population growth will require an additional 5.9 to 7.4 million acre-feet of water per year by 2030, if agricultural use remains constant. Current sources of water are not secure; the Colorado River supply for California is expected to decline and "environmental water uses" are likely to continue to compete with domestic and agricultural uses. There are several options available to help balance water use with supply in California in the immediate future. These include urban conservation measures, increased efficiency in agriculture, underground storage in groundwater basins, increased surface storage, recycling of municipal water, desalination, and reduction in losses from canals and conveyance.

There is substantial uncertainty regarding how climate change will affect hydrology in California. California encompasses many climates, from the very wet temperate forests of the north coastal ranges to the arid deserts of the southeast. How warmer temperatures will affect rainfall and stream flow patterns in each of these areas is difficult to predict. However, climatologists and hydrologists generally agree that we can expect greater variability and more extreme hydrologic events over time, including larger floods and more severe droughts. Greater climate variability has implications for aquatic biota, such as riparian communities dependent on floodplain processes which are structured by the frequency and depth of inundation. Water quality may also be affected by global climate change because of more intense rainfall events and increases in runoff and sedimentation.

Despite uncertainty, scientists generally agree that warmer temperatures will have major impacts on California's water supply. Warmer temperatures will increase the percentage of precipitation that occurs as rain rather than as snow. More rainfall and less snow will shift the timing of flows, from snowmelt yielding water from April through September to rain events from November through March. In this case, reservoirs would fill earlier and have to release water during the wet season. Managers would have to release water before the growing season or early in the growing season. Those releases would no longer be replenished by snowmelt. Even if the same amount of annual discharge from the mountains occurs, a shift from snowmelt to rain with anticipated climate change is likely to reduce the amount of water available for agriculture in much of the state.

In recent years, discussions about how to adapt to meet our future water needs have become more urgent. New dams have been suggested; some of these would occupy sites that have been proposed in the past, and others would be in new locations previously unplanned. Still others call for reducing water use and increasing efficiency by reconstructing decades-old leaky channels and shifting from thirsty crops to those that need less water or produce larger financial benefit with smaller yields.

How California deals with these pressures, and others as yet unanticipated, remains to be seen. Just as it is uncertain precisely how flow regime will change with changes in climate, the direction of the dialogue for finding solutions to these issues remains uncertain. One thing that Californians can count on is that water will remain at the center of economic, ecological, social, and policy discussions far into the future.

Explore!

VISIT A PERMANENT OR TEMPORARY WETLAND

Visit a wetland or a vernal pool and notice the changes in the plant communities near and far from the wetland. Document changes that you think might have occurred since European settlement. Look at an aerial photograph and in the field to see if you can determine whether the size, shape, or extent of the wetland has changed over time. For example, have some areas been filled for development? You can find wetlands by accessing the National Wetlands Inventory at http://www.fws.gov/nwi/.

VISIT A WASTE WATER TREATMENT PLANT
THAT USES PONDS FOR DECOMPOSITION

In addition to providing information about innovative new approaches to wastewater treatment and wetland creation, these ponds are almost always excellent places to go birding. Cities with these ponds include Arcata, Ukiah, Petaluma, Davis, Fresno, San Rafael, Santa Maria, and Ventura. *Please note* that these ponds are run by municipal agencies and vary in their level of preparedness for visitors. Call ahead to check.

VISIT THE BAY MODEL

The Bay Model is a three-dimensional working hydraulic model of San Francisco Bay and the Sacramento-San Joaquin River Delta. It is administered by the Army Corps of Engineers and located in Sausalito, across the Golden Gate Bridge from San Francisco. Find out more about it at www.spn.usace.army.mil/bmvc/.

HELP WITH WATER QUALITY MONITORING

Check with local stream restoration groups or watershed groups for opportunities to sample water quality. Some groups have a "first flush" event that collects water quality information during the first major rain event each fall.

**BUILD YOUR OWN HESTER-DENDY
AND SAMPLE BENTHIC MACROINVERTEBRATES**

This is so much fun, you won't believe it yields important results. With a small amount of instruction, you can learn to identify and sample benthic macroinvertebrates, which provide key information about water quality. As with other volunteer water quality sampling, check with local stream groups for information.

A Hester-Dendy is a simple piece of equipment you can build to catch macroinvertebrates for water sampling. Adopt-A-Stream has instructions on making one at www.adopt-a-stream.org/pdf/monitoring_tools/the_hestner.pdf. Utah State University Extension, http://extension.usu.edu/waterquality/files/uploads/PDF/Making%20_equipment.pdf, has nice information about building all kinds of simple water-monitoring equipment.

EXPLORE WHERE YOUR DRINKING WATER COMES FROM

Describe how drinking water arrives in your house, and identify at least two social or political positions on the issues that arise from that process. Make an argument in favor of and against each position. The Water Education Foundation's website, "Where does my water come from?" at www.water-ed.org/watersources, is a nice place to start.

4

Plants

Plants surround us, shelter us, feed us, and form the aesthetic and functional backdrop to our lives. Were it not for green plants, there would be no life as we know it on Earth. Despite their central importance to our lives, many of us are no more aware of the plants we live among than we are of billboards. Ask yourself these simple botanical Jeopardy questions: How many trees can you name on sight? What is the first bush to bloom in your yard each spring? Are the conifer trees on Mt. Lassen the same species as those you can find in the Sierra Nevada? Are they the same species as the trees in the mountains above Los Angeles?

Plants can be categorized into various groups or sets that share characteristics, life style traits, and adaptations to their environment. This chapter starts with huge generalities about all plants and gradually focuses in on specific traits of some of the important plants of California.

LIFESTYLES OF RICH AND FAMOUS PLANTS

Warm and wet conditions promote the growth of plants. Cool, cold, and dry conditions cause plants to slow down metabolically. Thus tropical rainforests are "ideal" spots for plants to grow. Most of the world, however, is not a tropical rainforest, so the story of plant adaptation is the story of the development of alternative lifestyles to cope with the diverse deviations from ideal climate conditions that the majority of the world presents.

Conifer trees in front of the Mt. Lassen volcano. Photo by Kerry Heise

Some plants live for a few months, others for many years. Indeed, the longest-lived organisms on Earth are plants. One species of Mediterranean sea grass (*Posidonia oceanica*) is one of the slowest-growing and longest-lived plants in existence, with some large clones estimated to be thousands of years old. Trees are perhaps the most familiar, archetypal plants. Trees generally grow from seeds, starting out as collections of a few cells and enlarging to become the most massive and the tallest organisms on Earth. Trees are said to be both perennial and woody. Perennial plants are those that live more than one year and generally pass an unfavorable season in a dormant or inactive state.

Trees can also be divided into those that are deciduous and those that are evergreen. Deciduous trees and shrubs lose their leaves during the unfavorable season, whereas evergreen trees and shrubs keep individual leaves for more than one growing season, and may be photosynthetically active during the unfavorable period.

Shrubs are another type of woody plant. They generally have more than one stem, whereas trees classically have only one main trunk. Shrubs generally keep to below 15 feet tall; trees are often much larger. Is the 25-foot-tall, single-trunked rhododendron in your neighbor's yard a tree or a shrub? Exceptions to these rules abound, so *shrub* and *tree* are general terms without precise distinctions.

The last category of woody plants of relevance to California naturalists is lianas, or woody vines. Most plants desire to maximize their exposure to sunlight. Essentially, they compete for sunlight. Trees compete by putting huge allocations of resources into growing a stem that allows them to overtop other plants. Lianas are cheaters: they utilize the structure of trees and shrubs to get to the canopy without making the investment in a large stem. There are four genera of lianas that are common in California: poison oak (*Toxicodendron*), wild grape (*Vitis*), honeysuckle (*Lonicera*), and virgin's bower (*Clematis*). These four plant genera illustrate the three mechanisms lianas use to climb: twining, tendrils, and adventitious roots. Honeysuckle stems wrap around the stem they climb: they twine. Poison oak can climb tree trunks or bare walls using sucker-like roots: adventitious roots. Grapes use the grappling hooks of the plant world: tendrils.

Annual plants are distinct from perennials in that they complete their life cycle in one growing season. They pass the unfavorable season as a seed. Those of you who have grown tomatoes from seed will be familiar with the concept. Tomatoes have an annual lifestyle: one good growing season and leave behind seeds. Such well-known spring wildflowers as Chinese houses (*Collinsia*), baby blue eyes (*Nemophila*), and popcorn flower (*Plagiobothrys*) are annuals, as are many of the plants that grow wild in the hills of California.

The California poppy is a familiar wildflower. Poppies are herbaceous (nonwoody) plants and they have a little secret: they grow as both annuals and herbaceous perennials! In favorable circumstances they switch from being an annual to being an herbaceous perennial. At the close of the favorable season, poppies may translocate carbon compounds and minerals to their roots. At the return of the favorable season, they may begin to grow once again, powered by the energy and nutrients stored in the roots, rather than starting from a seed. This phoenix-like rebirth driven by stored reserves is a major class of adaptation of California plants, referred to as the herbaceous perennial lifestyle. Examples of other plants with this lifestyle that may be familiar to you are soap root (*Chlorogalum*), blue dicks (*Dichelostemma*), and mule ears (*Wyethia*). Trees and shrubs are easy to tell from herbaceous plants. Annuals and perennials are more difficult to distinguish. Often you will need to expose the root or follow the plant's growth over the course of a year to distinguish an annual from a perennial.

The stored energy in a mariposa lily (*Calochortus*) bulb or a snake-root (*Sanicula*) tuber allows it to produce leaves much more quickly than the seed of an annual poppy, which must start from scratch to build a plant body by photosynthesis. Thus herbaceous perennials can overtop and exclude annuals in stable, predictable environments, like woodlands and shrublands. But in open and disturbed environments, annuals come into their own, playing on their ability to produce numerous seeds. Human activity, in maintaining many open and disturbed environments, has created a bonanza for annuals.

PARTS OF A PLANT

Plants grow by making stems. In order for a plant to produce a leaf, it must make a stem. Some stems are very contracted (think of a cactus), others more elongate and easily visible, but all plants must make stems to produce leaves. Leaves are usually the primary locality of photosynthesis, thus it behooves plants to make leaves. As the stem elongates, leaves are produced sequentially, from the near end of the stem out to the tip. At the base of each leaf is a remarkable structure, a bud. A bud is a clump of tissue specialized to be ready to grow a new stem, leaf, or flower. Buds are often visible at the base of the leaf. The easiest time to see buds on deciduous plants is during the dormant season. Often buds in this season are enlarged and prominent, but even during the growing season and on evergreen plants, buds are often discernible. Buds consist of the tissue that will become the new stem, leaf, or flower, surrounded and protected by one or many bracts or scales. The bracts and scales are evolutionarily modified leaves. They enclose the dormant bud tissue and protect it from weather extremes (cold, dry) and predators. When the new stem begins to grow, the bud scales relax and open to allow the new stem to elongate. Typically they fall from the plant and may be noticeable on the ground, or the bud scale scars they leave upon dropping may be visible or prominent on the stem.

As stems elongate, they produce successive leaves along their length. Leaves come in a startling variety of shapes and sizes and are arranged upon the stem in typical patterns. Leaves may be arrayed along a stem in alternate, opposite, or whorled fashion. The leaves themselves may be simple (undivided) or compound (divided). Leaves can also be very thin—needles are in fact a kind of leaf!

Flowers can be thought of as variations on a theme. The theme is four whorls of modified leaves, the sepals, petals, stamens, and pistil.

Flower buds of wild lilac (*Ceanothus*). Buds are condensed tissue ready to expand when the growing season begins. Photo by Lynn Watson, Santa Barbara

Forms of leaves. From left to right: bigleaf maple (*Acer macrophyllum*), simple leaf deeply palmately lobed; Pacific bleeding heart (*Dicentra formosa*), three-part compound leaf, deeply dissected; oceanspray (*Holodiscus discolor*), leaves simple, alternate, and toothed; snowberry (*Symphoricarpos albus* var. *laevigatus*), leaves simple, opposite, and toothed at all margins. Photo by Kerry Heise

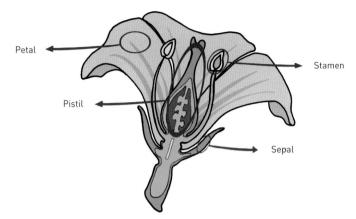

Parts of a flower. The critical parts every naturalist must be able to recognize are the sepals, petals, stamens, and pistil. Courtesy of Mariana Ruiz Villarreal

Very generally, the function of the sepals is to enclose and protect the inner parts: the petals, stamens, and pistil. Petals are the often highly colored part of the flower that signals to potential pollinators that "there may be a reward here, please investigate" and can be thought of as a kind of advertising. The stamens are the functionally "male" part; they are the site of pollen production. The pistil is the functionally "female" part, largely characterized by an ovary within which the seeds develop.

The function of flowers is to produce seeds. The function of seeds is to allow the plant to have progeny both locally and distantly. The intermediate step between flowers and seeds is the fruit. Fruits are the enlarged, mature ovaries that were present in the flower. Fruits come in a bewildering array of shapes and sizes, from tiny orchid fruits an inch long with 25,000 seeds to the baseball-sized fruits of the buckeye (*Aesculus*) with only one seed. The unifying theme is that all fruits are ripened ovaries.

Because plants have had millions of years to try different strategies for success (about 130 million or possibly more in the case of flowering plants), many different solutions to the mechanics of seed production have evolved. Every type of flower you see today has a unique, ancient lineage. The result is a bewildering array of different-looking flowers (about 250,000 kinds on Earth today). In some plants the sepals and petals are just alike and are called tepals (many lilies). Different parts of the plant may be modified to produce nectar: the leaves (*Prunus*), petals (*Ranunculus, Aquilegia*), sepals (*Ipomoea*), stamens (*Viola*), or base of the pistil.

What this means is that every flower in your garden or your local park is a mystery waiting for you to investigate it. Try dissecting a flower. Perhaps you'll start with a California poppy. Look for the sepals, petals, stamens, and pistil. Try to find an old poppy flower that has dropped its sepals, petals, and stamens, to see what the ovary looks like as the seeds develop.

Pollination

Functionally, producing seeds is the name of the game. To reproduce, plants need to put "male" and "female" parts together. That is, they must unite pollen with ovaries. For maximum effectiveness (that is, for the best rearrangement of genetic material), it is best to mate with another individual, not with yourself. (Yes! Plants have the option to mate with themselves!) Most plants attempt not to mate with themselves; they try to promote outcrossing. One of the best methods plants have developed to ensure outcrossing is to use animals to carry pollen from one plant to another. This system is a typical business deal, with payments (rewards) for services rendered, advertisement, and competition. Think of a bumblebee hovering around a manzanita (*Arctostaphylos*) flower in January. Why should it? For the reward. Manzanitas pay bumblebees with sugar water (nectar). Some flowers pay in nectar, others pay in pollen, a very few pay in oils, but there is no free lunch. To some extent everyone gets what they need or want. The bumblebee (pollinator) gets food for itself or its offspring. The plant gets transfer of pollen from one flower to another. Plants that use animals to transfer pollen must provide two functions: advertising and reward. They must attract the pollinator and reward it for its work. The advertising generally consists of gaudily colored sepals or petals or stamens. This is a visual attractant to cue the pollinator. Olfactory cues (smells) may also be used, either separately or in combination with visual cues. This is one of the great ancillary benefits of pollination: wonderful smells are produced that we can enjoy if we take time to smell the roses.

There are, however, plants that are pollinated in a different way. Some plants are pollinated entirely or in part by wind or water transport of pollen. Grasses are perhaps the most familiar example of a wind-pollinated plant. Because wind-pollinated plants do not need the services of animal transport agents, they can dispense with the costs of advertisement (pollinator attraction) and reward (pollinator payment). A quick look at a grass will show that most do not have colorful parts or smell good to attract an animal. A closer look would show that most grasses have dispensed with sepals and petals completely, and they do not have parts that produce nectar as a reward.

Seed Dispersal

One of the most fascinating aspects of plant morphology is the complex array of forms that have developed to transport seeds to suitable places for them to grow. Seeds can be transported externally when they are caught on the fur or feathers of mammals or birds. They can also be transported internally, as when bears eat manzanita berries and the seeds are pooped out in a great steaming heap on the other side of the mountain, or when birds eat elderberries (*Sambucus*) and the seeds fall thousands of feet to splat in a landslide. One of the most wonderfully whimsical seed dispersal systems you will see is dispersal by ants. Many plants in California, and more globally, produce seeds with an oil-rich food body (an eliasome) attached. Ants gather the seeds, eat the eliasome, and discard the seed, which then grows in its new home. California examples of ant dispersal are *Dicentra, Genista, Scoliopus, Trillium, Vancouveria,* and *Viola sempervirens.*

PLANT COMMUNITIES OF CALIFORNIA

Every individual plant is unique in its form and each species has a distinct set of environmental tolerances that influence where it can be found. When plants with similar environmental requirements are regularly found together, we call them a plant community. Such communities blend into one another, so the concept is useful mostly as a human construct to make it easier to talk about natural environments.

The plant communities of California are determined by the various plant species' genetic requirements and tolerances interacting with all of the aspects of the local environment. Climate, geology, and interaction with animals—notably elk, cattle, and people—influence the local and regional distribution of plants. Fire is also a huge factor in determining the distribution of plants. The broad treatment of plant communities that follows generalizes the plant communities of California into only a few, easily identifiable groups: beach vegetation (strand), grassland, salt marsh, freshwater marsh, coastal scrub and chaparral, mixed evergreen forest, oak woodland, riparian (or gallery) forest, coniferous forest (includes Douglas-fir forest, redwood forest, closed-cone pine forest, as well as other montane forest types), and hot deserts.

Beach vegetation, or strand, is the low, sparse, windswept carpet of plants occupying the sandy shore and the dunes and bluffs immediately adjacent to them. This group of plants is composed primarily of annual or herbaceous perennial plants. These plants must be able to put up with the thrashing delivered by ocean waves, high salinity, extreme winds, shifting substrate, and blowing sand. Many of these plants have very wide geographic ranges, with seeds that are dispersed by flotation in ocean currents up and down the Pacific Coast. This community is highly altered by people in many places, with seawalls, coastal homes and communities, and introduction of European beach grass being the main avenues of impact.

There is an abundance of grassland in California mostly composed of nonnative European and Asian annual grass species which often exists without much shrub or tree cover. The occurrence of grassland throughout the California Coast Ranges and Sierra foothills is intimately intertwined with historical land use, although there are some naturally treeless areas. Woodlands, forests, and chaparral have been cleared throughout the state for agriculture or pasture, usually by cutting and burning. The natural succession of grassland to brush to woodland or forest is retarded or suspended by grazing or burning. In most areas, grasslands return to shrublands and woodlands without fire or grazing. Wind-dispersed coyote brush (*Baccharis pilularis*) and bird-dispersed poison oak (*Toxicodendron diversilobum*) are usually the first colonizers, followed by trees such as oaks (*Quercus*), bay trees (*Umbellularia californica*), or Douglas-fir (*Pseudotsuga menziesii*).

This phenomenon is illustrated by the Golden Gate National Recreation Area. The land between the Golden Gate Bridge and Olema was a series of cattle ranches between 1820 and 1970. The ranches were first logged, then heavily grazed. Photos of the coastal slope from the 1950s and 1960s show expansive grasslands (cattle pastures). Since the land was purchased by the National Park Service in the 1970s, it has not been grazed. Coastal sage scrub has almost completely covered the former pastures and is now being invaded by Douglas-fir trees and bay trees, in part due to fire suppression.

A few areas where native grasses thrive still exist. Rangeland managers and restoration ecologists would like to replace exotic annual grasses with native grasses, as this increases the native biodiversity associated with these areas. In many grasslands, removing livestock and fire can cause overproduction of exotic annual grasses and result in the loss of native grasses and forbs (small broadleaf plants).

Many otherwise rare grassland species are found primarily on serpentine soils. These are generally unfriendly places for plants to grow unless, like some California native plants, species evolve to thrive in these conditions and thereby avoid competition with species less tolerant of these harsh soils. Serpentine soil areas support a higher ratio of native plants to introduced plants than nonnative grasslands. Areas with serpentine soils are great places to see incredible displays of brilliantly colored wildflowers.

Salt marsh is another community of herbaceous plants, those adapted to periodic inundation (flooding) by salt water, followed by exposure to extreme solar radiation. Salt marsh is further characterized by extremely low soil oxygen and high rates of soil deposition, thus the plants of salt marshes must be able to cope with regular inundation and burial. Salt marsh plants are twice daily inundated with salt water and must be able to cope with high soil salinity and low oxygen. Not so obviously, many salt marshes have creek channels running through them and may seasonally be flooded with freshwater, another extreme rigor to which marsh plants must be adapted. When you think of salt marshes, you want to include both the vegetated and bare areas (the mudflats, tidal channels, and stream channels). The bare mudflats and the vegetated areas are intimately linked and function together as parts of a system, with the vegetated areas occupying slightly higher elevations and performing primary production, and the bare areas at slightly lower levels, getting inundated more deeply, and supporting diverse communities of invertebrate consumers and decomposers.

Despite all of these seeming disadvantages, salt marshes are sites of very high primary plant productivity and behave as nurseries for fish and other inhabitants of the estuary environment. Salt marshes are typically very flat and occupy areas of high utility for human beings. Thus, salt marshes suffer greatly during development. Ninety percent of the original Bay-Delta salt marshes are now converted to other uses. Los Angeles and San Diego have similar histories of salt marsh loss. Salt marshes are perhaps the most threatened plant community of the California coastal zone.

Freshwater marsh is an assemblage of different microhabitats. It includes the giant tule beds of the primeval Central Valley, the complex sloughs and islands of the Delta, vernal pools imbedded in grass-

The Life of the Salt Marsh Bird's Beak

Flower stalk of salt marsh bird's beak (*Chloropyron maritimum*). The leaves are purple and covered with white crystals of excreted salt. Photo courtesy of Brad Kelley

One of the unique inhabitants of salt marshes of the Bay-Delta is the salt marsh bird's beak (*Chloropyron maritimum*), an inconspicuous annual plant known only from salt marsh habitats in coastal California. The salt marsh bird's beak has seeds that are stimulated to germinate when salinity is low. In high-rainfall years, when the "salt" marsh is mostly rinsed of salt by flows of freshwater, the bird's beak sprouts in abundance. In years of low rainfall, when salinity remains high, the bird's beak may sprout in very low numbers or not at all! The plant completes its life cycle (nine months) in "typical" salt marsh conditions as the rains pass, tides bring salinity levels back up, and day length increases.

lands, the wooded transitional marshes at the upstream edges of salt marshes, and the woody and herbaceous vegetation surrounding lakes. Anywhere seasonal or permanent standing freshwater is a primary factor in determining what plants grow on a site can be considered a freshwater marsh.

The plants of freshwater marshes, like those of salt marshes, often must cope with low soil oxygen. They also experience seasonally fluctuating water levels. Seasonally or permanently flooded areas exclude the great majority of plants and provide an opportunity to those that can cope with these conditions.

Prior to the damming, diking, and channelization of the Sacramento and San Joaquin Rivers and most of their major tributaries, these great streams flooded much of the Central Valley annually during the wet season. Controlling these rivers has made possible one of the greatest, most productive agricultural enterprises in history, and has eliminated huge, expansive, productive wetlands. When the big rivers of the Great Valley flooded each year, they filled many off-channel basins with water to depths of 3 to 12 feet for three to six months. As the floods receded, the basins gradually dried down, so by the end of September they were baked hardpans of dry, cracked soil. These basins were populated with humongous stands of tules (*Schoenoplectus*).

Another unique feature of the large, flat river valleys of California is the development of small, shallow basins (vernal pools) on a variety of terraces and low spots in the valleys and surrounding foothills. These basins fill with water a few inches to a foot in depth, dry gradually, and support a unique flora of annual plants growing in concentric rings determined by water depth.

Anywhere a river or creek enters a lake, a salt marsh, or a larger river, freshwater may pond seasonally or permanently. These "transitional marshes" are often wooded with willows (*Salix*), alders (*Alnus*), ash (*Fraxinus*), maple (*Acer*), or sycamore (*Platanus*). Beneath these deciduous trees you will find the herbaceous vegetation of a marsh: cattails (*Typha*), tules, sedges (*Carex*), and rushes (*Juncus*).

All of these marsh habitats are extremely important to wildlife, from the great flocks of migratory waterfowl found in seasonal wetlands of the Central Valley; to beavers, muskrats, and rails in transitional marshes; to the endemic delta green ground beetle (*Elaphrus viridis*) which occurs only in association with Central Valley vernal pools in Solano County.

Coastal scrub and chaparral are brush communities, characterized by dense stands of shrubs 3 to 15 feet tall. The shrubs are usually close together and intricately branched enough to make human passage difficult or impossible. Bears, deer, pigs, coyotes, gray fox, wood rats, and rabbits, however, move through them with ease. The two main discernible types of brush communities are coastal scrub, near the ocean, and chaparral in hotter, dryer, more interior sites. In the interior (away from the coast, chaparral) the herbaceous layer is often depauperate, although near the coast (coastal scrub) the herbaceous plants between the shrubs may form the majority of the biomass.

Chaparral is often composed of nearly pure stands of manzanita (*Arctostaphylos*) 8 to 15 feet tall. In other areas, the cover is a mix of manzanita, chamise (*Adenostoma fasciculatum*), wild lilac (*Ceanothus*), scrub oak (*Quercus*), and bush monkey flower (*Mimulus aurantiacus*). Chamise and bush monkey flower commonly form pure stands. Chaparral occurs on hot, south-facing slopes and on hillsides characterized by impoverished soil such as heavy clay or thin, rocky soil. Chaparral is often the aggregation of woody plants that will first colonize a disturbed area, especially after a fire. Manzanita seeds are known for their ability to remain viable through long periods of dormancy (50–75 years!). Mature stands of chaparral provide a shaded seedbed for their successors, oak woodland and coniferous forest. Chaparral shrubs, especially chamise, provide excellent deer browse, and their growth is often retarded by the "hedging" effect of this browsing. Coastal scrub generally lacks manzanita and chamise, rarely rises above 8 feet in height, and is usually dominated by coyote brush, coastal sage (*Artemisia californica*), California blackberry (*Rubus ursinus*), flowering current (*Ribes sanguineum*), and sticky monkey flower (*Mimulus aurantiacus*).

Mixed evergreen forest is a composite of many different trees, including oaks, bay, Douglas-fir, madrone, tan oak, and others. This forest forms dense stands with adjacent trees touching each other's canopies. Mixed evergreen forests occupy sites subject to frequent or infrequent, often intense, fires. Ability to stump sprout after fire as well as leathery, hard, often spiny, evergreen leaves are the prime attributes of this community type. All plant communities intermix with other community types to a greater or lesser extent, but botanists do recognize a wide variety of community types and species associations. The mixed evergreen forest grades into and borders conifer forest, oak woodland, and grassland. In many places distinguishing them is somewhat arbitrary. Old forests and ancient trees are difficult to find in this community type, since the stands are very fire prone, and individual trees often succumb to the fires that exclude conifers from the site.

There is a very odd word you must learn if you want to be a California naturalist: *sclerophyllous*. The word comes from the Greek roots *sclero* (hard) and *phyllon* (leaf). Sclerophyllous plants are those

Mediterranean Climate and California Plant Communities

Mediterranean-type climates are characterized by cool, wet winters and hot, dry summers. In North America, this climate type extends from southern Oregon to northern Baja California. Plant distribution varies across the climate type: drier conditions shape the sclerophyllous scrub vegetation and chaparral in the south, while centrally, more moist conditions prevail, producing vast areas of oak-dominated woodland and grassland.

Areas that share Mediterranean climate with California are Chile, the Mediterranean basin, South Africa, and southwestern Australia. Plants from other Mediterranean climate regions often flourish in California because of their adaptations to a similar climate and the absence of evolved predators to control their numbers. Examples include *Eucalyptus* (a native of Australia), Cape ivy (South Africa), and French broom (the Mediterranean). These plants cause substantial loss of habitat. The Global Mediterranean Action Network (www.mediterraneanaction.net) provides these facts:

- About 20 percent of all known vascular plants species grow in Mediterranean climate regions, though these regions represent only 2.2 percent of the Earth's land surface.
- The California–Baja California region supports more plant species than Canada and the central and northeastern United States combined, while supporting a disproportionately large number of people. Covering just 1 percent of the United States, the region contains 10 percent of the population.
- Perhaps 24 percent of California's 5,900 plant species are endemic. About 17 percent are nonnative.
- The proportion of habitat destroyed in the Mediterranean biome is greater than in tropical rainforests.

with hard leaves, often with short internodes and marginal spines. The hard, evergreen leaves of coast live oak (*Quercus agrifolia*) are classically sclerophyllous, as are those of the other evergreen oaks, madrones, bay trees, and many of the shrubs that occur in chaparral. The needles of pine trees and Douglas-firs can also be considered sclerophyllous. Sclerophyllous plants are thought to have developed in response to increasing aridity. Over time (20 million years), as California became increasingly arid, many species of plants were excluded—that is, they went extinct or were extirpated from California. Others changed; they evolved in response to the changing climate and developed adaptations

Sclerophyllous leaves of hoary manzanita (*Arctostaphylos canescens*).
Sclerophyllous leaves are hard, waxy, usually simple, and untoothed. The red
objects are the "little apples," the immature manzanita fruit. Photo by Kerry Heise

to resist draught. Hard, evergreen (sclerophyllous) leaves is one such
adaptation. The waxy coating on many sclerophyllous leaves, reduced
numbers of stomates, and having stomates only on the lower surface
of the leaf all help minimize water loss through the leaf surface. These
abilities are critical in the Mediterranean type climate California shares
with Chile, the Mediterranean region, South Africa, and southwestern
Australia. All of these other areas with Mediterranean climate also
have vegetation types dominated by sclerophyllous plants, so if you
learn the concept here, it will serve you well in your travels to these
other Mediterranean climate areas.

Oak woodland is perhaps the most widespread and characteristic plant community in California. The term is usually reserved for
the lands covered in deciduous oaks, with hillsides clothed in evergreen oaks falling under the banner of mixed evergreen forest. Oak
woodland is rich and variable in its floristic makeup, shares dominance
among five tree species, and has the richest, most diverse shrubby and
herbaceous understory of any forest type. Oak woodland also seems to
harbor the greatest variety of native perennial herbs of any community.

California's oak woodlands are amazingly rich biologically. They provide habitat to 120 species of mammals, 147 species of birds, 60 species of amphibians and reptiles, and 5,000 species of insects and arachnids. Astonishingly, 1 acre of oak woodland can contain between 10 and 100 million individual insects and other invertebrates! In addition, oak woodlands provide watershed protection, open space, and opportunities for recreation.

Oak woodland can be dense or savanna-like. On cool north-facing slopes, the deciduous Oregon oak (*Q. garryana*) is often abundant in Northern California. It is the only California oak that continues north to Oregon, Washington, and British Columbia, where it seems to appreciate the increased rainfall. Oregon oaks can be thought of as our most moisture-loving oak. Blue oak (*Q. douglasii*) is the dominant oak on many extremely hot, arid sites, and in fact forms a "bathtub ring" around the Central Valley, essentially mapping the rain shadow areas in three dimensions. It is the diametric opposite of Oregon oak, specializing in the most arid sites that support large trees. Valley oak (*Q. lobata*) is abundant on deep soils of flats at low to medium elevations. It grows to enormous proportions in the deep, rich soils of valley bottoms, especially along creeks. Valley oaks also have the ability to survive flooding, often growing in areas where water stands for months during the wet season.

Oak woodland provides a variety of habitats for other plants, including those with deep shade, light shade, sunny openings between widely spaced trees, and seasonal shade below deciduous trees as well as branches where epiphytic lichens and mosses perch. Perhaps the seasonal change of light penetration into these deciduous forests is the most salient characteristic, accounting for the preponderance of herbaceous perennials and shrubs in the forest understory.

Once established, oaks become highly resistant to fires. Thick bark allows California oaks to withstand even moderately intense fires with little damage. When fire destroys foliage or small branches, oaks are capable of epicormic sprouting: they force out new shoots from larger branches and re-create their small branches and leaves quickly. When the entire trunk and major branches are killed, oak trees will often sprout from the burned stump and roots. They are highly fire-resistant trees, occurring in a landscape that has evolved with frequent fires as one of the signature conditions of life.

Native Americans reached population densities in California greater than those of any other nonagricultural people in the world. Acorns, the large, single-seeded fruits of oaks, were one of the primary resources that made this amazing population density possible.

Riparian forest is found along riverbanks and other bodies of water. The floodplains of the Sacramento, Salinas, Los Angeles, and other large and small rivers and streams are often lined with deciduous trees. The names of these trees read like a catalogue of eastern deciduous forest genera: *Acer, Alnus, Fraxinus, Platanus.* These are genera that do not do well in the hot, dry hills of California. Essentially, these trees are hiding in the cracks, escaping the severe draught that descends on California every June by living on the banks of streams. None of these riparian trees have the adaptations to aridity so widespread in other California plants. They don't need to! They have their roots down in the permanent water source that allows them to transpire as much as they want to, with more water immediately available to replace that which was lost.

The coniferous forest is characterized by evergreen cone-bearing trees (conifers) with one or more species sharing dominance. In much of California, the Douglas-fir is an important species of different coniferous forest communities. In places, especially in the fog zone along the coast, Douglas-firs share dominance with the unique California relict, the sequoia, or coast redwood (*Sequoia sempervirens*). At the dryer extremes, Douglas-firs cohabit with draught- and fire-adapted conifers like the knobcone pine (*Pinus attenuata*). They may also interdigitate (interlock) with or border the coastal pine, or Bishop pine (*Pinus muricata*). Douglas-fir trees live in dynamic equilibrium with the plant communities that surround them. Douglas-firs constantly throw seeds into mixed evergreen forests, oak woodlands, chaparral, and grassland in an attempt to take over these communities' land holdings. Douglas-fir trees will take advantage of the partial shade provided by oaks or manzanitas, seed beneath them, and grow up through them. The Douglas-firs then shade out the other species, eventually killing them. Fire interrupts and/or reverses these changes, as young Douglas-firs are killed outright by fire while oaks sprout from trunk or stump and manzanitas sprout readily from seeds or burls. Large (60-plus years in age), thick-barked Douglas-fir trees are impervious to ground fires, but they succumb to crown fires.

There is a class of coniferous trees in California that illustrates how closely adapted to fire the flora of California is. These trees, called closed-cone pines or fire pines, produce cones (woody, seed-bearing structures) that don't open the first year. The cones and the seeds they contain are stored on the tree, often for many years. When a fire enters the stand, the closed-cone pines burst into flame, actually exacerbating the fire with flammable chemicals stored in their needles and bark. The entire stand is destroyed, but the fire has another effect. It allows the cones to open, releasing the stored seeds, which sprout in the now open and fertilized habitat following the fire, and the stand is renewed. What this leads to is even-aged stands of trees over large patches of landscape.

Redwoods are one of the signature trees of California. Virtually everyone has heard of them, most Californians have seen and perhaps walked in a redwood forest, and many of us have them growing as cultivated ornamentals within a block or two of our houses. Redwoods are conifers, like the Douglas-fir and the fire pines. Redwoods are also paleoendemics—a species with a range that is a small remnant of a former much larger geographic distribution. Redwoods have a long evolutionary history and a great fossil record. Fossils of redwoods have been found far beyond the current, relict (surviving) range of redwoods. Redwood fossils are known from throughout the western United States and Canada, as well as in Europe, Greenland, Alaska, and China. The oldest known redwood fossils date back 160 million years!

The Sierra Nevada range provides a clear example of how elevation and other environmental factors, such as latitude, aspect, parent material, and soil, determine the types of trees that grow in a certain place. On the west slope of the Sierra, forests generally arrange themselves in broad elevational belts dominated by one or several tree species. Imagine a hike from the Central Valley floor, somewhere east of Fresno, to the top of the Sierran crest. You would start in oak woodlands and grasslands of the lower foothills, which give way to conifers such as Douglas-fir, ponderosa pine (*Pinus ponderosa*), white fir (*Abies concolor*), and sugar pine (*P. lambertiana*). As you climb higher, these species are replaced by forests of red fir (*A. magnifica*), Jeffery pine (*P. jeffreyi*), and lodgepole pine (*P. contorta* ssp. *murrayana*). Higher still, you find yourself in a subalpine forest of mountain hemlock (*Tsuga mertensiana*), western white pine (*P. monticola*), whitebark pine (*P. albicaulis*), foxtail pine (*P. balfouriana*), and limber pine (*P. flexilis*). The subalpine forests consist of short trees shaped and pruned by the heavy snow and high winds of their high-elevation habitat.

California's hot deserts, the Mojave, Colorado, and Sonoran Deserts, located in the southeast portion of the state, are primarily scrub-dominated landscapes. The three deserts are distinguished by their climates. The Mojave Desert, located farthest north, is influenced primarily by winter rain from the Pacific. The hotter, subtropical Colorado and Sonoran Deserts receive moisture from convection storms during the summer months (July–September), in addition to infrequent Pacific winter storms. Creosote bush (*Larrea tridentata*), white burr sage (*Ambrosia dumosa*), and brittle bush (*Encelia farinosa*) form vast areas of scrub vegetation across all these deserts, especially in well-drained washes, bajadas, and alluvial fans. Distinctive features of the Mojave Desert include woodlands of Joshua tree (*Yucca brevifolia*), black brush scrub (*Coleogyne ramosissima*), and salt-tolerant shrubs of the genus *Atriplex*.

PLANTS AND PEOPLE

People do many things with plants, including move them around. When we move to a new home, we commonly bring plants from the old place. Chinese workers brought tree of heaven (*Ailanthus altissima*) seeds to California to remind them of the lives they left behind in China. Tree of heaven is now widespread in California, with clusters of trees often marking sites of former Chinese habitation. We also bring and import plants of agricultural or horticultural importance. This is quite a two-edged sword. On the one hand, importing avocado plants from Mexico adds a delightful item to our diet and commerce. On the other hand, *Eucalyptus* trees, imported from Australia for ornament and in the mistaken notion that they could be grown for lumber to make railroad ties, have become noxious weeds along the coast of California, where they seed readily and form large, expanding stands that exclude native California plants.

Walk over to your spice shelf and look at all of the choices you are faced with to season your meals: salt, pepper, nutmeg, cinnamon, turmeric, allspice, cloves, and on and on. Now ask yourself which of these spices were available to native Californians as they lived for over 10,000 years in California before the arrival of Europeans in 1492. Here is the list: bay leaves, bay nuts, and a few odd roots you probably haven't heard of and certainly haven't eaten. Perhaps native Californians acquired paprika or cayenne by trade from Mexico, but probably not, or if so in very limited quantities. The point is that the world we take for granted is hugely shaped by the intentional and acci-

Some Important Invasive Species in California

Yellow star thistle. Photo courtesy of George Hartwell

Arundo. Photo courtesy of Joseph M. DiTomaso

California has nearly 5,000 native plant species, the most of any state in the United States. Over 200 invasive species are threats to California's wildlands and native plant species. Invasive species are second only to development in eliminating native habitat. Some of these are below.

Arundo donax L. (arundo, giant reed)
Arundo invades riparian areas, drying up groundwater and displacing native vegetation. Winter rains can distribute reproductive parts of this plant down the creek.

Tamarix spp. (tamarisk, salt cedar)
Tamarisk invasions have numerous impacts, including clogging streams, drying up wetlands, and increasing the salinity of soil. About 1.5 million acres in the US Southwest have been invaded by tamarisk.

Delairea odorata (Cape ivy)
Cape ivy takes over large swaths of riparian areas by growing in a solid blanket that kills other vegetation.

Genista monspessulana (French broom)
French broom is highly destructive to native plants and can cover whole hillsides. Despite this, it is still sold as an ornamental in gardening stores.

Centaurea solstitialis L. (yellow star thistle)
Yellow star thistle can be found in over 15 million acres in California, including rangelands, native grasslands, orchards, vineyards, pastures, roadsides, and wasteland areas.

Aegilops sp. (goat grass)
Goat grass is of concern because it has the duel ability to hybridize with winter wheat and to invade serpentine soils. Invasion of serpentine soils is a concern, as those soils also harbor many species endemic to California.

dental movement of plants from one continent to another. When we move plants and plant products on such a massive scale, there are inevitably stowaways, unintended hitchhikers who make the journey with the intended contents.

Because people have taken plants with them as they have moved around the world, the world we inhabit today is a composite of elements from diverse regions. Most everyone would agree that it is a good thing that rice from Southeast Asia is now available to grow in the Central Valley of California, which is one of the most productive rice-growing regions in the world. Many people would also be delighted that they can grow rhododendrons from the Himalayas in their yard. What most people don't realize is that transporting plants for agriculture and horticulture can impact native plant and animal communities. For example, transporting cultivated *Rhododendron* plants from Europe was probably the way the water mold *Phytophthora ramorum*, which causes sudden oak death, arrived in California.

We have a series of technical terms to designate the status of plants relative to geography. Native plants are those thought to be native or original to a region. Redwoods can be called many names, including endemic, paleoendemic, and native to coastal California and southwestern Oregon. French broom (*Genista monspessulana*), on the other hand, is a nonnative. Before people brought it to California as a horticultural plant, French broom did not occur in California.

Because *Eucalyptus globulus* and French broom are capable of growing, setting seed, and reproducing successfully in California without the help of people, we consider them both nonnative and naturalized. Nonnative plants like these that have successfully become naturalized and have attracted the attention of people as problematic in one way or another are termed invasive plants or invasive exotics. In extreme cases, where naturalized nonnative plants have important economic impacts or negative financial consequences, usually by disrupting agriculture, they reach the ultimate status of being termed noxious weeds.

Native American Plant Uses

Native Americans recognized that in California one of the most stable, abundant, storable food resources available to them were the fruits of oak trees, acorns. There is abundant evidence that native Californians harvested and stored great quantities of acorns, processed them into staple food items, and revered them in their religious worldview.

Native American Plant Uses

Indigenous people of California knew the regional flora so well that they were able to make their living from the land without importing agricultural crops from other regions. As we learn about their discoveries regarding which plants heal, which plants can be used to make music, which plants tie burdens, and which plants nourish bodies, we gain greater appreciation of California's native people and for native plants.

Today, Native Americans still gather native plants and fungi, conduct business in tribal councils, and carry on ancient traditions. Some of the traditional ecological knowledge concerning plant, fungi, and animal species that historically occupied specific habitats, as well as former burning practices and harvesting strategies, rests in the memories of elderly native people and longtime non-Indian residents. This vast body of traditional ecological knowledge could be used to improve natural resource management. For example, ethnographic interviews with elders of the Salinan have revealed that blue oak areas within the traditional territory of the Salinan were managed with fire to decrease insects and diseases. Reconstruction of the Salinan burning regime (season, frequency, observed fire behavior, extent, and slope), in combination with information on the insects' life history characteristics, may help managers evaluate the effectiveness of burning for biological control.

To preserve this kind of information, the hundreds of species that were historically useful to two tribes, the Nor-Rel-Muk of northwestern California and the Salinan of the Central Coast, are being assembled into an ethnobotanical information system (EIS). A key feature of the EIS is that it will allow the user to query the system to answer specific questions on topics such as indigenous harvesting strategies (e.g., season, frequency) and management methods (e.g., pruning, burning, sowing, weeding).

Tribes throughout California are interested in rekindling their historic relationships with nature. Organizations and government agencies are beginning to recognize the value of indigenous knowledge and its latent, largely unexplored, and potentially enormous contributions to contemporary society. Interest in the management practices of indigenous people has increased since the realization that many of our so-called pristine environments were greatly affected by Native Americans. Further exploration into traditional Native American land management practices may help us restore California's precious natural and cultural heritage.

Adapted from M. Kat Anderson. "The Ethnobiology of California's Oak Woodlands." UC Oak Woodland Conservation Workgroup, http://ucanr.org/sites/oak_range/.

Although native Californians didn't "plant" oak trees, they very much "tended" them. One of the forms of TLC native Californians applied to the oak trees they intended to harvest was to burn around and beneath them! Fire was a primary "agricultural" tool in pre-European California. Broadcast burning was practiced on a grand scale, and probably for multiple purposes. One of the effects of repeated burning, in many places on an annual basis, was to reduce or eliminate shrubs from the oak woodland understory. This had the effect of making travel easier, facilitated hunting by opening up visual corridors, and made the collection of acorns simpler by clearing the ground the acorns would fall on. More broadly, repeated burning opened meadows and increased their size. Grasslands were another of the resource-harvest areas native Californians relied on, for digging liliaceous bulbs and for harvesting the seeds of annuals and herbaceous perennials. Perhaps the second most important plant food resource in California was pinole, a mixture of the seeds of a variety of herbaceous plants collected by beating seed heads into baskets.

There is a plant common in coastal California called Indian plum, or oso berry (*Oemleria cerasiformis*). The fruits of this shrub were highly sought after and were considered a delicacy. This fact is a testament to the scarcity of choices native Californians had compared with modern Americans. Indian plums are small, with a single, large seed. The taste is initially sweet, but there is a strong, bitter aftertaste. Most people, when encouraged to try them, will not ask for a second one.

Another layer of interdependence native Californians had with plants was their use of plants for tools and fibers. The baskets used to collect and store both pinole and acorns were made from various plant fibers, including willow, sedge, iris, hazelnut, ninebark, and redbud. Basket making in California reached levels of technical skill unsurpassed anywhere on Earth. Baskets were woven that were watertight! Basket making also intersected the realm of the mystical when designs for a basket were found in a weaver's dreams. Digging sticks for harvesting liliaceous bulbs were crafted of mountain mahogany and toyon. Arrows were made of the straight stems of oceanspray. Houses and temporary shelters were made from a wide variety of plants, depending on the species available at a particular site.

We continue to depend on and interact with plants in numerous and sometimes surprising ways. California has been transformed since the arrival of Euro-Americans, with the damming of rivers for irrigation and flood control, the removal of oak woodlands, the plowing of the Central Valley for agriculture, the elimination of elk, and extensive grazing being perhaps the most noticeable. We have imported an astonishing array of plants to California from all corners of the world. California is a plant enthusiast's dream come true. The variety of plants available for agriculture, horticulture, crafts, and study is truly remarkable.

CALIFORNIA'S PLANT COMMUNITIES AND CLIMATE CHANGE

Climate in much of California is predicted to become warmer and drier as a result of global accumulation of greenhouse gasses. This will affect native plant communities and populations. Blue oak–gray pine woodland may increase, and valley oak range is predicted to shrink. Reductions in water availability could impact vernal pools, ponds, wetlands, and spawning tributaries of rivers, impacting amphibians and fish, among other fauna. Fire risk will increase with increased temperature and decreased moisture; at the same time, fire suppression is likely to continue at the urban-wildland interface, leading to buildup of fuels and a greater potential for catastrophic fires in the future.

Climate change is already influencing the distribution of plant communities in California. For example, the downslope edges of forests in the Sierra Nevada have been shown to be creeping to higher elevations. What is unclear is how extreme the changes will be. Changes in species distributions, community composition, and dominant cover types are likely. These vegetation changes will influence the distribution of animals as well as ecosystem processes such as nutrient cycling.

The effects of climate change on plant communities include

- Shifting of species ranges to the north
- A loss of species in Southern California
- An increase in invasive species
- Increases in drought-tolerate species
- Sea level rise, which will alter coastal plant communities, erode beaches, and inundate tidal areas, marshes, and wetlands

A more in-depth discussion of the effects of climate change and California's natural communities can be found in the Climate Change section of Chapter 7.

Explore!

TAKE A CREEK WALK

Walk a local creek. Can you identify the riparian plants? (Beware of poison oak!!) Can you tell where the riparian community ends and the upland community begins? If you don't want to walk alone, contact a local park or preserve, creek association, the California Native Plant Society, or a Sierra Club or Audubon chapter for information about creek walks.

LEARN ABOUT A LOCAL PLANT COMMUNITY

Choose a piece of land you care about, such as your own property, a local oak woodland, a redwood grove, a creek, a wetland, or a local park. Spend a day walking and sketching it and writing down what you notice. Then learn its history. Your local library, the county clerk's office, and the park or preserve's administration offices will have historical records, but you may find that the best source of information is oral history. Ask someone who has lived in the area for a long time about that land.

VOLUNTEER AT A NATIVE PLANT NURSERY

This is a fun way to learn local plants and also learn about local plant issues in your community. Look in the phone book, ask at conventional nurseries, or call your local California Native Plant Society chapter (www.cnps.org) to find a native plant nursery.

EXPLORE YOUR BACKYARD

Spend a half hour in your backyard without any interruptions. Take a journal and write down and/or draw what you see, hear, smell. Survey the plants and make note of any you can't identify. Pick three to learn more about. Then go to a local park and see if you can find any plants that are the same as the ones in your yard.

PARTICIPATE IN A RESTORATION PROJECT

Restoration projects will get you pulling weeds, planting native plants, and if you are lucky, collecting seeds. They are fun and a great way to increase your knowledge of local plants. Check with local parks and creek "friends of" associations to see if they hold regular restoration days.

PRESS PLANTS

Pressing plants is another great way to get to know local plants. To make a small field plant press, cut two 8½ inch by 11 inch pieces of cardboard and place layers of newspaper between the cardboard.

(continued)

Explore! *(continued)*

Collect the stem with attached leaves and, if at all possible, flowers and/or fruits, and place them on the newspaper, cover with several pieces of newspaper and cardboard, and wrap rubber bands around the bunch. A more complete guide for "How to collected, press, and mount plants" is available from Montana State University Extension at http://msuextension.org/publications/AgandNaturalResources/M T198359AG.pdf.

LANDSCAPE WITH NATIVE PLANTS AND WILDFLOWERS IN YOUR YARD

About 30 to 60 percent of urban freshwater is used for maintaining US lawns, along with the application of 67 million pounds of synthetic pesticides. Native landscaping makes your yard unique and attractive to native fauna such as butterflies. The California Native Plant Society website (www.cnps.org/cnps/horticulture/brochure .php) and the Nature Conservancy website (www.growingnative .com) have excellent information to get you started.

MAKE ART ABOUT PLANTS

Sit in a natural place you love and write a poem or a song, draw a picture, make a painting, or take a photograph of something that inspires you. Try to incorporate naturalist details into your work, such as the shape of the leaves, pollinators, insects that use the plants, seeds, or whatever you notice and feel drawn to.

5

Forest, Woodland, and Range Resources and Management

Forests compel us because they play so many different roles in our society. They are places of beauty and refuge, often inspiring awe and a connection to something greater than ourselves. They provide shade and habitat for birds, insects, fish, amphibians, and reptiles. They sequester carbon. They are the source of wood, a hugely important natural resource that we depend on for lumber, paper, and fuel. For these reasons, feelings about forests and their uses run deep.

Forests and woodlands are defined as large tracts of land that have at least 10 percent tree cover. California has nearly 33 million acres of forests—about a third of the state's total acreage. In California there are two principal types of forests: those primarily covered with conifers (trees bearing cones) such as redwoods, Douglas-firs, and pines; and those primarily covered with broadleaf hardwoods, mostly oaks. Both of these forest types provide vital services to the state's residents, including wildlife habitat, water storage, wood products, recreational opportunities, and scenery. Another increasingly recognized value of forests is their ability to store carbon, helping to offset the adverse impacts of our releasing vast amounts of carbon dioxide and other greenhouse gases into the atmosphere.

Coniferous and broadleaf forests are very different. In the Sierra Nevada and southern California mountains, conifer forests generally occur at higher elevations than oak woodlands. The areas where conifers grow are often colder and wetter than hardwood forests. Conifers

A coastal watershed. Looking down the Garcia River from the headwaters to the distant ocean. Most of the watershed is covered in mixed evergreen forest. Photo by Kerry Heise

are evergreen, and broadleaf trees are often deciduous, so the amounts of light that can penetrate the two types of canopy are very different, especially after the hardwoods' leaves have dropped. Often conifer stands are dense, with little sunlight penetrating to the ground, so there are few understory plants. Conifers generally grow faster, and the wood products produced, including lumber and paper, are more valuable. The trees in conifer forests can grow to enormous size. Coastal redwoods, for instance, can be over 300 feet tall, with a diameter of over 20 feet. Walking into a dark, cool mature redwood stand makes one feel small and insignificant next to these vertical giants.

Although there are private timber companies that own conifer forests, a higher percentage of conifer forest land is publicly owned and managed by the US Forest Service, the US Bureau of Land Management, and both federal and California park services. In contrast, approximately 80 percent of oak woodlands in California are privately owned.

Oak woodlands occur at lower elevations, where it is usually hotter

Blue oak savanna after the rainy season, when widely spaced blue oaks have all leafed out. Photo courtesy of Greg Damron, www.wildvinestudios.com

and drier. There is far less harvesting for wood products, and the products that are produced, such as firewood, are generally lower in value. While there are certainly dense oak woodlands on favorable sites, many oak woodlands are characterized by widely spaced trees and a vigorous understory of grasses and forbs. Many of us are more comfortable walking in open woodlands where there is plenty of light and we can readily see, which may hark back to a time when seeing predators was essential for survival. The primary agricultural product in these lower-elevation forests is forage for domestic livestock, not timber.

HISTORY OF CALIFORNIA FORESTS AND THEIR MANAGEMENT

When Europeans first began settling in California in the early- to mid-1800s, the forests appeared vast, pristine, massive, and endless. Up to that point, the forests had been impacted, and managed, by the native Californians, who had lived here for at least 10,000 years. Early Europeans saw mixed conifer forests in the Sierra Nevada that contained up to a dozen tree species, and coastal forests that contained massive Douglas-firs and awe-inspiring redwoods. These forests were diverse in species and in the ages and sizes of their trees. During these

Oak Woodlands in Peril

Though the majority of Californians live in close proximity to oak woodlands, few people realize the ecological and economic importance of oak woodland habitat or the frightening rate at which it is disappearing. Many factors threaten the integrity of oak woodlands, but the number one threat remains development: housing development, agricultural and vineyard conversion, and tree cutting for firewood and forage. These types of land use lead to high rates of habitat loss and fragmentation that are likely to continue. The Fire and Resource Assessment Program (FRAP) estimates that from 1990 to 2000, approximately 167,000 acres of oak woodland were developed for residential use and that another 9.7 million acres are estimated to be developed to some degree in the next 40 years. Land-use planning generally takes place at a local or regional level, where it can be affected by local political and financial influences. Conservation of oak woodlands, therefore, presents a challenge to local stakeholders, regional planners, and elected officials to create solutions to complex ecological and social problems.

early years, wood products were generally taken by high-grading, that is, removing just the biggest and best trees, which limited impact on the forest communities.

The available technology largely dictated how and where harvesting took place. In the early years, in addition to oxen and horses, water was commonly used to transport logs, so logging was concentrated near rivers. In coastal forests, harvested trees were temporarily stored near streams, and "splash dams" were built to collect sufficient water to carry trees downstream in the spring. The torrents of water rushing from opened splash dams removed boulders, spawning gravels (used by salmon and steelhead), large woody debris, and even nearby trees. They also tended to widen streams and hasten erosion. The effects of the rush of water and logs downstream can still be seen in the form of scoured stream beds. Even today, some of these streams have low habitat complexity, and they support fewer juvenile salmonids as a result.

When railroads became available to transport raw materials, harvesting took place where access was easy and the rail transport cheap. It was often easiest to take all of the trees at these places, so clear-cutting—a harvesting system that removes all of the trees on a tract of land—became common. This was not an intended silvicultural practice

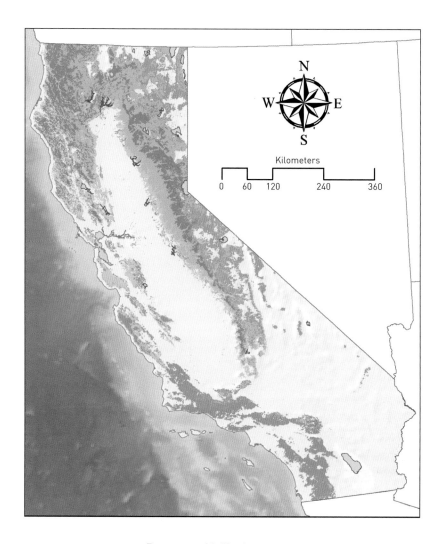

Forest cover of California

▧	Chaparral	▧	Pinyon-juniper
▧	Douglas-fir	▧	Ponderosa pine
▧	Fir-spruce	▢	Redwood
▢	Lodgepole pine	▢	Western hardwoods

California forest cover types. The white areas are not forested. Adapted from the US Geological Survey (controlling establishment, composition, and growth of forests). It was just the most expedient method of tree removal. After clear-cutting, people relied on natural regeneration to restock the harvested areas, but few people were really looking far ahead.

Around the beginning of the twentieth century, forests no longer seemed inexhaustible, and people began to have concerns about wood supplies, watershed protection, and the effects of insects and disease. Huge wildfires occurred during this period, which led to rules for treating slash (wood left behind after tree cutting) in order to protect the increasingly valuable timber stock. In part as a result of these impacts came a growing belief that the government should get involved in forest protection and management. Under the leadership and guidance of Gifford Pinchot, the father of American forestry, the US Forest Service was created and a network of National Forests was established. The number expanded rapidly and, compared with other regions of the country, California had extensive National Forests. Forest Service lands were opened for public use, including timber harvesting, grazing, mining, and recreation.

By the early twentieth century, many people felt that good stewardship was essential and hoped that government ownership would help protect forests into the future. Pinchot recognized that forests provided multiple benefits and championed wise use of resources among competing interests. In addition to promoting multiple use, Pinchot felt that forestry should be science based and that the critical factor for determining successful management was the greatest good for the greatest number of people for the longest time. Under his leadership, some of the worst practices, in terms of adverse impacts on the environment (e.g., hydraulic mining), were outlawed on National Forest lands. Pinchot's convictions brought him into conflict with those more interested in exploiting forest resources for profit. His multiple-use philosophy also brought him into conflict with those, like John Muir, who advocated increased protection for forest resources. Muir felt that publicly owned forests should not be used for resource exploitation and that people in extractive industries, such as mining and lumber, should look elsewhere for their products. Muir's ideas led to the creation of the National Park system. Both the conservation and the preservation principles championed by Pinchot and Muir influenced forest management for generations.

After the Second World War, demand for wood products increased dramatically and harvesting skyrocketed, fueled largely by increases

Gifford Pinchot (1865–1946)

Gifford Pinchot. Photo courtesy of the US Forest Service, Grey Towers National Historic Site

Gifford Pinchot was the first chief of the US Forest Service and the father of American forestry. His father suggested he study forestry. Pinchot later stated, "I had no more conception of what it meant to be a forester than the man in the moon. . . . But at least a forester worked in the woods and with the woods—and I loved the woods and everything about them." Pinchot vastly expanded the number of forest preserves, professionalized management of them under the principle of "the greatest good for the greatest number," and emphasized forest management that focused on the long term. He popularized the concept of conservation of natural resources, in the sense of using them wisely.

in home construction. From 1950 to 1966, for instance, twice as much timber was cut as in the previous 45 years. Both private industry and the Forest Service took up the challenge to ensure production of wood products and were very successful in providing lumber. They built roads into previously roadless areas and developed high-yield forestry practices that included the clear-cutting of old-growth forests.

During this period, not only conifer forests but also oak woodlands were impacted by human activities. Between 1945 and 1970, approximately 2 million acres of woodlands and chaparral in California were cleared of woody vegetation to create grazing land. While clearing usually did result in some forage increases, the benefits often didn't last much more than a decade, while the adverse impacts—including soil erosion, degraded wildlife habitat, and treeless landscapes—remain with us today. Fortunately such clearing for range improvement is largely a thing of the past, although in the last decade there has been an

John Muir (1838–1914)

The clearest way into the Universe is through a forest wilderness.
—John Muir

John Muir. Photo courtesy of the National Park Service

The National Park Service website calls John Muir the father of the National Park Service: "John Muir was many things, inventor, immigrant, botanist, glaciologist, writer, co-founder of the Sierra Club, fruit rancher. But it was John Muir's love of nature, and the preservation of it, that we can thank him for today. Muir convinced President Teddy Roosevelt to protect Yosemite (including Yosemite Valley), Sequoia & Kings Canyon, Grand Canyon and Mt. Rainier as National Parks."

Muir was born in Scotland but became one of California's most prolific and ardent naturalists. Muir is best known for his unsuccessful fight to prevent the damming of Hetch Hetchy Valley in Yosemite, which inspired preservation efforts across the country. Muir and Gifford Pinchot were initially friends but became rivals when their philosophical differences became clear, with Pinchot supporting "multiple uses" of forests and Muir opposing tree harvest, mining, and grazing. Muir's point of view became known as preservation, while Pinchot's became known as conservation.

increase in clearing of oak woodlands and chaparral to convert these lands to intensive agriculture, such as vineyards, and for suburban and rural residential development.

In the 1960s the environmental movement was born, and the public grew increasingly aware of the way conifer and hardwood forests were being mismanaged. Environmentalists opposed the clear-cutting of conifers. While it was usually the cheapest and easiest harvest method, it created an eyesore, adversely affected fisheries and wildlife habitat, and was responsible for increases in erosion and sedimentation, especially on steep slopes. There was also concern about how other forest management practices were affecting environmental resources. Rachel Carson's book *Silent Spring* awakened the public to the dangers of pesticide use, and people became concerned that herbicides sprayed in forests to kill unwanted vegetation could get into waterways and impact wildlife and human health. Environmentalists also became concerned that old-growth stands were being cut at an alarming rate. There was an emerging understanding that forests—especially old-growth forests—are more than just assemblages of large trees or supplies of timber, but also storehouses of biological diversity. Forests were also recognized as special places that provide inspiration and renewal. For all these reasons, efforts began to protect forestlands.

The precursor to the Endangered Species Act (ESA) was passed by Congress in 1966, and the ESA was passed in 1973. It was aimed at protecting species that were threatened with extinction, and it provided a vehicle for opponents of the prevailing forest management practices to challenge them in court. Since some wildlife species, such as the northern spotted owl and the marbled murrelet, require large old trees for hunting and breeding, the courts ruled that existing forest management practices were insufficient to guarantee these species' survival. This ruling and other legal challenges helped to trigger changes that led to new and different approaches to forest management. The impacts on wildlife became a frequent determining factor in timber harvest decisions, and ultimately there were fewer and smaller harvest areas and more retention of old-growth trees. However, many people felt that not enough had changed. Some individuals sat or even camped out in trees to protect them from being cut down, and others tried to stop logging on private lands by physically blocking vehicles or interfering in other ways. In addition, legal challenges to proposed logging were vigorous and often successful.

Such challenges led to a transformation in the way forests are managed. On federal lands, ecosystem management became public policy. The underlying principles of ecosystem management are that biodiversity and ecosystem health should be managed at the landscape level, not the stand level; processes such as nutrient and water cycling are critical to take into account; and the emphasis should be on the ecosystem as a whole, not on products such as timber or on individual wildlife species. Ecosystem management also takes into account the fact that people are part of the equation and that management must be socially acceptable, as well as ecologically based.

Working Together: The Redwood Forest Foundation

The Redwood Forest Foundation is an example of how people with different backgrounds and interests can come together for a common goal and can change how local forest resources are managed. For decades the communities in the redwood region along California's North Coast experienced conflict and argument over the logging of the forests. The conflict was partly due to the fact that decisions affecting local communities were often made by absentee, corporate landowners. In 1997, a nonprofit organization calling itself the Redwood Forest Foundation, Inc. (RFFI) was formed. Its stated mission was "to acquire, protect, restore, and manage forestlands and other related resources in the Redwood Region for the long-term benefit of the communities located there." It began by building a diverse board of directors, including people who had often been adversaries in forest conflicts. The directors included representatives from the timber industry (a mill owner and Registered Professional Foresters), community activist groups (Earth First! and the Sierra Club), the banking community (a stockbroker, a banker), and the University of California Cooperative Extension. They set out to create a new structure of ownership and community partnering unprecedented in the region. The RFFI established county-based advisory committees that played the traditional "shareholder" roles in its decision-making process. These committees also reflected the many talents and diverse experiences of the local communities.

In June 2007, 10 years after its formation, the RFFI acquired nearly 51,000 acres of coastal redwood lands in northwestern Mendocino County, with $65 million in financing from Bank of America. The bank's enthusiasm for working with RFFI was due largely to the community-oriented structure of RFFI's board and the credibility of its members and advisors. The structure of the loan included provisions to protect the forests and prevent overharvesting of timber in order to reduce debt. "This is the beginning of a new era for our local community," said Art Harwood, president of RFFI. "We are banding together to protect and manage our forests. We are pulling together private capital, and the hopes and aspirations of people from all walks of life to create a bright beacon for our future. We are doing this by ending the 30 years of fighting, and focusing on what unites us."

The RFFI illustrates the fact that forest management in California is changing dramatically. In the past, forest managers often focused almost exclusively on timber production. Today, new organizations such as the RFFI realize that cooperation among competing interests is often crucial if they want to manage forests so that they provide critical habitat, increase biodiversity, and improve regional economic vitality.

Contributed by Greg Giusti, Forest Advisor, UC Cooperative Extension.

Today, the debate about how to manage forests in California continues. The Forest Service and Bureau of Land Management are now both dedicated to practicing ecosystem-based management. As a result, harvesting has been greatly reduced on public lands, and large areas of old-growth and mature (late-succession) forests have been set aside. Laws have been passed that regulate timber harvest on federal, state, and private lands. This has resulted in an increased emphasis on "uneven-aged management" and an attempt to make forests more diverse, with a greater range in age and size classes, species, and adequate dead material, both as standing snags and as dead and down wood. Forested areas are also increasingly linked via habitat corridors that wide-ranging wildlife species can use to travel between areas, so the impacts of timber harvesting are minimized.

In the last several decades, there have been dramatic changes in the management of oak woodlands as well. In the early 1980s, there were calls for increased state regulation and for rules that would limit the cutting of oaks and other hardwood species. However, the California Board of Forestry was reluctant to adopt statewide regulation and instead required counties to develop conservation practices to protect oak woodland resources. These local policies have been applied with mixed success. Woodland habitat is still being lost as oak woodland is converted to agricultural land and used for housing and commercial development.

From a social standpoint, public land managers now recognize that they must consider the effects of forest management on people and communities and that they should have input into the decisions that affect them. There are also efforts to operate more at the landscape level and to bring together public and private forest owners and managers for cooperative decision making. Numerous watershed-protection groups, in both woodlands and conifer forests, have been established to address mutual problems and develop innovative solutions (see Collaborative Conservation in Chapter 8). And there is a general belief that forest management should be flexible or adaptive, not rigid, and management practices should be modified if something doesn't work or if science or experience provides new information leading to a different approach.

FOREST DYNAMICS

Forests are dynamic habitats. Through both human and natural disturbances, these plant communities are in continual flux. The composition of species within a stand changes, depending on the age of the forest and the time span between disturbances, with smaller-magnitude disturbances having greater impacts as the stand matures. For example, all else being equal, a less dense coniferous forest that had recently burned wouldn't have enough fuel for a hot-burning crown fire, so it would do less damage than a fire in a more mature forest that hadn't seen human or natural disturbances for 10 or more years.

As forests grow and develop, they change the environment. On a site that has not previously borne vegetation, such as a recent lava flow or an exposed slope after a landslide, plants may be exposed to full sunlight. Initially, only plants that can tolerate high light levels become established. Those that can't will simply not survive. However, as these light-loving plants begin to grow and occupy the site, they reduce the amount of light reaching the ground. Eventually a different cohort of plants begins to grow in the understory—those that can tolerate high levels of shade. Other changes in the environment can also affect community composition. For instance, some sites are initially deficient in nitrogen. Many pioneer species (the first ones to grow) have nodules on their roots that let them fix nitrogen, that is, convert nitrogen in the soil to a form that plants can use. California examples include alder (*Alnus*) and buckbrush (*Ceanothus*). Eventually the fixed nitrogen increases the fertility of the soil and other plants begin to grow there. While plants affect each other and the available resources, it is often the frequency and duration of the disturbances in any given forest that dictate the community composition.

There have been many studies on forest succession to try to predict changes in the composition or structure of forest communities following disturbances such as logging and fire. These studies have found that it can be hard to generalize the path of change; there are many site and landscape characteristics that influence a forest's response to disturbance.

Forests change slowly or rapidly, depending on the disturbances that occur. As a budding naturalist, take time to notice the size of the trees in a forest stand, as well as what makes up the understory, and think about how past disturbances such as grazing, fire, and logging may have influenced what you see.

Forest change can also occur because of disease. When disease organisms are moved from continent to continent by people, they can dramatically alter forest ecosystems. Chestnut blight, for example, was a fungus accidentally imported on nursery trees to the eastern United

Sudden Oak Death and the Gold-Spotted Oak Borer

Sudden oak death (SOD) is a disease that affects several native California oak species in both coastal woodlands and coniferous forests. It is caused by *Phytophthora ramorum*, a fungus-like water mold that causes bark cankers that can girdle and kill mature trees. Since its appearance in California in 1995, SOD has killed hundreds of thousands of tanbark oak, coast live oak, California black oak, Shreve's oak, and canyon live oak trees. SOD has been confirmed in 14 coastal counties, extending from Monterey to Humboldt, but it appears that conditions farther inland are too hot and dry to permit its spread there. Elevated mortality of oaks raises concerns about habitat degradation, invasive species, and increased risk of wildfires.

"As if life wasn't tough enough already for California's oaks," a University of California flyer bemoans, "a new pest has emerged in the last several years. This pest, called the gold-spotted oak borer or GSOB (*Agrilus auroguttatus*, who some refer to as the Golden SOB!!) has been killing thousands of oaks in the mountains in central San Diego County. Experts think the GSOB arrived in the last few years. To date it has attacked coast live oaks (*Quercus agrifolia*), California black oaks (*Q. kelloggii*) and canyon live oaks (*Q. chrysolepis*). The Golden SOB attacks large, vigorous, healthy trees, including urban trees in people's yards."

Firewood has emerged as an important vector for the spread of several invasive species, including *Phytophthora ramorum* and the "golden SOB." Federal, state, and local resource managers are working to raise public awareness as a part of their effort to prevent the spread of pest species through the movement of firewood. Do your part and don't move oak firewood out of local areas! For more information, visit www.gsob.org.

States around 1900. In about 40 years, it killed almost all of the chestnuts in the eastern deciduous forests, forever changing the look, feel, and function of those forests. Chestnuts used to be the largest and most abundant trees in many eastern forests and grew to a diameter of 14 feet! Now they are gone.

We are currently in the initial stages of what may be California's version of chestnut blight. A fungus, probably imported accidentally on cultivated rhododendrons from Germany, is dramatically changing the structure of coastal oak woodlands by killing millions of tan oaks and coast live oaks. Will our grandchildren grow up without ever smelling the distinctive tang of blooming tan oaks in June? On an even larger scale, the combination of white pine blister rust (accidentally introduced by foresters) and mountain pine beetles is devastating western North American stands of whitebark pine (*Pinus albicaulis*). The tree's range is expected to shrink by 70 percent within two decades, and the US Fish and Wildlife Service has determined that it may be in danger of extinction.

CALIFORNIA FORESTS AND WILDFIRE

Fires have always occurred in California and have been instrumental in shaping forested landscapes. Prior to European settlement, fires were intentionally set by Native Americans. There was a widespread recognition by Native Americans that regular burning of forests was beneficial for a variety of reasons: it made hunting easier, stimulated the growth of plants used in basket weaving, made it easier to collect acorns and other forest products (mushrooms, berries), and reduced the likelihood of catastrophic fires. Early ranchers regularly burned their lands—especially oak woodlands—to improve forage production. But about 100 years ago, fire management practices in California dramatically changed, and the era of Gifford Pinchot and Smokey the Bear began. This largely resulted from dismay at the loss of timber resources in massive wildfires near the beginning of the twentieth century. It was reasoned that if wildfires could be put out soon after they started, they would be contained and losses would be reduced. Firefighters were very successful at their job, and as a result, fire as a natural ecosystem process was dramatically reduced.

Many decades passed before people saw a downside to such effective fire suppression. In the past, frequent low-intensity fires had opened up the understories of forests and left fewer shrubs and dead wood, without destroying many large trees. The recent elimination of frequent fires caused dramatic ecosystem changes. In middle-elevation conifer forests, shade-tolerant species such as true firs, previously held in check by regular burning, became much more common. Shade-intolerant species such as ponderosa pine became more rare. Dead material on the forest floor built up, and ladder fuels—those fuels that allow a fire to move from the ground to the tops of trees—increased. Similar, though not as dramatic, changes occurred in oak woodlands as dead material accumulated in the understory and shrub species increased in some areas. In some low-elevation forests, especially in coastal foothills, the removal of fire caused a conversion from savanna-like woodlands to

Rethinking How We Live with Fire

Fire has been an important and necessary ecological process in much of California for many thousands of years, and it will remain so for many more. Wildfires, like other natural hazards on the landscapes we inhabit, are therefore phenomena we must learn to live with. After decades of suppressing wildfires, we now struggle to reintroduce them safely. At the most basic level, however, the current "fire problem" exists primarily because we have developed in ways and in locations that are vulnerable to this natural hazard. We need to rethink how we live with fire.

Fire spread is a physical process affected by many factors. Different combinations of these factors can produce different fire behaviors and varying rates of propagation across the landscape. As "fire weather" gets worse (i.e., higher temperatures, lower humidities, and greater wind speeds), characteristics of fuels (i.e., amounts and spatial patterns of biomass) become less important in controlling how and where a fire may spread. When winds are so strong that long-range "spotting" occurs, blowing burning embers far ahead of a wildfire, the influence of fuel-related factors is greatly diminished. Thus, there is a natural tradeoff between the importance of fuels characteristics and weather conditions; not surprisingly, a similar tradeoff occurs between topography and varying weather conditions. All of these factors will still impact how a wildfire spreads in a given situation, but their relative importance can vary greatly.

Given an understanding of the different controls on fire spread, we can begin to assess the usefulness of fuel treatments on the landscape, whether through prescribed burning to reduce biomass levels or by some other means. A general conclusion is that the effectiveness of treated patches of vegetation will vary, depending on weather conditions. Under the mildest weather conditions, a fire might reach such a treated area and simply go out, due to a lack of flammable material. Even in more hazardous weather conditions, this part of the landscape might still be used by suppression forces, as fire intensities could be low enough to safely work there. Under extreme fire weather conditions, such as the Santa Ana winds that occur each fall, these treatments may only constrain fire spread in a minimal way—if at all—and they are not safe locations for fire suppression forces.

Ultimately, in a world of scarce resources, complicated environmental regulations, and sprawling development, the effectiveness of fuel treatments is limited to certain strategic locations on the landscape. Such locations may be at or near urban-wildland interfaces,

(continued)

Rethinking How We Live with Fire *(continued)*

where they can be the last line of defense in suppressing a wildfire. As we rethink further how to live with fire, we will require more retrofits to existing homes and neighborhoods. This will involve alterations to vegetation around structures, updates to certain building materials and designs, and better development of evacuation procedures.

Excerpted from Max Moritz, 2005. "Rethinking How We Live with Fire," pp 103–105 in *Fire, Chaparral, and Survival in Southern California*, Richard B. Halsey, ed. Sunbelt Publications, San Diego.

forests dominated by conifers, especially Douglas-fir. A consequence of these changes is that when fires do start in California forests—especially during periods of low humidity, high temperatures, and strong winds—they are much more difficult to control, and they tend to burn the tree canopies rather than only near the ground. Some of these fires have become catastrophic stand-destroying fires that have burned large, established trees as well as homes and other property.

Today it is recognized that the structural changes in forests need to be reversed if we are to reduce catastrophic fires. Prescribed fire, as well as thinning and removal of understory plants, are tools to make forests "fire safe." The enormous efforts required, as well as the staggering costs, prevent these treatments from becoming commonplace, so we are likely to continue experiencing massive forest fires in California in the immediate future.

FRAGMENTATION OF FORESTS

Another recent trend impacting California's forests is fragmentation, as large tracts of land are sold and subdivided. Some of these lands continue to be managed as commercial forests, but many are converted to home sites with a range of factors that were previously absent: roads, buildings, noise, and pets. These changes alter the character of the forest, adversely affect wildlife movement, alter scenery, and impair ecosystem processes. The trend toward fragmentation is especially evident in oak woodlands as people move from densely populated urban areas to seek the beauty and solitude that woodlands provide. While development pressures are less in coniferous forests, they still exist and

Urban and agricultural landscape, Sonoma County. Vineyards, orchards, pastures, reservoirs, and roads penetrate and replace oak woodlands. Dense industrial and housing development on the flat valley margins. Animals and plants are separated into fragments of natural habitat. Photo by Adina Merenlender

bring with them a range of problems. In addition to impacting wildlife species that need protected, interior habitat, fragmentation in coniferous forests can reduce management options. For instance, it becomes increasingly difficult to conduct prescribed fires if houses are scattered throughout the forest.

Private land conservation tools can provide incentives to prevent habitat loss and fragmentation while maintaining compatible land-use practices and revenue from compatible activities such as sustainable forestry or livestock production. One such commonly used tool is the conservation easement, an incentive-based approach that relies on continued private ownership and management of land with an easement attached to the title that limits some development or other activities on the land. Easements typically cost less than fully acquiring the land for protection purposes and perhaps more importantly leave the management costs and opportunities for other activities on the land to the private landowner while at the same time maintaining most of the land as undeveloped.

Zoning laws that require large minimum parcel sizes in wildland areas also help protect forests. But as more and more people move into California, there is greater pressure to change zoning and to fragment the forests. In Nevada County, for example, the median size of land-holdings in 1957 was 551 acres, but by 2001 it was only 8.9 acres. The pressure to change zoning is particularly intense where large sums of money can be made by the sale or development of land. Improved land-use planning, acquisition of conservation easements, and other private land-conservation tools are needed if large forest and woodland parcels are to be protected, allowing them to continue to provide critical goods and services to the people of California.

CARBON SEQUESTRATION

California has become a leader in committing to reducing greenhouse gas emissions that contribute to climate change. One new approach has been to promote a cap-and-trade system in which those generating CO_2 emissions (polluters) must buy carbon offsets (ways to compensate) equal to the amount of carbon they emit. Since forests store carbon in trees, those owning forestland have recently been able to "sell" carbon credits to emitters. While this approach is new and it is hard to predict how effective it will be in actually slowing climate change, California and its California Air Resources Board are at the forefront of implementing this approach. One significant outcome could be to increase the number of acres of forest put into conservation easements and maintained as forests which store and sequester carbon from the atmosphere. By leveraging income from carbon credits to finance the purchase of conservation easements, it may be possible to protect forestlands from development or overharvesting. Whatever the outcome of cap-and-trade programs on climate change, these discussions further demonstrate the critical role forests play in environmental health.

The forests of California are certainly very different today than they were 200 years ago when Europeans first arrived. There are fewer forests and more even-aged stands. The trees in these stands are, in general, younger and smaller. The species composition has changed as a century of fire exclusion has caused an increase in shade-tolerant species, as well as a tremendous buildup of fuel. This has greatly increased the risk of catastrophic fires and caused foresters to rethink fire suppression and the roles both natural and prescribed fire play in forest management.

Milling has also changed as the logs removed from conifer forests have become smaller. Many lumber mills have closed, forcing people

How Forests Sequester Carbon

The process of photosynthesis combines atmospheric carbon dioxide with water, releasing oxygen into the atmosphere and incorporating the carbon atoms into the cells of plants. Forest soils also capture carbon. Trees, unlike annual plants that die and decompose yearly, are long-lived plants that develop a large biomass, thereby capturing large amounts of carbon over many decades. Thus, a forest ecosystem can capture and retain large volumes of carbon over hundreds of years.

Forests operate both as vehicles for capturing carbon and as carbon reservoirs. Forests sequester carbon roughly proportional to the forest's growth in biomass. An old-growth forest acts as a reservoir, holding large volumes of carbon for hundreds of years. The Intergovernmental Panel on Climate Change (IPCC) states that forest management directed at carbon sequestration could make a significant difference in global carbon sequestration over the near and medium term. Strategies include reduction of tropical deforestation, forest expansion, increases in forest density, and sequestering carbon in long-lived wood products.

Adapted from Roger Sedjo, 2001. "Forest Carbon Sequestration: Some Issues for Forest Investments." RFF Discussion paper 01-34, Resources for the Future, Washington, DC.

out of work and causing social and economic upheaval in a number of forest-based communities. With the high demand for raw logs from overseas, from China in particular, there is little incentive for local mills to cut lumber for local or international markets. Those remaining in the milling business have had to modify their equipment, to accommodate smaller log sizes and newer products such as particleboard, oriented strand board, and laminated beams, which have a higher market value.

Other recent changes include an increase in interest in forest certification—an assessment of whether individual forests are being managed sustainably—and in new commodities harvested from the forest: specialty products such as mushrooms, fir boughs, moss, and ferns have gained importance. There is now greater public input into decision making, and the effects of management actions on local people and communities are factored into the decision-making process. There is greater landscape, rather than stand-level, planning, as well as efforts to protect habitats rather than individual wildlife species.

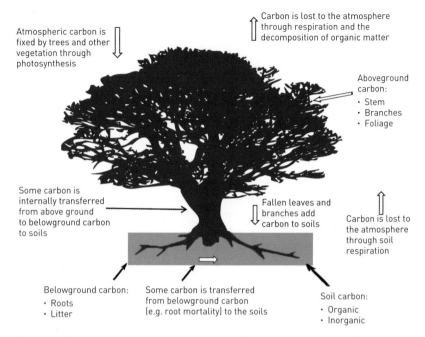

Atmospheric carbon is fixed by trees and other vegetation through photosynthesis

Carbon is lost to the atmosphere through respiration and the decomposition of organic matter

Aboveground carbon:
· Stem
· Branches
· Foliage

Some carbon is internally transferred from above ground to belowground carbon to soils

Fallen leaves and branches add carbon to soils

Carbon is lost to the atmosphere through soil respiration

Belowground carbon:
· Roots
· Litter

Some carbon is transferred from belowground carbon (e.g. root mortality) to the soils

Soil carbon:
· Organic
· Inorganic

Carbon in living systems. Carbon moves among living organisms, the soil, and the atmosphere. Photosynthesis harvests carbon from the atmosphere and stores (sequesters) it in living and dead organisms and in soil. Decomposition releases carbon to the atmosphere. Adapted from the US Environmental Protection Agency

Though the forests and woodlands of California are not what they were in the presettlement era, they are still the dominant feature in large portions of California and are still awe inspiring. They are revered for their majesty and beauty and appreciated for their complexity and productivity.

RANGELANDS AND LIVESTOCK GRAZING MANAGEMENT

The most common use of California's rangelands has been livestock grazing, and livestock continue to have strong cultural and economic value and to play an important role in land management. Domestic cattle, sheep, and horses arrived with the Spanish colonists in 1769, and by the early 1800s livestock grazing was widespread throughout California. During the Gold Rush, livestock grazing boomed because of an increased demand for meat, and by the late 1800s there were about 3 million cattle and 6 million sheep on California's grasslands.

Restoring California's Native Grasses

California's grasslands were once vegetated by native perennial grasses. But during the last 200 years, exotic annual grasses from Europe started taking over, and now only 2 percent of the state's grasslands are vegetated by native perennial grasses. There are about 300 species of native grasses, which began to get displaced when Spaniards settled in California in the 1700s, bringing livestock and new land practices. Annual grasses took over in the 1800s, possibly because of overgrazing.

A study of three grass fields 30 miles west of Sacramento, California, was conducted to increase our understanding of how well revegetation with native grasses works. One field contains annual grasses, one is a newly restored field of native grasses, and the third has contained native grasses for 10 years. "We're looking at various methods, such as using controlled fires, applying herbicides, and determining what species grow best in which areas of California," says Stephen M. Griffith with the USDA.

Unlike annual grasses, perennial grasses turn green faster, stay green longer, and produce more biomass which can benefit livestock and wildlife. This equates to more protein and higher value forage for both wildlife and livestock. The site that contained annual grass had significantly fewer tons per acre of aboveground plant biomass accumulation than the two plots that were restored to native grasses. Native grasses integrate better with other plants. That diversity of plants attracts wildlife not found in annual grasses. "We've noticed a significant change in biodiversity," says California farmer John Anderson about the native planting experiments. Furthermore, native grasses improve soil and limit erosion.

One problem is that native-grass seed is very expensive. It may cost $40 a pound, while turfgrass seed is about 50 cents a pound. Perhaps showing the positive effects of native grasslands will influence supply and demand and make native grass more affordable.

Adapted from David Elstein, May 2004. *Agricultural Research.*

The US Department of Agriculture has estimated that about 5.2 million head of cattle (and 500,000 sheep) are in the state today, making California the fifth largest cattle-producing state in the nation. The California cattle industry is valued at over $2 billion from around 11,800 ranches across the state. Less than 10 percent of the cattle in California are raised in large feedlots, emphasizing the importance of California's range resources for cattle production.

The spread of cattle grazing was accompanied by the spread of non-native grasses and other invasive species, many of which decreased the quality of the forage. This is a concern for ranchers, as cattle depend on quality grassland production during the fall when the grasses begin to green, throughout the slow winter period of growth, and into spring when forage plants grow rapidly before dying off during the dry summer. It's important to manage livestock in a way that leaves enough residual dry matter after the growing season. This material ensures the next year's crop of grasses because it acts as a mulch to increase soil organic matter and promote plant germination and growth.

The amount of residue remaining on the ground is an important measure. Ranchers use it as a gauge to determine "stocking rates" and to manage livestock in ways that maintain rangeland quality while increasing animal weight. Stocking rate is the number of animals of each type that graze an area of land for a specific period of time. The animal unit month (AUM) is the most common measure of stocking rate, with an animal unit commonly defined as one mature (1,000-pound) cow. An AUM equals the amount of forage required for a 1,000-pound cow to maintain its weight for one month. Rangelands have different carrying capacities—the number of animals that can be raised year after year without damage to range resources—depending on soil quality, rainfall, slope, tree canopy cover, and the grazing and management history of the site. These influence grassland composition and hence overall productivity. Excessive grazing results in low amounts of residual dry matter and can promote the growth of less desirable forage species and lower total production of rangelands.

Cattle grazing on private land helps preserve 20 million acres of open rangeland landscapes. Today, there is a concerted effort by many California range managers to improve rangeland productivity by adding native perennial grass recovery to the overall grazing program. Equally important, land trusts are actively working to conserve rangelands as open space. They can prevent development by purchasing these lands or through partial purchase as part of conservation easements and other agreements.

CONSERVATION BIOLOGY

Conservation biology is a relatively new and interdisciplinary science. It has its roots in ecology and wildlife management and emerged from the realization that the Earth is in a biodiversity crisis. Its focus is on main-

All You Need to Know to Be a Principled Ecologist

- All species in ecological systems are dependent upon other species for their existence.
- The organisms in ecological systems nearly always act to maximize their individual fitness (reproductive success), not to benefit the population, community, or ecosystem.
- Change is a commonality at all levels of organization.
- While each successively larger scale is composed of the units of the next smaller scale, it possesses properties unique to that scale.
- Ecosystems are altered by human manipulations, and these changes are often irreversible.
- The abundance and distribution of a species will depend on its interaction with other species and with the abiotic environment: soils, wind, temperature, light, water, geologic formations, natural and human-induced disturbances.

Adapted from Mary Orland. "Principles of Ecology." *Essays on Wildlife Conservation* (Peter Moyle and Douglas Kelt, eds.) at www.marinebio.org.

taining the Earth's biodiversity, including natural ecological and evolutionary processes. To achieve this goal, conservation biologists work at all scales of life, from genes to ecosystems. There is increasing recognition among conservation biologists that social science is integral to providing solutions for the biodiversity crises. This includes working with indigenous people, land-use planning, landscape architecture, political ecology, and other disciplines. Michael Soulé, who helped found the Society for Conservation Biology, characterized conservation biology as a "crisis discipline," in which tactical decisions must sometimes be made in the face of uncertain knowledge. The discipline has developed ways to address complex environmental issues with dynamic solutions based on scientific research.

How is it, exactly, that human activity impacts natural communities? Does cutting an oak or patch of oaks diminish the value of the remaining woodland? It depends. Rarely do such acts happen in isolation. It is the overall pattern of change that dictates the level of impact on a plant community or on a population of animals that depend on those plants. Certainly, human activities across all scales, from local harvesting to global climate change, can result in loss of individual spe-

Ecological Values and Land Use

The Ecological Society of America (ESA) has prepared a set of basic guidelines that provide a conceptual framework for land-use planning. They recommend that the following checklist of factors should be considered in making land-use decisions:

1. Examine the impacts of local decisions in a regional context.
2. Plan for long-term change and unexpected events.
3. Preserve rare landscape elements, critical habitats, and associated species.
4. Avoid land uses that deplete natural resources over a broad area.
5. Retain large contiguous or connected areas that contain critical habitats.
6. Minimize the introduction and spread of nonnative species.
7. Avoid or compensate for effects of development on ecological processes.
8. Implement land-use and land-management practices that are compatible with the natural potential of the area.

Excerpted from V. H. Dale, et al., 2000. "Ecological Principles and Guidelines for Managing the Use of Land." *Ecological Applications* 10(3): 639–670.

cies and/or loss of habitat. But it is often the pattern of habitat loss that has accumulating effects on the quality of a community.

When a patch of continuous habitat is broken up into many small patches, a process called fragmentation, the remaining patches may not be able to support all of the species the original patch did. Even when habitat loss is due to natural causes such as hurricanes or earthquakes, smaller habitat patches contain fewer species, as well as fewer specialists (i.e., species that depend on specific habitat, foods, or other limiting factors in order to survive). This change in habitat patch size, with a reduction in interior or core habitat and an increase in edge habitat, has implications for the conservation of biodiversity.

Size and isolation of patches are two of the most important factors affecting whether species persist in an area after fragmentation. Larger fragments support larger numbers of species. The relative isolation of those patches from one another is important because, ultimately, many species that require large areas to maintain functional populations need to move among the remaining habitat patches to survive, whether many

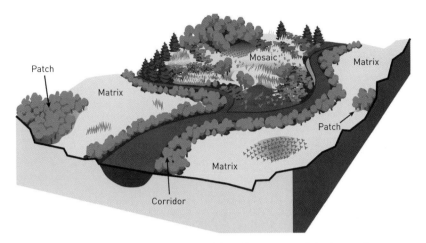

Fragmentation vocabulary: study this model until you can explain the words *matrix*, *mosaic*, *patch*, and *corridor*. Courtesy of the Federal Interagency Stream Restoration Working Group (FISRWG)

Community fragmentation

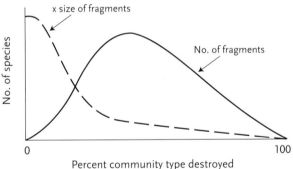

Community fragmentation. The number of species decreases as the number of fragments increases. The number of species also decreases as the size of fragments decreases. From *Corridor Ecology*, by Jodi A. Hilty, William Z. Lidicker, and Adina M. Merenlender. Copyright © 2006 Jodi A. Hilty, William Z. Lidicker, and Adina M. Merenlender. Reproduced by permission of Island Press, Washington, DC small patches or several large patches of habitat remain. Patch size and location relative to one another as well as how permeable the landscape is between patches determine habitat connectivity, a measure of the extent to which plants and animals can move among habitat patches. High levels of habitat connectivity may lessen some impacts of fragmentation by allowing individuals or populations to use more than one habitat patch, thus helping species persist in a region. Valley oak woodland is a good example of this concept. Because habitat loss has occurred across a large portion of this community's historical range, many of the remaining valley oak woodlands are small, isolated patches of habitat. This means that any future loss of habitat will further reduce the number of functional habitat patches, decrease connectivity, and increase the decline of species dependent on valley oak wodlands.

What does this mean for the future of conservation in California? Scientists throughout California and beyond have been looking into this question. Using the principles of conservation biology, scientists have begun to put together a picture of the existing resources and their biogeographical relationships to each other. What are the quality, size, and characteristics of a particular habitat? Where is it located in relation to other similar habitat? Is it at high risk for conversion for development or agriculture? Is it a functional patch of habitat, or has community integrity already been compromised? These are some of the questions that scientists will continue to address to help set priorities for conservation, patterns of development, and principles of resource management.

Explore!

VISIT A NEARBY STATE OR NATIONAL FOREST OR PARK

Go to the visitor's center and find out what, if any, silvicultural practices have influenced the landscape, then look for the "evidence" in the trees and understory.

VISIT UNUSUAL FORESTS

We are so fortunate to live in a state with some of the world's largest and most amazing trees and forests. Don't let more time pass without visiting some of them! Good places to start include these:

- The Mendocino Staircase Pygmy Forest at Jughandle State Reserve has a series of terraces, each with its own ecology, and one featuring pygmy trees.

- Redwood National Park is the home of some of the tallest coast redwoods (*Sequoia sempervirens*).

- Prairie Creek Redwoods State Park is home to giant redwoods and the tallest Sitka spruce (*Picea sitchensis*).

- Sequoia and Kings Canyon National Parks are home to the largest trees on Earth, including a giant sequoia (*Sequoiadendron giganteum*) called General Sherman.

- Demonstration forests are operated by CAL FIRE throughout the state for research on forest management techniques. There are eight, and they're also open to the public. Site locations can be found at www.fire.ca.gov/resource_mgt/resource_mgt_state forests.php.

ENGAGING IN LOCAL LAND-USE PLANNING

Learn about land use, zoning, and development in your area. Who are the stakeholders and what are their positions? What is the history of land use and development? What does your county's general plan say about development of rural parcels? Research zoning, grading, and tree preservation ordinances to see what protections these policies afford woodlands and forestlands. For the politically inclined, attend the meetings of your planning commission, city council, or county supervisors.

PLANT TREES

Planting trees is an excellent way to learn local trees and help preserve forest resources. Many county, state, and federal parks and forests, as well as California ReLeaf, American Forests, and the Arbor Day Foundation, have organized events.

FEEL THE SPIRIT OF THE FOREST

Forests have a way of taking us into a spiritual state of mind, and many religions have some way of honoring or celebrating trees. Research the history and rituals of your spiritual practice and get involved when the tree holiday comes along: organize a hike, plant trees, share nature poetry, or revive some ancient practice that has been long forgotten.

GET CREATIVE

Spend some time alone in a beautiful forest environment and create a piece of art based on your experience—a song, a story, photographs, poems. In the fall, weave garlands of fallen leaves.

6

Animals

Most animals on Earth are dependent on the sun for their energy needs. They derive their energy by eating plants and other photosynthetic organisms which are capable of capturing the sun's energy and transforming it into a form that is useful to animals. With the exception of the few species that rely on Earth's interior energy at spots like deep-sea hydrothermal vents, animals directly or indirectly depend on plants for their livelihood. This pattern is universal and explains the energy relationships among organisms elegantly, so it is helpful to think of all of the animals on Earth in terms of these energy relationships: as either primary consumers (animals that eat photosynthetic organisms) or predators (animals that eat other animals). Important but often misplaced in the array of organisms are those that eat and recycle dead matter: detritivores (primary consumers that eat plants after the plants are dead), scavengers (predators that eat dead animals), and microbes (bacteria, yeasts, and others). These categories can be much further divided and fine-tuned, and there are animals that don't fit well. For instance, is a dung beetle that rolls up and buries small balls of mammal feces and lays its eggs on the balls a predator or a scavenger? But, for the most part these terms describe well the energy relationships of the great majority of animals.

Predation and competition among animals for resources (food, shelter) are important ecological properties that structure animal communities. A classic example of predator-prey interactions is the snowshoe

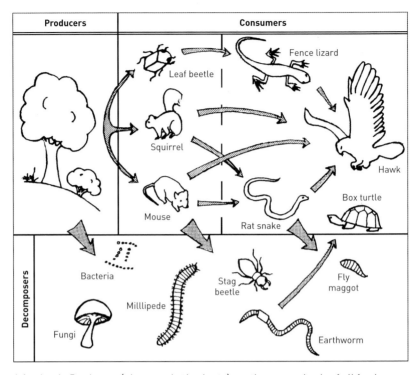

Producers	Consumers

Leaf beetle

Fence lizard

Squirrel

Hawk

Mouse

Box turtle

Rat snake

Decomposers

Bacteria

Stag beetle

Fly maggot

Milllipede

Fungi

Earthworm

A food web. Producers (photosynthetic plants) are the energy basis of all food chains. From *Conservation Planning: Preserving Ecosystems in Open Space Networks*, Agriculture and Natural Resources publication 3370. Copyright UC Regents, used by permission

hare and the Canadian lynx, in which the population of the two animals is tightly linked. Abundance or scarcity of snowshoe hares regulates lynx populations and vice versa: when the population of hares is high, the population of lynx increases as well until the point where predation by the lynx starts to decrease the hare population. The lynx population then follows with a decline, the snowshoe hare population rebounds, and the cycle begins again.

An important concept for understanding the energy relationships among organisms is the food web. A food web graphically describes the many interconnected energy relationships among the plants, herbivores, carnivores, and decomposers in a given system. The arrows in the graphic represent the direction of energy transfer, that is, who is eaten by whom. Look at the food web diagram and try to identify the primary producers, primary consumers, and secondary consumers.

Which is an herbivore? Is there an omnivore? Notice how the mouse, for example, is a food source for three different animals. Although a food web is always oversimplified, it attempts to convey the complex interactions that take place in nature.

Animals can be categorized in a variety of other ways in addition to energy relationships: by their lifestyles and activity patterns, their ecological functions, their reproductive strategies, and their unique and wonderful adaptations. For example, all of the animals on Earth can be categorized according to when they are active. Most animals have a typical time of day for being active and a habitual time to rest or hide. Those that graze or hunt during the day are called diurnal, like cows and swallows. Those that are active at night are nocturnal, with examples being raccoons and spotted owls. There is another group that is not as clear-cut as the above—those that are most active at dawn and dusk but may be somewhat active into the day or the night. They are called crepuscular. Examples might be coyotes, nighthawks, and hawk moths. On a longer scale, some animals are active year-round (people, elk, sharks), while others take a metabolic vacation during the unfavorable season. This time off can look very different for different kinds of animals.

Many people will be familiar with the idea of hibernation, where an animal becomes inactive; its body temperature, respiration rate, and heart rate are reduced; and its metabolism is greatly slowed down, usually in relation to cold temperatures and short day length. Hibernation is an example of an endothermic (warm-blooded) mammal taking an extended break. Other examples of metabolic change that may be less familiar are birds and bats going into a state of torpor for half the day (birds overnight, bats during the day). In the torpid state, birds or bats exhibit reduced core temperatures and lower heart and respiration rates, but the state lasts only about 12 hours. This ability apparently helps these small endotherms to conserve energy. Essentially, while they sleep, they save the cost of heating for flight activity the following day. Examples of hibernation in exothermic (cold-blooded) animals are far more dramatic, with frogs spending the winter below the ice in a frozen lake and fish frozen into blocks of ice being perhaps the most extreme. Many exothermic vertebrates spend extended periods being inactive, either during the cold, short days of winter (hibernation) or during the hot, dry days of summer (estivation). Red-legged frogs, slender salamanders, and many others retreat to deep underground cavities to avoid desiccation during the six-month California dry season. In

Why We Need Sea Otters and Other Top Carnivores

Sea otter (Enhydra lutris) near Morro Bay, California. Photo courtesy of Michael L. Baird, flickr.bairdphotos.com

Sea otters have not had an easy time of it along the North Pacific Coast. By 1900, populations were decimated by the fur trade. Protective efforts have revived populations, but from Alaska to Southern California, sea otters are under new pressure from human threats. Members of the commercial shellfish industry propose an otter hunt to reduce competition for clams, mussels, and abalone. There is even a bill in Congress proposing that the sea otter fur trade be resumed in some areas. But this push-back on otters ignores the food web and its connection with the carbon cycle.

Sea otters are top predators in the marine food chain and have a critical effect on trophic levels below them. In addition to other shellfish, they eat sea urchins, which feed on kelp. Kelp makes up the forest of the sea, providing habitat and food for myriad other life-forms. When sea otters are missing from the coastal reefs, unchecked urchin numbers feed on the kelp until there isn't any more. No kelp eventually means small fish and shellfish go too. The productivity of the marine system without its top predator is vastly curtailed. This means far less quarry for the human hunters as well.

Plant life, including kelp, additionally contributes important functioning to the atmospheric carbon cycle. Plants produce oxygen and sequester carbon. Otters help keep kelp levels healthy, which in turn helps balance the marine ecosystem, which impacts carbon uptake. We need otters, and not for their fur.

Mary Ellen Hannibal, 2012. meh@znet.com.

the lowlands of California, estivation is more common and important, while in the higher-elevation areas of the Sierra Nevada, Cascades, and Southern California mountains, hibernation is more important. Another approach to avoiding the unfavorable season is to have a life cycle oriented around the seasons, and pass the unfavorable season as a hard-shelled egg, a desiccation-resistant pupa, or an inactive grub. Insects have specialized for all of these techniques, and spiders, centipedes, and millipedes exhibit some of them.

Another way to group animals is to think about their method of reproduction. All animals must reproduce themselves, and most do it through sexual reproduction. The variety of schemes animals have come up with to exploit this opportunity is an entire course in itself (sociobiology), only briefly treated here. Most insects, spiders, amphibians, fish, reptiles, and many small mammals give minimal physical inheritance (energy, biomass) and no parental care to their offspring. Essentially, they bet on producing so many young that some will survive with minimal inheritance, even if the majority does not. The most contrasting approach is to produce only one offspring at a time; give it huge gifts of protein, fat, and carbohydrates; care for it for multiple years; and expect that added physical support and parental care will maximize reproductive success. This strategy is followed by many of the largest mammals, including elk, cougars, and elephant seals. There is a continuum of possibilities between these two extremes; many different points along the spectrum have been tried, and multiple exceptions exist within evolutionary groups, but it is helpful to think of most animals as following either the "many offspring, little parental care" approach or the "few offspring, intensive care" approach.

It is important to remember that life on Earth arose in the ocean, and only much later were various forms of life able to colonize the great land masses. Thus all terrestrial life on Earth, which we consider the norm, is in fact highly specialized and derived from aquatic forms. Much of the selection pressure that constrains the forms of animals on land today is related to the difficulty of existing in a terrestrial habitat and coping with water loss. Insects are characterized by having a hard outer shell (an exoskeleton) made of chitin. It can be argued that the most important evolutionary function of the insect exoskeleton is to retain moisture. The skin of humans is far less efficient than an insect exoskeleton at impeding water loss. Nonetheless, one of the main functions of our skin is to keep us from drying out.

Animals are terrific architects of the environment. Grasslands and

Ladybird beetle winter congregation. Ladybird beetles
migrate to winter hibernation masses, feed on aphids, and
are chemically protected. The farthest right beetle has spread
its elytra. H. Vannoy Davis © California Academy of Sciences

meadows remain grasslands and meadows mostly because, in North
America, bison, elk, and gophers keep them that way. Without the grazing and trampling effect of large mammals, and the soil-rotating effect
of small burrowing mammals, most meadows would soon become
shrublands and woodlands.

Beavers are a startling example of animals that manipulate habitat
to suit their needs. In addition to felling trees and opening up grazing
habitat to sunlight, beavers dam creeks and small rivers, turning river
habitat into pond or lake habitat. Not only are the beavers affected, but
the water temperature and water chemistry, the aquatic plants, the fish,
and every other aspect of the habitat is altered. Whole suites of organisms are excluded or invited when a beaver dams a river. Animals are
largely responsible for the destruction and recycling of plants (decomposition). Without the beetles that eat dead trees, the entire world
would be a giant pick-up-sticks-like maze of fallen, dead, undecom-
posed trees.

Perhaps the most enthralling aspect of watching wildlife is the
diversity of behaviors one sees. From cormorants fluttering their gular
pouches to release heat, to the head butting of elk to establish a dominance hierarchy, animal behavior is wild and wonderful. Each animal will display behaviors of some kind, from sitting quietly to avoid
detection to making dramatic noises or movements that serve a suite

Bull elk sparring to establish dominance. The dominant male (bull) elk controls and mates with all females in a harem. Antlers are shed annually. Gerald and Buff Corsi © California Academy of Sciences

of evolutionary or life history needs. Behavior is a large and fascinating topic. Read avidly and spend time observing animals closely. The rewards are legion.

EVOLUTIONARY GROUPS

One last way to think about animals is by their evolutionary groups, the sets of who is related to whom. Although scientists today are far from

KINGDOMS OF LIVING THINGS IN THE LINNAEAN CLASSIFICATION SYSTEM

Kingdom	Structural Organization	Methods of Nutrition	Types of Organisms	Total Species (estimated)
Monera	Small, single prokaryotic cell (nucleus not enclosed by a membrane)	Absorb or photosynthesize food	Bacteria, blue-green algae, and spirochetes	1 million
Protista	Large, single eukaryotic cell (nucleus enclosed by a membrane)	Absorb, ingest, and/or photosynthesize food	Protozoans and algae	600,000
Fungi	Multicellular, filamentous forms with specialized eukaryotic cells	Absorb food	Fungi, molds, mushrooms, yeasts, and mildews	1.5 million
Plantae	Multicellular forms with specialized eukaryotic cells without their own means of locomotion	Photosynthesize food	Mosses, ferns, nonflowering plants, and flowering plants	320,000
Animalia	Multicellular forms with specialized eukaryotic cells with their own means of locomotion	Ingest food	Sponges, worms, invertebrates, fish, amphibians, reptiles, birds, and mammals	9.8 million

unanimous in using the "five kingdom" scheme to describe the diversity of life on Earth, it is useful. The five groups are prokaryotes (called Monera in the table), protists (Protista), plants (Plantae), fungi, and animals (Animalia). Prokaryotes have simple cellular structure, lacking organelles or a nucleus, and usually reproduce asexually. Prokaryotes include bacteria and cyanobacteria, formerly known as blue-green algae. A few prokaryotes may be slightly familiar thanks to the diseases they cause, such as *Streptococcus pyogenes* that is the source of strep throat. The other four groups are all eukaryotes, with organelles and a nuclear envelope in their cellular structure. The eukaryotes can be divided into three easily recognized categories (fungi, plants, and animals) plus the mostly unicellular protists.

The division of kingdoms is clearly artificial in some ways, stressing large multicellular animals and plants. At the root of the tree of life there is tremendous diversity among unicellular organisms that the five kingdom scheme does not recognize. This system divides animals into two major groups: invertebrates and vertebrates. Invertebrates include the worms, clams, spiders, scorpions, millipedes, centipedes, insects, and many other forms. The invertebrates are by far the larger group, in terms of total number of species and in terms of global biomass, yet generally receive less attention than vertebrates.

Vertebrates are the group with fish, birds, frogs, mammals, toads, turtles, lizards, snakes, crocodilians, salamanders, and dinosaurs. The principal feature distinguishing these two great groups is the presence or absence of a bony or cartilaginous backbone: vertebrates have one, invertebrates do not. Invertebrates generally utilize an outer shell, or exoskeleton, to provide the functions vertebrates accomplish with internal bony or cartilaginous structures.

INVERTEBRATES

The invertebrate world is as strange as any Hollywood horror movie, if not more so. Within the great group of invertebrates, evolution appears to proceed along a simple line: the differentiation of a segmented body plan. Imagine the most ancient ancestor of spiders, crabs, millipedes, and beetles looking like a simple, undifferentiated worm with legs. The body is externally supported, with internal organs like lungs, circulatory system, and muscles being attached to the exoskeleton. It is bilaterally symmetrical, with each segment of the body bearing one pair of appendages.

Click beetle. Head and thorax are merged. Antennae are beaded, with triangular beads, the first much larger. Eyes protrude from the side of the head. Six segmented legs. Elytra cover the abdomen, hiding the folded wings below them. © Joyce Gross, http://joycegross.com

Each of the modern forms has been derived by taking the original body plan and reducing, increasing, or merging the number of segments and modifying the appendages for specific functions. Thus, the one pair of antennae on a moth are ultimately derived from one segment of the ancestral invertebrate, with the appendages (legs) highly modified for sensory purposes. The spider body plan consists of two main regions, the cephalothorax and the abdomen. The cephalothorax is the body part that carries the four pairs of legs and can be thought of as four ancestral segments merged into one, with the retention of all four pairs of appendages as legs. Similarly, the fangs of a spider and the mandibles of a beetle represent modified segments, with the appendages (legs) being specialized for food acquisition purposes.

There may be a few people whose "folk taxonomy" lumps all "creepie-crawlies" into the group insects. Actually, the invertebrates are a highly diverse lineage, and insects are only one of the types of invertebrates: spiders, crabs, scorpions, and many other invertebrates are not insects. To help distinguish these taxonomic groups, the following sections will outline each of the major invertebrate cousins, identify special reasons for noticing them, describe a few of the distinguishing features of these groups, and highlight a few of the most common organisms and the patterns they exemplify.

Centipedes are perhaps the invertebrate most superficially like an ancestral arthropod, and they are good organisms to use in imagining the ancestral invertebrate body plan. They are strongly segmented, with all segments except those in the head region bearing only one set of jointed legs. Thus, they exhibit little evidence of merging or modification of segments. Centipedes are flattened, which facilitates their habit of living under rocks, logs, and bark and moving through tight spaces. Unlike insects, centipedes have no waxy coating on the exoskeleton, thus they are highly susceptible to drying out (desiccation). For

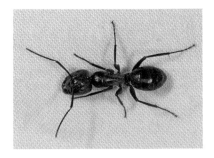

Ant. Head (left), thorax and abdomen (right) visible. Six legs attached to the thorax, with six distinct segments, final segment with paired claws. Head wider than the thorax. Antennae attached to the head, basal segment far longer than the others. © Joyce Gross, http://joycegross.com

this reason they are strictly nocturnal, prefer to live in damp micro-habitats, or are active only during appropriate climatic conditions. In other words, they are found in the moist forests in northwestern California, as well as under rocks and garbage cans in the wet season in most of California, but they go deeper underground and become inactive in the dry season. The centipede head bears a pair of appendages highly modified for chemical and tactile sensory function (antennae) but has no eyes or only simple eyes (ocelli) that tell light from dark but do not resolve an image. So these highly active, fast-moving predators are blind! They hunt by smell and feel. They take one to three years to grow from an egg to an adult, then live three to six additional years. This is a long-lived invertebrate! For this reason, they make good pets. Although adult centipedes may have 15 to 99 pairs of legs (but always an odd number of pairs), they are born with only 3 to 7 pairs. With each molt they add pairs of legs until they reach adulthood.

Millipedes are another classic, segmented arthropod, but this time a detritivore-herbivore with two pairs of legs per segment. Thus, this animal exhibits a simple variation on the segmented-worm-with-legs theme: merging without reduction. Each modern segment of a milli-pede's body represents two ancestral segments that have become one, with the appendages (legs) from both ancestral segments retained. Millipedes are cylindrical animals, contrasting sharply with the flat-tened centipedes. Millipedes are thought to be among the first animals to have colonized terrestrial habitats during the Silurian period (439–408 mya). The oldest known fossil of a land animal, *Pneumodesmus newmani*, was a 1-centimeter-long millipede. There are about 10,000 species of millipedes globally.

Crustaceans are a distinctive group of largely aquatic inverte-brates that include well-known macroscopic forms like crabs, lobsters, shrimp, crawdads (also called crayfish), and sow bugs (also called pill

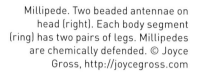

Millipede. Two beaded antennae on head (right). Each body segment (ring) has two pairs of legs. Millipedes are chemically defended. © Joyce Gross, http://joycegross.com

bugs). Crustaceans also include ecologically important microscopic forms that inhabit freshwater, especially ponds, and form an important part of aquatic food chains (fairy shrimp, water fleas, copepods, and ostracods). One of the distinctions of the crustaceans, being largely aquatic, is that most of them breathe by means of gills. Unlike the millipedes, centipedes, and insects, which breathe through small holes (spiracles) in their exoskeletons, crabs and their allies have special organs that can be external or internal and provide a surface for gas exchange.

Spiders are one of the larger, more successful groups of arthropods, with perhaps 40,000 species on Earth. They are prominent in most habitats and easily observed, and for these reasons they can be very attractive to naturalists. Spiders have two body segments, the cephalothorax and the abdomen. The cephalothorax carries the four pairs of legs, the eight eyes (!), and the chelicerae (fangs). Under the abdomen, toward the rear, are the (usually six) spinnerets, through which silk is emitted. Spiders have a relatively simple life history. They hatch from eggs as tiny versions of the adult. They then shed their exoskeletons to grow larger.

Virtually all spiders have venom glands which they use to subdue prey or for defense. In most spiders the venom is delivered via hollow fangs, each with a hole near the tip. Most spiders are too small to successfully inject venom through human skin, and most of the spiders whose fangs are large enough to penetrate our skin have innocuous venom. There are two spiders in North America which are dangerously poisonous, the black widow and the brown recluse. The black widow is widespread in the United States, but the brown recluse is not present in California.

Insects are the most successful group of organisms on Earth, as measured in terms of number of species or biomass. The estimates of the number of species of insects vary wildly, between 2.5 and 30 million.

Wolf spider with multiple young clinging to its abdomen (left). Look for eight legs, eight eyes, a pair of palps (short, leg-like appendages), and bristles on the legs. © Joyce Gross, http://joycegross.com

The buzz of a honeybee, the sting of a yellow jacket, the beauty of butterflies, the buzz of cicadas are all familiar parts of daily life.

Insects have such different approaches to life than mammals that it is mind boggling to contemplate them. The insect body plan is an exoskeleton divided into three segments, the head, thorax (chest), and abdomen (belly). On the head are the sensory and feeding structures, the modified legs that have become antennae and mouthparts. The thorax carries the three pairs of legs, and usually one or two pairs of wings. The abdomen is appendage-less but carries the reproductive parts, which function through the tip (distal end) of the abdomen.

Insects exhibit complex life cycles. Each species has a lifestyle that is slightly different, but insect life cycles can be grouped into two broad categories: complete and incomplete metamorphosis. Complete metamorphosis is the classic insect life cycle exemplified by butterflies: egg to grub (larva), grub to pupa (chrysalis, or cocoon), pupa to adult. This life cycle (termed holometabolous) is shared by butterflies, moths, beetles, flies, caddis flies, fleas, and wasps. Adult insects do not grow. This fact bares repeating, as it is crucial to an understanding of insect life cycle adaptations: adult insects do not grow, nor do they ever shed their shells again. If one loses a leg, it is gone, never to be regrown. This is unlike spiders, which continue to shed their shells throughout their lives and may regrow lost limbs.

Incomplete metamorphosis is also termed gradual development. In insects exhibiting incomplete metamorphosis, the form that hatches from the egg looks like a small, wingless version of the adult. It then sheds its shell several times, growing larger with each shed (each molt). On the final shed, new structures are added, including wings and reproductive organs. Incomplete metamorphosis is practiced by grasshoppers, aphids, stinkbugs, roaches, and silverfish. There is one major variation on the theme of incomplete metamorphosis, that of

Honeybee on sage. Honeybees are not native to the New World and are the most important pollinators of agricultural crops in the world. Photo by Kathy Keatley Garvey, courtesy of UC Agriculture and Natural Resources

some aquatic insects like dragonflies, damselflies, and mayflies (hemimetabolous insects). Hemimetabolous insects grow through a series of molts, but the juveniles look quite unlike the adult form, being wingless and adapted to an underwater life very different from that of the adults. Hemimetabolous insects pass through a "transforming stage." In this stage they are nonfeeding, relying on stored resources to produce the wings and reproductive organs necessary for their next life stage. Reliance on stored resources to power transformation is the same as in insects with complete metamorphosis. The difference between hemimetabolous insects and insects with complete metamorphosis is that in hemimetabolous insects, the transformative (pre-imago) stage is mobile, unlike in a butterfly or wasp, which is immobile in its cocoon.

Insects have hit upon two great keys that have allowed them to become so diverse and ecologically important: complex life cycles and flight. Flight allows insects to colonize distant lands, cross water barriers, pass over mountains, and skip over deserts to find suitable habitat beyond. Flight also gives the advantage of transportation to safe hiding, nesting, and overwintering sites, and escaping enemies. Many insects have incorporated flight into their mating and hunting strate-

Where Are the Bees?

Honeybees are essential to the production of many of our favorite foods. They pollinate about a third of human food plants, including almonds, apples, onions, carrots, avocados, and strawberries. Massive bee disappearances are decimating honeybee populations across North America and Europe, causing a serious disruption to the crops that they pollinate. The condition is known as colony collapse disorder (CCD) because the colonies are found with most or all of their adults missing. The reasons for CCD are not yet fully understood, but recent research suggests that exposure to a class of pesticides called neonicotinoids may be the primary culprit, though other stressors such as malnutrition and disease may also play a role.

gies. They evolved flight about 250 million years ago (mya), some 100 million years ahead of birds, and perhaps 200 million years before the only flying mammals, bats, took to the air.

Complex life cycles, where the juvenile may occupy a very different niche than the adult does, are another key to insect success. Consider for a moment a dragonfly hovering above a pond. The adult is winged and lives on the air, hunting, mating, and escaping predators by flight. The juvenile stage is a wingless, wormlike animal that lives in the mud on the bottom of the pond, ambushing passing bugs for its sustenance! Another example is wood-boring beetles, whose soft-bodied larvae bore through and around logs, eating cellulose for dinner, excavating a tunnel to live in, and avoiding desiccation by hiding in the cool, dark, moist tunnel. Meanwhile, the adults fly from place to place in the open air, seeking mates and laying eggs. In some insects success is achieved by separating the foraging strategies of the adult and the juvenile: mom eats tofu, kids eat burgers, as in dragonflies. In others the entire responsibility for eating is delegated to the juvenile form, while the adults concentrate on reproduction. Adult mayflies, for instance, live only to mate; they do not eat. Butterflies and moths are similar; the adults are simply mating machines. The larvae eat to gain weight; the adults sip only water or nectar to keep from drying out or to procure a few calories.

Another unique advantage of complex life cycles is that insects have four chances to evolve strategies for avoiding seasonally unfavorable climatic conditions. They can, and do, use any of the four stages of their development as a resting stage, when they hunker down and wait for favorable climatic conditions to return. They can rest (be in diapause) as an egg, a larva, a pupa (cocoon), or as an adult.

VERTEBRATES

Many of us have some idea of which mammals are living in our vicinity, but can you imagine which reptiles live within a mile of your house? How many kinds of frogs have you seen or heard? Do you know what fish swim past your town each year? Mammals, reptiles, amphibians, and fish share a common characteristic: they have spinal cords protected in a bony tube. The novel adaptations shared by all vertebrates, especially the internal, bony skeleton used to support organs and muscles, separates this group of animals from the invertebrates. Pause for a moment now to think whether you can construct a family tree for vertebrates based on what you already know about them. Think what is most closely related to what, and which evolved from which? Here are the players: snakes, fish, mammals, crocodilians, salamanders, birds, turtles, frogs, and lizards.

After thinking about it for a while, take a look at the family tree illustration (cladogram). The first major branch on this tree is fish, which are ancestral to all four-legged creatures (tetrapods). The first tetrapods (four-legged creatures) to distinguish themselves were the amphibians: the frogs, salamanders, and caecilians. Fish and amphibians are distinguished from all further tetrapods by laying nonamniotic (single-layer) eggs. Fish and amphibians are nonamniotic; all other tetrapods have amniotic eggs (eggs with a multi-layered skin). Amniotic eggs were a huge advance in the colonization of land in that they allowed amniotes to produce eggs that survived in more and more extreme (dry) environments, as exemplified by the reptiles and birds.

The last group branching off gives rise to the mammals, with their unique suite of adaptations, notably hair and the production of milk in mammary glands (lactation) to nourish offspring. A technical character that separates mammals from the other tetrapods is possession of three temporal fenestrae. The skulls of mammals, dinosaurs, and reptiles have holes behind the eye sockets called temporal fenestrae. Mammals have three temporal fenestrae; turtles have no temporal fenestrae; and crocodilians, birds, lizards, and snakes have two tem-

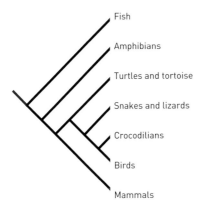

Fish

Amphibians

Turtles and tortoise

Snakes and lizards

Crocodilians

Birds

Mammals

Vertebrate evolution. The branching diagram (cladogram) shows degrees of relationship and ancestry. Groups that branch off together share more traits in common and are inferred to be more closely related.

poral fenestrae. So lack of temporal fenestrae, plus the unique presence of a shell, separates the turtle lineage. The crocodilian and bird groups are separated from the snakes and lizards group by single versus double penises. Yes, lizards and snakes have paired penises! On the crocodilian and bird branches, crocodilians differ from birds (and dinosaurs) in being ectothermic (relying on external surroundings to regulate body temperature) and in having a bony hard palate. Birds separate from dinosaurs, their immediate ancestors (not shown), by the presence of a unique throat modification (the syrinx) that facilitates song, the absence of a jawbone, and lack of teeth. Birds are best thought of as the living descendants of dinosaurs. Birds are, essentially, dinosaurs without teeth! Snakes and lizards are closely related and roamed the Earth long before dinosaurs. In fact, snakes ate dinosaur eggs just the way they enjoy lizard and bird eggs today. The most striking adaptation of snakes, loss of legs, has arisen multiple times. Lizards have also evolved in slightly different guises multiple times.

The family tree of vertebrates just presented is one of various versions that are argued about in academic circles with great vigor. Please don't feel beholden to it. The idea is not to present perfect knowledge to you as truth but to encourage you to think about the world, your prior knowledge, your beliefs and assumptions and to then test them against the facts (evidence). Science is an evidence-based approach to understanding the world! The phylogeny presented is discussed as though one or two unique derived characteristics constitute the defining changes of each lineage. Actually, each lineage is supported by numerous technical character changes. For instance, mammals exhibit unique derived characteristics beyond the three temporal fenestrae, including jugal teeth with two roots, dentary-squamosal jaw articulation, sebaceous glands at the bases of hairs, and sweat glands. The introduction above is, by necessity, vastly simplified.

Fish

Fish are one of the most ancient life-forms still extant on Earth. Fish first evolved in the oceans and later colonized rivers, lakes, and other aquatic habitats on land. Fish in continental rivers and lakes are great subjects for biogeography studies because their habitat boundaries are so clear-cut. Fish in a lake don't generally walk across land to another lake.

Most animals use oxygen to power their activities, and the ways animals obtain oxygen are critical to their survival. Fish extract oxygen from water through the use of gills. Water is taken in, generally through the mouth, passes over the gills where oxygen is extracted, and passes out through gill slits. This one-way passage of water over the gills can be continuous and can be powered by swimming (in sharks) or by "pumping" (in most bony fish). Since fish live in water and need to move in three dimensions, buoyancy is important in determining their vertical position in the water column. Fish solve this problem in two ways. Dense-bodied fish use their pectoral fins to create lift the way wings are used on airplanes. Unfortunately for these fish, they must keep moving to stay afloat, and they can't swim backwards or hover. The more widespread adaptation fish employ is to have portions of their body that are less dense than water, which allows the fish to rise. Some fish use gasses contained in a gas bladder (swim bladder) to maintain buoyancy, while others use lipids dispersed throughout their bodies. The incompressibility of lipids (as compared to gas in a gas bladder) allows greater movement at greater depths without the need to compensate for pressure changes.

Fish reproduce in a way that may be surprising. In most fish, the female lays eggs that are unfertilized. After the eggs have left the female's body, the male squirts sperm on the eggs. The female and male may never touch in the process of reproduction! Other fish do exhibit internal fertilization, especially sculpins, sharks, skates, and rays. A few marine fish produce leathery egg cases that sometimes wash up on a beach, and a few sharks give birth to live young feeding on a placenta-like structure.

Evolutionarily, there are three broad groups of fish in California and

Salmonids and California's Rivers

Many Californians are surprised to learn that salmon and steelhead may be living right in their neighborhood creeks. In fact, five species of Pacific salmon, as well as steelhead and lamprey, are native to California and were once abundant here. While dams, fishing, development, pollution, and erosion have taken a toll, small populations can still be found today in coastal rivers and creeks up and down the state. To thrive anadromous fish need

- Barrier-free migration paths to spawning areas
- Clean, cold water
- Continuous, consistent water flows
- Tree cover on stream banks

Adapted from *Agua Pura: Exploring Salmon and Steelhead in California Communities*, UC ANR Catalog (Pub. 8422).

its nearshore waters: jawless fish (hagfish and lampreys), cartilaginous fish (sharks, rays, and chimeras), and bony fish. The most "primitive" surviving vertebrates on Earth are the hagfish and lampreys. These cylindrical, eellike fish are members of the jawless group and are further characterized by having pore-like gill openings along the sides, lacking scales, and lacking pectoral or pelvic fins. Hagfish are rarely-seen bottom-dwelling, deep-water marine forms. Lampreys are born in freshwater, but most species are anadromous; they migrate to the ocean where they spend part of their lives feeding and growing, then return to rivers to breed. Most species are parasitic or predatory, attaching to the sides of fish or marine mammals and sucking blood or ripping flesh from them. Lampreys may use an anticoagulant to promote blood flow.

Sharks and rays are probably familiar to most of us, at least conceptually. Who hasn't seen movie or television footage of a shark? Some of our most beloved films star sharks, if not always in a way that accurately portrays their natural history. Sharks and rays are members of the second major group, the cartilaginous fish. The skeleton to which their muscles are attached is made of cartilage, not bone. They are further differentiated from bony fish by having multiple external gill openings (sharks, five to seven; bony fish, one). Shark skin also differs from that of bony fish. Most bony fish have overlapping scales covering their bodies, while sharks have toothlike denticles which give them a characteristic rough texture.

Rays differ from sharks in being strongly flattened for bottom dwelling, and in having their pectoral fins attached to their heads to form a characteristic "disk" shape. Rays don't intake water through their mouths for respiration, but rather through an opening (spiracle) on the upper surface of the "face," which facilitates life on a muddy or sandy bottom. Sharks and rays are generally marine dwellers, though a few enter freshwater. Rays have evolved novel adaptations, including a barbed sting (stingrays) and the ability to produce electric current (electric rays) to defend themselves.

The third group in the cartilaginous fish category is the chimeras. These are ancient, deep-water marine forms rarely seen. They have one external gill opening; smooth, scaleless, slippery skin; and a large, rabbit-like head!

Most familiar forms of fish such as trout, salmon, and aquarium fish fall into the third evolutionary category, the bony fish. Bony fish occur in virtually all waters of the world from high altitude (4,828 meters) to deep-sea trenches 11,000 meters below sea level! This group includes the brilliantly colored coral reef fish, the strange monsters of the deep ocean, and most of the fish commonly eaten or cast after for sport. One of the adaptations that evolved in many bony fish is the ability to exploit both fresh and salt water during different portions of their life cycle. This ability to be anadromous is illustrated by salmon, whose eggs hatch in streams. The fry (small fish) move downstream to the ocean, where they feed and grow for one to five years. The fully grown adult salmon then swim back up the river in which they were born to spawn (mate and lay eggs). The adults die after spawning, and their carcasses fertilize the river and the adjacent forests. These complex interactions between rivers and the ocean have important consequences for three ecosystems. For instance, bears, raccoons, and trees along rivers where salmon spawn derive much of the nitrogen in their tissues from marine sources! In other words, salmon are harvesting marine resources and delivering them to fertilize freshwater and terrestrial ecosystems!

Amphibians

Amphi- means "both," and *-bio* (*-bian*) means "life," so *amphibians* are animals that have "both lives," who live their lives both on land and in water. Many amphibians spend much of their lives "on land" (that is, in nonaquatic, terrestrial habitats) but "return" to water to breed.

The Pacific tree frog (*Pseudacris regilla*) is a great example. Tree frogs spend much of their time hunting or estivating far from water, but when it is time to breed, the males and females meet in ponds, lakes, and streams where they court, copulate, and deposit eggs to develop in the aquatic environment. Tree frogs would be unable to breed without puddles, ponds, and streams. Fertilization would be impaired, or their egg masses would dry out. When the eggs hatch, the resulting tadpoles require freshwater in which to swim, scrape algae from plant stems for sustenance, and hide from predators. Thus, important portions of amphibian life cycles may take place in both aquatic and terrestrial habitats.

Not all amphibians are so closely tied to ponds, lakes, and streams for reproduction. Many woodland salamanders have cut the tie to breeding in aquatic habitats and lay egg masses in moist cavities in logs or under rocks. This adaptation probably developed as a result of another widespread amphibian adaptation: small home ranges. Many small, slow-moving salamanders spend their entire lives within a few-square-meters patch of forest. The small, black, slender salamander (*Batrachoseps*) under the garbage can on a wet winter morning may never move more than 4 meters from that spot during its entire life! So many patches of potential habitat are far from water that some amphibians evolved ways to cut their ties to water in order to exploit them.

One of the important ecological characteristics of amphibians is soft, moist, water-permeable skin. Because amphibians lose water through their skin at about the same rate that water evaporates from a glass, they are in extreme danger of drying to death. Amphibians lose water through their skin far faster than other terrestrial vertebrates like snakes, lizards, birds, and mammals with relatively water-retentive skin. For this reason, amphibians have a suite of behavioral and life history traits that protect them from drying up. Often they are active only during the wet season, and they sit out the dry season in a protected, cool, moist microsite, like 2 feet underground in a gopher burrow. Typically they are active aboveground only at night, or during a rainstorm. One of the more fantastic adaptations along this line is "drinking by the seat of your pants." Western toads, which live in relatively hot, dry habitats and are active at night during the dry season, have the ability to expose a patch of thin skin between their hind legs (the "seat patch" or "pelvic patch") to bits of moisture, like dew on grass at dawn or damp soil. They absorb moisture through this "seat patch" in place of directly drinking.

Amphibians: Earth's First Responders

Because amphibians complete important life cycle events both on land and in the water, they often are among the first vertebrates affected by environmental changes and pollution. Unfortunately, amphibians provided the first well-documented example of an extinction that may have been caused by climate change due to global warming. The golden toad (*Bufo periglenes*) of Monteverde, Costa Rica, was apparently driven to extinction by the drying of its cloud forest habitat. The drying was caused by the increase in elevation of the cloud masses that pushed against the mountaintops.

Amphibian defensive chemistry is highly developed. Western toads (*Anaxyrus boreas*) and northwestern salamanders (*Ambystoma gracile*) have large, swollen areas on their skin (parotid glands) that hold defensive chemicals that can be excreted over their bodies as a milky ooze when threatened. These defensive chemicals may kill small predators (snakes or shrews) or sicken larger ones (raccoons or skunks). An interesting human application of amphibian defensive chemistry is the use of parotid gland secretions from the Sonoran desert toad (*Bufo alvarius*), which contain hallucinogenic tryptamines. People have been known to smoke toad as a way of altering their perception of reality! Perhaps the salamander most familiar to many Californians will be the newt (*Taricha*), whose skin contains one of the most potent neurotoxins known, tetrodotoxin. The toxin is actually synthesized by a bacterium living on the skin of the salamander, not by the salamander itself, but nevertheless the animal is rendered deadly poisonous. At least one animal, the western terrestrial garter snake (*Thamnophis elegans*), has evolutionarily "learned" to detoxify the tetrodotoxin and preys on newts throughout much of the newt range. On Vancouver Island, BC, where the snake is absent, newts are far less toxic, indicating that an arms race between the newt and the snake may have driven the newt to extreme levels of toxicity.

Dinosaurs

Dinosaurs raise a topic every naturalist must come to terms with: extinction. Like individuals, species usually have a "life span," and 99.99 percent of all the species that have ever roamed the Earth are now extinct.

Or, as David Raup of the University of Chicago has said, "to a first approximation, all species are extinct." Apparently the statistical (average) life span of a species is about a million years. Dinosaurs roamed the Earth, and in some ways dominated the terrestrial sphere, for about 80 million years. Then, about 65 million years ago, they all suddenly died out—very suddenly. The dinosaurs dominated the Earth until a 10-kilometers-in-diameter meteor hit the Earth in the shallow Cretaceous seas off of the coast of Mexico near the Yucatan Peninsula. This impact set off a chain of events that wiped out about 70 percent of the species that existed on Earth at the time, including most of the dinosaurs.

The extinction event of 65 mya (when the Cretaceous period ended and the Tertiary period began) is perhaps the best known of the many major extinction events that have interrupted the course of life on this planet, but certainly not the most dramatic. That title probably belongs to the Permian-Triassic extinction event of 245 mya when about 97 percent of all species on Earth died in a terrific spasm of global warming. Temperatures were driven by greenhouse gasses to 160°F! The beginning and ending of "geologic" periods are generally defined by extinction events.

Birds

Amphibians have moist, porous skin. Mammals have hair growing from their skin. Reptiles have scaly skin. Birds have feathers growing from their skin. These huge generalities that many schoolchildren know are actually good markers for some of the evolutionary and ecological distinctions of the major groups of vertebrates. Birds are the descendants of dinosaurs. They are characterized by the possession of feathers, an evolutionary novelty no other group of organisms has invented. Birds use feathers to stay warm or dry (insulation), to advertise to potential mates, to blend into their environment (camouflage), and perhaps most distinctly, to fly. Flight is so central to birds' fundamental nature that many other physiological structures can be traced to the ability to fly. Why do birds have so many neck vertebrae, far more than mammals? To be able to reach body parts with their bill to scratch or preen. People would use a hand, but birds don't have one. Their forelimbs are dedicated to flight! Why do birds have a lightweight bill with a bony core and a cover of keratin, but no teeth? To reduce weight for flight. Why do all birds lay external eggs, and why has no bird developed live birth? To quickly get rid of weight to facili-

Naturalists at Work

A great way to become familiar with birds, and nature observation in general, is in your backyard. Watch the birds nesting under your eaves and drinking from your birdbath. Or start by sitting in your yard for five minutes with your eyes closed and focusing on the sounds around you. Then open your eyes and spend another five minutes without moving. With eyes open, and still listening intently, see if you can locate any of the birds you hear. If you repeat this exercise a couple of times each week or daily, within a year you will be an accomplished birder. There are many aids to learning birdsongs: your friends; your fellow naturalists; books; CDs of local or regional birdsongs; and numerous websites with birdsongs, photos, and videos. Use all of your resources! The most important is personal experience, so practice on your own!

tate flight. In fact, the combined weight of all the feathers on a bird is often twice the combined weight of all of the bones. What does that indicate about a bird's priorities?

Flight also explains much about bird behavior. Birds fly to escape terrestrial predators like coyotes and snakes. Birds fly to avoid the unfavorable season in temperate latitudes (we call this migration). Birds are able to nest high in trees, on vertical cliff walls, on nearshore rocks, and inside hollow dead snags. And yet turkey vultures choose to nest on the ground, often at the base of a hollow tree trunk. Kingfishers and bank swallows dig tunnels in vertical dirt walls, and many birds weave bags or "socks" in which to nest, for instance bush tits. Some birds, such as penguins, ostriches, and kiwis, have evolved other ways to get around. The variety of strategies the 9,000 species of birds alive today have evolved to cope with the opportunities and challenges offered by the environment are nearly endless.

A second novel adaptation of birds is the use of song to communicate. The syrinx in a bird's throat is a unique, derived characteristic, not shared with other groups of vertebrates. It both helps to define birds and gives them the ability to sing. Birds sing or call to attract mates; to define and defend territory; to warn of the presence of predators; and to promote cohesion in social groups, like foraging flocks and family groups.

Most songbirds learn their songs, but for some birds, such as the tyrant flycatchers in North America, their songs are innate. For birds that learn their songs, the kind of "teacher" they have is terrifically important. If a band-tailed pigeon is raised in captivity by mourning dove parents, it will sing the song of the mourning dove. Separate populations of birds of the same species will sing different *dialects* of the same song. The white-crowned sparrows of the San Francisco Bay Area are well studied in this regard, with the dialect of birds born in San Francisco differing from those born in Berkeley or Marin County. Another nuance in birdsong is that the same bird will sing slightly differently at different times of year, and at different times of day. When the red-breasted nuthatches begin to sing in the spring, they often sound like they don't know what a red-breasted nuthatch is supposed to sound like. It takes them a week or two of trying to get it right. And no two robins' songs are exactly alike. Every robin song is new and live, and may be different from any other. Many brilliant people have spent the majority of their lives learning about birdsong and not gotten to the end of it.

Lizards and Snakes

It is easy to take living on land pretty much for granted, but life on land is the great evolutionary feat that led to much of the diversity of life on Earth today. The great innovations that made life on land possible are related to surviving hot, dry conditions. The first tetrapods on land were the amphibians, which are constrained by need of moisture to reproduce. The great innovation of further vertebrates was the amniotic egg, which is porous to gasses but retains water, thus allowing birds, crocodiles, turtles, lizards, snakes, and mammals to invade increasingly dry habitats. Another pivotal adaptation lizards and snakes have developed is dry, scale-covered skin that retards moisture loss. Lizards and snakes are unlike birds, crocodiles, and turtles in that lizards and snakes separate the water from their waste products to avoid losing it in disposing of the waste. Lizard or snake scat (poop) is composed of two separate parts: a dark part made of the insect exoskeletons or mouse skin and bones or whatever else the lizard or snake ate; and a white, powdery or pasty portion composed of uric acid. This is distinctive, and very different from the excrement of birds, turtles, or crocodiles. Uric acid is one of the basic waste products vertebrates must excrete. Most do this by urinating. They pass a lot of water to lose a little uric acid. Lizards and snakes spend time and metabolic energy separating the uric acid from the water, retain the precious water, and dump the uric acid as paste or powder.

Another huge difference between lizards and snakes versus mammals and birds is their metabolic rates. In order for birds and mammals to be fast and active, they must have a high metabolic rate. For birds to fly, they must beat their wings rapidly and continuously, thus producing an extreme oxygen demand. Compare this with a rattlesnake that may lie without moving for days, waiting for an unsuspecting rabbit to pass within striking distance. The energy demands are very different. Don't be tempted to think of lizards and snakes as inferior or primitive because they are ectothermic or poikilothermic. Ectotherms are actually, in some ways, at an advantage with their "undemanding" metabolism. Birds and mammals use about 80 percent of the calories in their food simply to maintain their constant body temperature. Thus, lizards and snakes can survive on about one-tenth the food birds and mammals need. When food is scarce or unavailable, lizards and snakes can wait for abundance to return, whereas birds have to fly to Central America. In many habitats the biomass of lizards and snakes combined is larger than that of birds and mammals combined, in part because their smaller metabolic demands require less energy from the ecosystem.

Snakes exhibit a suite of traits that distinguish them from other vertebrates and characterize them ecologically: they are extraordinarily mysterious, eat infrequent but large meals, and depend on smell rather than sight or sound for most of their information about the world. Snakes are also typically limbless: although fossil snakes and a few basal snakes have a rudimentary pelvis and hind limbs, no living snake has a pectoral girdle or forelimbs. Snakes and lizards also have paired penises (hemipenes), a derived adaptation shared with no other group of vertebrates. Both lizards and snakes shed their skin to renew it, a marked contrast to birds, which regrow individual feathers, and mammals, which regrow individual hairs. Most lizards shed their skin irregularly, dropping small, ragged patches over the course of a week or two. Snakes (and alligator lizards) loosen their skin as a whole package, break it loose at the mouth, and then crawl out in as little as five minutes, leaving the inside-out skin with the tail pointing in the direction the shedder departed. Lizards have external ear openings and eyelids, whereas snakes never do. These are useful characteristics for distinguishing a legless lizard (of which there are many) from a snake. Snakes also have paired glands in the tail (cloacal scent glands) that produce

Pacific gopher snake (*Pituophis catenifer catenifer*), Pepperwood Preserve. Photo courtesy of Greg Damron, www.wild vinestudios.com

foul-smelling liquids. These cloacal scent glands may have evolved to deter predators when the mouth is otherwise occupied (i.e., in swallowing). Neither lizards nor any other vertebrate possess cloacal scent glands. A few snakes (boas, pythons, pit vipers) use heat (infrared radiation) to gain information about the world. A pit viper (such as a rattlesnake) may actually form an image in its brain based on infrared radiation. The pit viper's infrared image would be analogous to the visual image derived from light that the eye-brain system produces.

Perhaps the most important attribute of snakes is their devotion to chemical cues to navigate and negotiate their worlds. Although snakes have nostrils for breathing, smell (i.e., chemical perception through the nostril) is unimportant to them. Snakes have a deeply forked tongue which they flick as they travel. When the tongue is retracted after each flick, each fork tip (called a tine) is carefully placed in a special pocket on the roof of the mouth. The chemicals gathered on the outward flick are thus transferred to these pockets, which are remarkably sensitive to chemical cues. The entire apparatus is termed the Jacobson's organ, or vomeronasal organ, and is shared among snakes and a few lizards. When a snake (or monitor lizard) flicks its tongue, the two tines reach widely to each side. The tines separate to gather spatially different chemical cues. This allows the snake to perceive concentration differences from side to side and, for instance, follow the stronger scent trail to a prey item or potential mate.

Lizards seem to be the ancestors of snakes, or said another way, snakes seem to be very specialized lizards. Lizard and snake eggs are soft and leathery, unlike the hard, breakable eggs of birds. In California, lizards are desert specialists, with far more species and greater numbers of individuals in hot, dry habitats than in cool, moist forests. One of the unique attributes of lizards is the ability to lose and regrow their tails. Lizards do this so commonly that they have special joints in the tail vertebrae to facilitate tail loss. Lizards have a special mechanism for stopping the flow of blood at the lost joint. The tail, meanwhile, may wriggle frantically when separated from the body, distracting the predator from the other potential food item nearby. Lizards regrow their tails over time. The tail loss tendency seems to be an adaptation to high rates of predation: better to lose a tail than die! Many lizards establish and defend territories, marking them with chemicals produced by scent glands located on the legs. The territory is commonly defended with ritualized threat displays that involve doing push-ups on prominent perches to show off brightly colored belly scales that are normally invisible when the lizard is not displaying.

Mammals

People have a love-hate relationship with animals. On the one hand, 60 percent of Americans live with dogs or cats and love them but fear rats. Tourists pay good money for the chance to see a whale or a polar bear and value that experience highly, but they ignore squirrels. But how many of us take the time to watch a spider weaving a web on a bush in the garden or are willing to share our living space with dangerous animals? The California state mammal, the grizzly bear, has been extirpated from California, Oregon, Washington, Utah, New Mexico, Arizona, and most of Idaho and Montana. The current political dialogues surrounding resurgent mountain lion populations and the return of wolves to Washington and Oregon are examples of the difficulty people have allowing dangerous animals to coexist with us. The fear and the facts do not always match up: though numerous people are afraid of wolves as scary predators, how many have been killed in North America by wolves since records have been kept? Zero!

Mammals differ from other vertebrates by having skin with hair; by nourishing their young with milk produced in mammary glands; and by having diverse tooth types. Like feathers in birds, hairs are a mammalian invention. Hairs are used to keep warm and cool, to advertise and for camouflage, much as are the feathers of birds. Even marine

Reversal of Fortune: Bats

Bats provide a great example of how society's perceptions of wildlife can change. In the 1950s and 1960s, bats were commonly viewed in America as pests or as dangerous carriers of rabies. This is factually inaccurate; bats almost never transmit rabies to people. Far from being pests, they are among the most helpful, efficient protectors of our health and agricultural production. A single bat may eat 1,200 insects in one hour! Without bats we would be overwhelmed by mosquitoes, which, unlike bats, are serious, dangerous transmitters of disease to humans. Bats also protect our agricultural crops by gobbling down the insects that would otherwise consume them. Since about 1975, there has been a huge reversal of the image of bats in the American public mind. People now fly across the country for the purpose of watching bats fly out of their daytime roosts at sunset, a knockout sight. The popular image of bats also differs depending on where you were raised. In Chinese culture, bats are revered as a symbol of health, long life, prosperity, love of virtue, and a tranquil, natural death.

mammals (whales, dolphins, seals, otters) have at least some hair at some point in their life cycle. Many, perhaps most, mammals also use hairs for sensory purposes: they feel with them. The hairs about the face normally called whiskers on cats and dogs are actually long, stiff, sensory hairs. Although the hairs are "dead" (they have no nerve cells within them), nerve cells attached to the base of each whisker transmit important information about the near environment. Whiskers can tell a bobcat that it is about to touch a tree or a spiny blackberry stem before the animal bumps into those things with more sensitive features like its nose or mouth.

Most people will be familiar with the idea of lactation: feeding offspring with a rich, sweet, liquid food for the first days or months of life. This is another typically mammalian trait. Even whales and dolphins, which nurse their young underwater, rely on this method.

Teeth in most nonmammalian vertebrates are relatively uniform. Although snake teeth and lizard teeth may look quite different from each other, all the teeth in an individual lizard's or snake's mouth are basically the same. Mammals have diversified teeth for different functions: the grinding teeth of a grazer like a deer look very different from the tearing teeth of a predator like a coyote. One mammal may even have two or three very different tooth styles: the chisel-like front teeth of the beaver look and function very differently than its rear grinding teeth. The tooth specializations of mammals represent specific evolutionary adaptations, which are central to the habitats and niches mammals have been able to occupy.

There are three main evolutionary groups of mammals: monotremes, marsupials, and placentals. The monotremes stretch the idea of what a mammal is, since they give birth by laying eggs! There are two extant genera of monotremes, the spiny echidna of New Guinea and the duck-billed platypus of Australia. In monotremes the eggs are placed in a marsupial-like pouch where they hatch and the infants are fed milk. Monotremes further distinguish themselves from other mammals by lack of teeth! Monotremes also have a combined urogenital opening, a cloaca, like birds, amphibians, and reptiles. Monotremes are a good illustration of the idea that for every generality about how the world works, nature has produced an exception. *Always* is a word naturalists should be cautious about using!

Marsupials should be familiar to many through popular culture: just picture a mother kangaroo with a joey sitting looking out of her pouch. Marsupials reached their greatest diversity in Australia, New Zealand, and New Guinea where different lineages of marsupials occupied all of the ecological niches of mammalian browsers, grazers, predators, and burrowers. There was even a "marsupial wolf" (the thylacine) which was driven extinct by Euro-American bounty hunting in 1936. Although marsupials are associated with Australia, South America also had a wonderful radiation of marsupials. Most of them were driven extinct when placental mammals invaded South America approximately 3 million years ago when the Panamanian land bridge arose, separating the Atlantic from the Pacific and connecting North and South America. However, one South American marsupial flourished and invaded North America: the "Virginia opossum." In marsupials, the young are born very early in development and migrate to a "pouch" (marsupium) where they are fed milk and grow. Like monotremes, marsupials have a cloaca.

The third and final group of mammals is the placentals, by far the most diverse lineage of mammals, and the dominant group of vertebrates on the planet today. In placental mammals the young undergo considerable development within the body of the mother. They are nourished by a specialized organ, the placenta, which allows food, oxygen, and waste products to pass between mother and offspring. The digestive tract has been completely separated from urinary and genital organs, thus placental mammals are unique among vertebrates in lacking a cloaca.

HUMAN ACTIVITY AND DOMESTIC AND INTRODUCED ANIMALS

We share the Earth with animals as pets, neighbors, and competitors. Human activity influences wildlife populations in two ways: through changes in land use and through the introduction of domesticated and other animals. Changes in land use alter habitat by removing it (development, clear-cuts) or through habitat fragmentation or simplification. All of these activities favor some wildlife species over others. Species that favor open spaces and edge habitat tend to thrive, while species that require lots of cover, cooler temperatures, or continuous habitat tend to suffer.

Some fauna were introduced intentionally as work animals or pets. Some were introduced accidentally as hitchhikers in ships or cargo. Many introduced animals live with relatively little impact on the environment, while others compete so strongly with native species that they eliminate them from their native ranges. One example is the bullfrog. Bullfrogs were brought to California as a food source but made their way into wildlands where they quickly spread. Bullfrogs prey upon native species of insects, frogs, turtles, and fish. In locations throughout California and much of the western United States, bullfrogs have led to the decline or displacement of native amphibians. Invasive species do not always originate from distant places. For example, the Sacramento pike minnow is native to the Sacramento area but has become invasive in the nearby Eel River, where it has impacted populations of salmon and steelhead.

Domesticated animals, when not managed properly, can also have a deleterious effect on native species and the environment. One fairly well-known example is the effect of cats on songbirds. Dr. Stanley Temple of the University of Wisconsin estimates that 20 to 150 million songbirds are killed each year by rural cats in that state alone. Some domesticated animals have become well established or naturalized in the wild. A good example are feral pigs in California's woodlands, which are a concern for land managers because of rooting activities that churn up large amounts of ground. There are also potential impacts for woodland species conservation, because pigs are nonnative predators. In fact, 40 percent of the pigs studied in the Diablo Range, California, had native vertebrate prey in their stomachs, which totaled to 167 individuals, demonstrating that the impacts of pigs extends to small mammal and other vertebrate consumption.

Explore!

VISIT A MIGRATORY PATHWAY STOPOVER

As an important stretch of the Pacific Flyway, California is one of the best places in the country to watch migrating birds. Great places include the Marin Headlands, the islands in Channel Islands National Park (take a boat out of Ventura), and Monterey Bay. Other ideas include an Audubon sanctuary, a wildlife refuge, an estuary, or even the local sewage treatment plant ponds.

Monarch butterflies migrate to California to overwinter. Good places to see them include Natural Bridges State Beach in Santa Cruz, Monarch Grove Sanctuary in Pacific Grove, Pismo Beach Monarch Grove, Ellwood Main Monarch Grove and Coronado Butterfly Preserve in Goleta, and Camino Real Park in Ventura.

VISIT A WILDLIFE REFUGE, NATURE CENTER, OR NATURAL HISTORY MUSEUM

The best way to hone naturalist skills is to take a field guide, some binoculars, and a notebook and head out to a wildlife refuge. Local refuges can be found on the US Fish and Wildlife website, at www.fws.gov/refuges/refugeLocatorMaps/california.html.

Also visit one of California's many nature centers or natural history museums, such as the California Academy of Sciences in San Francisco, the Pacific Grove Natural History Museum, the Santa Barbara Museum of Natural History, the Natural History Museum of Los Angeles County and the La Brea Tar Pits, and the San Diego Natural History Museum. California also has many outstanding local nature centers. You can find a list at http://en.wikipedia.org/wiki/List_of_nature_centers_in_the_United_States#California.

GO TO A NATIVE PLANT GARDEN AND FOLLOW THE POLLINATORS

First, try to identify as many plants as you can. Then find a native bee and see what plants it pollinates. The California Native Plant Society has a list of native plant gardens at www.cnps.org/cnps/horticulture/garden_links.php. The Urban Bee Gardens website, http://nature.berkeley.edu/urbanbeegardens/, has some photos and also suggestions for watching bees safely.

PARTICIPATE IN THE CHRISTMAS BIRD CENSUS

Every December, the National Audubon Society engages thousands of citizen scientist volunteers all over the country to conduct a bird census in their local area. To get involved, contact your local Audubon chapter or go to www.audubon.org/bird/cbc/.

TRACK AN ANIMAL AND IDENTIFY SCAT

Learn the tracks and scat of common mammals and birds in your area and try to identify them as you hike. Keep a journal of what you found, and draw tracks you come across.

LEARN ABOUT ALTERNATIVES FOR PEST CONTROL

Most pest control techniques involve the use of poisons to kill the undesired creatures. Those poisons have the unfortunate tendency to end up in the water system and often don't solve the problem. Natural pest control attempts to solve the root of the problem. (Is there is a hole that needs to be plugged? Standing or leaking water?) And it utilizes less toxic or nontoxic methods. You can learn more at the University of California's Integrated Pest Management website, www.ipm.ucdavis.edu.

7

Energy and Global Environmental Issues

Energy is a fundamental unifying concept for physical and biological scientists because it drives all Earth systems. Energy is neither created nor destroyed, it simply changes form. Therefore, energy can never be "used up." When nuclear fusion in the dense gas cloud of the sun releases the energy of the atom, it transforms that energy to various forms of electromagnetic energy. The exact amount of energy that was held in the nuclear bonds of the hydrogen or helium atoms reacting in the sun is the amount released as light, heat, and other forms of energy.

FORMS AND SOURCES OF ENERGY

Forms of Energy

Energy exists in a variety of forms. We know and are familiar with electromagnetic energy as light, heat, radio waves, television signals, and microwaves. Importantly, energy can be converted from one form to another. Nuclear energy of atoms of the sun is converted to electromagnetic energy, which is captured by plants and stored as chemical energy. Chemical energy stored in food is used to power the mechanical movements of activity—to walk, open doors, hunt. Mechanical energy is used to move cars, open bottles, and crack nuts with a nutcracker. Mechanical energy is the force that dug the Grand Canyon and that powers turbines to create electricity at hydroelectric dams. Thermal energy is what we commonly experience as heat. Electrical energy is converted to thermal energy in toasters and ovens to prepare the chemical energy in food. The chemical energy derived from the food is converted to the mechanical energy of pushing down the toaster button. Energy is commonly converted from one form to another throughout our lives every day. Thinking about these transformations or conversions helps elucidate the energetic basis of life on Earth.

Potential and Kinetic Energy

One way to imagine energy never being created or destroyed, but rather changing form, is to hold a ball at shoulder height. The ball is full of potential energy, the energy of position. If the ball drops, it has the power (the energy) to bounce if it hits the floor. Even though the ball is not moving when held at shoulder height, we think of it as having energy by virtue of its position in space. When the ball is dropped, its potential energy is transformed to the energy of motion, kinetic energy. The ball's speed increases all the way to the floor as its potential energy is completely transformed to kinetic energy. What happens when the ball hits the floor? Suddenly its kinetic energy (the energy of motion) is transformed again. Some of the kinetic energy of the falling ball is transformed to mechanical energy, sound; some of the kinetic energy of the falling ball is transformed to light (a sensitive enough device might even be able to detect it); and some of the kinetic energy of the falling ball is transformed to heat (thermal energy). Dribble a basketball in one place on the floor for a few minutes, then feel the floor. It will be slightly warmer than the floor a few feet away. Most of the kinetic energy of the falling ball will be transformed to elastic potential energy, represented by the deforming or compressing of one side of the ball. This elastic deformation is what stores the energy that will power the rise (the bounce) of the ball back toward your hand. But will a ball ever bounce all the way back to the point from which it was dropped? It can't, because some of its original potential energy has been transformed to heat, sound, and light.

Sources of Energy

Energy on Earth is derived from two sources: geothermal heat generated within the core of the planet and electromagnetic energy coming from the sun, most notably heat and light.

Energy within the Earth

Earth's interior is not a simple homogeneous mass of solid rock. There is quite a lot of variation among layers, in terms of composition, density, and phase (liquid vs solid). The Earth's core is a tremendous source of heat—some theorize that the Earth's core is hotter than the surface of the sun, around 5,500°C! This intense heat is derived primarily from two sources, primordial heat and radioactive decay.

Primordial Heat. The Earth was first formed 4.5 billion years ago by bits of rock and dust coalescing as they orbited the sun, and these bits of rock contained a certain amount of energy. As the rocks piled up deeper and deeper, some of that energy was trapped. Some of the kinetic energy of the rocks' motion was also converted to thermal energy (heat), and thus huge amounts of energy were trapped deep in the core of the developing Earth as heat. This heat, coupled with heat generated by radioactive decay in the core, has been enough to keep the outer core in a liquid state, despite the great pressure the material is under. Heat conduction from the outer core drives the convective flow of the solid but ductile mantle, and ultimately plate tectonics, on the surface of the Earth.

Radioactive Decay. The heat produced by radioactive decay of, for example, potassium 40, uranium 238, uranium 235, and thorium 232, combined with the original heat from the Earth's formation, drives the global geological cycle, including the motions of tectonic plates and the continents that ride as components of those plates, the eruption of volcanoes, the thundering of earthquakes, and the uplifting of mountains. The Earth is constantly releasing the heat stored and produced deep within its core. How quickly the core heat of the Earth is lost depends on a number of factors, including the production of heat through radioactive decay, which diminishes over time, distance to the surface, materials the heat must travel through to reach the surface, and the insulating properties of the mantle and atmosphere. The moon, Mars, and Venus are geologically dead because they have lost all of their internal heat. Thanks to the insulating properties of the crust, the Earth will probably retain its core heat until long after the sun swells to swallow it. If the Earth's internal heat were all dissipated, like the moon's has been, the motions of the continents would end. Volcanoes would no longer erupt and add to the land surface area, and the continents

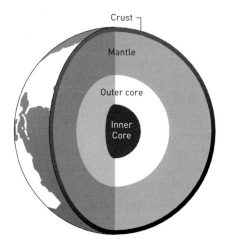

Internal structure of the Earth. Not to scale; the crust should be far thinner but is drawn so that it will show. Used with permission from the National Energy Education Development Project, www.need.org

would eventually be washed away by erosion into the oceans and not be rebuilt.

Energy from the Sun

In order to carry out any activity—waking up, walking, breathing, eating, flying, hunting, mating—energy is required. Virtually all of the energy driving the common biological world is derived from nuclear reactions taking place within the sun. The sun is composed of hydrogen and helium, which are involved in continuous nuclear reactions. Nuclear fusion means the joining of two atoms, while nuclear fission is the splitting of the atomic nucleus. Both fusion and fission liberate huge amounts of energy. The sun is a giant ball of gasses undergoing continuous fusion reactions. The nuclear reactions of the sun send vast amounts of energy out into space as electromagnetic waves, which are captured by photosynthetic organisms and drive all life on Earth.

THE ENERGETIC BASIS OF LIFE

When the sun's energy arrives on the Earth, it is transformed in two key ways. Some of the solar energy is used to change water from solid to liquid or from liquid to gas. Water, perhaps the most amazing molecule on Earth, can exist in three states, or phases: solid ice, liquid water, and gaseous vapor. Transforming water from solid ice to liquid water (a phase change) or from liquid to gaseous water vapor (another

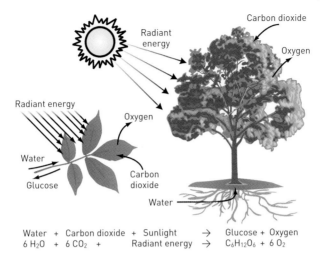

Water + Carbon dioxide + Sunlight → Glucose + Oxygen
$6\,H_2O$ + $6\,CO_2$ + Radiant energy → $C_6H_{12}O_6$ + $6\,O_2$

Photosynthesis is the energetic basis of all life on Earth.
Without green plants there would be no life as we know it.
Used with permission from the National Energy Education
Development Project, www.need.org

phase change) requires large amounts of energy. On Earth, water is
one of the primary acceptors of energy from the sun. Without the sun's
continuous energy input, all the water on Earth would gradually lose
its energy to the dark void of space and freeze. The various transformations of water from one phase to another drive the planetary climate system. The energy transformations of water from ice (solid) to
river (liquid) to water vapor (a gas which condenses into clouds) to rain
(liquid) or snow (solid) are examples of some of the primary determi-
nants of the physical conditions we take for granted, and upon which
life depends.

The second form of energy transformation on Earth is when the
sun's electromagnetic radiation is transformed to the energy of chemical bonds in living systems. This is a fact that is easy to overlook, but
without plants' ability to convert the sun's energy, there would be virtually no life on Earth. Photosynthesis is the second energy transformation upon which almost all life depends. Green plants and algae
use the sun's energy to build chemicals capable of storing that energy.
The primary chemical used to store the sun's energy and to power life
is glucose ($C_6H_{12}O_6$). Glucose is the transportable form of energy in
biological systems. It is used to drive the process of aerobic respiration, where glucose reacts with oxygen to release energy, carbon diox-

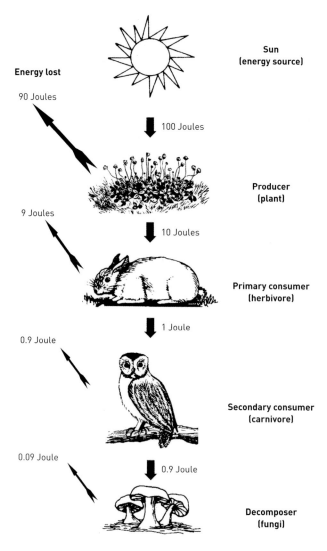

Sun
(energy source)

Energy lost

90 Joules

100 Joules

Producer
(plant)

9 Joules

10 Joules

Primary consumer
(herbivore)

1 Joule

0.9 Joule

Secondary consumer
(carnivore)

0.09 Joule

0.9 Joule

Decomposer
(fungi)

Energy loss in a food chain: 90 percent of the usable energy
in an organism is lost at each step. The 90 percent is converted to heat and other unrecoverable forms of energy.
Adapted from the University of Maine Cooperative Extension's
Connections to Our Earth: Leader's Guide, Orono, Maine, 1995

ide, and water. Respiration provides energy for all the cell's activities. Glucose supplies the energy for growth, reproduction, and all other aspects of biological activity. In sum, the sun's energy is captured in the cells of green plants, and those plants then provide the chemical energy to drive all other forms of life on Earth. There are interesting exceptions to life relying on photosynthesis, such as complex communities found in deep-sea hydrothermal vents where no sunlight reaches. Life at these vents begins with the thermal energy being released from deep within the planet. Organisms there convert energy into food in a process known as chemosynthesis.

Energy transformations in biological systems are inefficient. Each time a rabbit eats some grass, only about 10 percent of the energy stored in the grass is converted to usable energy in the animal. When a rattlesnake eats the rabbit, about 10 percent of the energy is successfully captured by the snake. When a coyote or a red-tailed hawk then eats the snake, the energy "loss" is similarly about 90 percent. Each time energy is exchanged in a food web, the loss in conversion is about 90 percent. This is a terrific limiting factor on the number of trophic levels a food web can support. It is the reason food chains almost never go beyond four or five transformations. It is more energetically efficient when people eat grains, vegetables, and fruits as compared with eating meat. Because the food source has gone through fewer transformations, less energy has been converted to unusable forms. Each time energy is converted in a food web, the "lost" 90 percent is used to heat the air or in other ways that are not useful. No energy goes away. We call this "energy loss," but it is really not a loss of energy but a degradation of a highly usable form of energy to a much less usable form.

ENERGY USE BY PEOPLE

People are masters of turning the chemical bonds of matter into energy. Energy warms our homes. It powers cars, the trucks that bring food, and the tractors that grow food. Electrical energy powers computers, radios, washing machines, and water heaters. Virtually everything about human life is intimately bound to energy use, though the dominant forms of energy have changed over the millennia.

The two most common forms of energy Americans are familiar with are electricity and gasoline. Electricity is the flow of electrons. To generate electricity requires setting electrons in motion. An electric generator is a device that changes mechanical energy to electrical energy.

Most large-scale electric generation is done using a turbine powered by wind, water, coal, or natural gas. The power sources for turning the turbine differ, but once a turbine is set in motion, the mechanical energy of the rotating shaft can be used to generate electricity. Gasoline perhaps shouldn't be referred to as a form of energy. Technically, gasoline is a potential source of energy. Only when the gas is burned and the controlled explosion is converted to mechanical energy (the movement of the piston) can the original source (the gas) be used to power useful work.

About 90 percent of the energy used by people globally is generated by burning fossil fuels. Fossil fuels are carbon-rich compounds formed from the fossilized bodies of ancient plants and animals. Ancient plants captured the sun's energy and then were buried for huge spans of time. Fossil fuels are the most concentrated and therefore the most convenient form of energy on Earth. Unfortunately, fossil fuels are not renewable on a time scale of interest to humans. Essentially, there is only so much oil in the ground. Although it is not known exactly how much oil is in the ground, we know that the supply is limited. For this reason, fossil fuels are termed nonrenewable resources. Unlike the energy of the sun, which arrives on Earth at a constant rate essentially in perpetuity, fossil fuels are a one-time bonanza.

Fossil fuels come in three general forms: oil, coal, and natural gas. They have, for about a century, been the main energy source powering society. Fossil fuels are inexpensive to obtain and convenient to transport and store. The technology to transform fossil fuels to electricity is simple and well developed. Unfortunately, within 100 years the quantities of petroleum and natural gas available will be largely depleted. World coal supplies are projected to last about 400 years at present rates of consumption. Estimations of fossil fuels reserves are, however, not a simple calculation but a complex interplay of what is in the ground, future demand, production technology, and price (i.e., the incentive to go after increasingly difficult-to-obtain reserves).

Coal is a solid and is extracted from the earth using digging and mining techniques and heavy machinery. Coal is used for firing power plants to produce electricity, and for steel production. Oil is a liquid, procured by drilling and pumping, and is used to produce gasoline, diesel fuel, and plastic products. Natural gas (methane) is the gaseous form of high-energy fossil carbon and will be familiar to many as the cleanest-burning form of home heating energy. About half of the natural gas used in California is used to fire power plants to make electricity.

California currently has no coal-fired power plants. This is commendable in terms of maintaining air quality. Coal is a dirty source of energy, and coal-fired power plants are notorious contributors to both global carbon issues and regional air quality issues. California imports electricity from coal-fired power plants as far away as Utah and Wyoming, essentially exporting air pollution to neighboring states with less stringent air quality regulations. However, new EPA rules for coal-fired plants and California's Assembly Bill 32 to reduce greenhouse gas levels have led California utilities to reduce the amount of energy imported from coal-fired plants. In California, power plants fired with natural gas (methane) provide about 40 percent of the electricity used in the state. This is advantageous in that natural gas is the cleanest-burning fossil fuel. The disadvantage of using natural gas for producing electricity is that it is an inefficient use of the natural gas, compared with using it directly to heat homes. Only about half of the energy stored in a given volume of natural gas is captured as electricity in a power plant, whereas burning it to heat a home can be 96 percent efficient.

The extraction and use of coal, oil, and natural gas create undesirable by-products. Coal extraction (coal mining) is highly dangerous work and employs methods, such as mountaintop removal, with extreme environmental consequences. Oil extraction and transportation can produce accidents that seriously contaminate sensitive ecosystems. Most notoriously, extraction and combustion of the carbon-rich molecules which store energy in fossil fuels produce CO_2 (carbon dioxide), a greenhouse gas. Natural gas is methane (CH_4), itself a potent greenhouse gas. Both CO_2 and methane are primary contributors to climate change. Ethanol burns more cleanly than gasoline in terms of particulates but similarly produces CO_2 emissions which may eventually be unacceptable in a warming world.

Another form of nonrenewable energy is nuclear power. The best estimates are that the current relatively modest rate of consumption of uranium 235 (U-235, the "fuel" used in nuclear reactors) could continue for between 100 and 200 years. If the rate of consumption of U-235 were dramatically increased by building many more nuclear power plants, the global supply of U-235 would be depleted more quickly. Nuclear power is clean in the sense that operating the power plants does not emit carbon dioxide and thus does not contribute to global warming. However, like fossil fuels, nuclear power is a nonrenewable form of energy and supplies of U-235 will eventually be exhausted.

More immediate drawbacks to nuclear power are the cost; the highly dangerous, long-lived radioactive waste produced in the process; and the possibility of a nuclear meltdown. The first generation of nuclear power plants was made economical through federal subsidies to the industry. As the subsidies have been withdrawn and power companies have had to face the entire cost of design, permitting, operation, and decommissioning of highly complex facilities, nuclear power has looked less economically attractive.

Nuclear waste may remain highly toxic for 600 years or more. Many engineers argue that the technical problems of storing dangerous nuclear waste are surmountable, but locating a storage area for the waste presents huge political and social problems. (Who wants a nuclear waste site nearby?)

Another problem associated with nuclear power plants is the highly technical process of running them safely. When the process is not carefully monitored and controlled, the outcome can lead to events such as the meltdown at Chernobyl in 1986. In addition, uncontrollable events such as the combination of a giant earthquake and a tsunami can overwhelm even plants that have backup systems, as was the case in Japan in 2011.

Geothermal energy is a clean, non-carbon-emitting power source that in some ways straddles the border between a renewable and a nonrenewable energy source. The mass of heat trapped in the interior of the Earth would essentially be inexhaustible if it were all available to be tapped. However, the portion accessible from the surface is small and often distant from major metropolitan areas where the power is needed. The technology used to transform the Earth's heat to usable forms, generally electricity, seems to make geothermal energy more like nonrenewable than renewable resources. In New Zealand, for instance, most electricity was produced by geothermal generation for about 30 years, but these sources have been depleted and are no longer of economic utility. Iceland, on the other hand, runs almost completely on geothermal power provided by superficial hot water vents likely to be available far into the future.

Geothermal has minor problems associated with disposal of contaminated water, which could probably be overcome with the proper attention to technology. Another challenge for geothermal energy is that the potential resource is sometimes located in some of the most pristine park lands (such as Yellowstone), where people will object to industrial development.

Wood for fuel also straddles the border between renewable and non-renewable. Wood is the primary cooking and heating fuel for much of the world. Trees are a renewable resource but not necessarily within the time frame needed for the people who depend on them. In many parts of the world, wood needs exceed supply, and wood gatherers have to travel farther and farther from home to find enough fuel. The collection of wood as an energy source is associated with the denuding of hillsides, leading to habitat destruction, soil erosion, and flooding. The burning of wood also produces CO_2, a greenhouse gas.

The renewable forms of energy available to humans include solar, wind, hydroelectric, wave, and tidal. While fossil fuels are concentrated forms of energy, renewables are dilute sources of energy. The cost of collecting dilute sources of energy can be high, so as long as fossil fuels remain cheap, renewable sources can compete economically only with subsidies.

Solar power has huge potential, for both small-scale and industrial applications. Solar energy can be trapped in many forms, from small-scale home water heaters, to industrial-strength solar arrays in the desert that use curved mirrors to heat water which turns turbines to generate electricity. Houses and office buildings can be heated passively by orienting windows to capture solar energy. Another method of capturing the sun's energy directly is with solar cells, which capture the sun's electromagnetic energy and convert it directly to electricity.

Solar is a clean source of power that does not emit carbon during the operation phase. All sources of power emit carbon during the manufacturing phase (e.g., making solar panels), thus the common term *carbon neutral* is somewhat misleading and is not used here. Solar is a renewable source of power, and the prognosis for the sun to rise tomorrow is good. Solar power is currently expensive compared with fossil fuels, but that is partly due to subsidies that benefit oil companies. The cost structure of these competing sources of energy is changing as technology improves and growing demand facilitates mass production of solar equipment and technology. The comparative cost of solar energy may change as costs associated with global warming become more explicitly attached to the burning of fossil fuels.

Solar energy is currently one of the most promising new ways to generate power. However, utility-scale solar farms use a lot of land, and when that means covering extensive amounts of fragile desert ecosystems, this presents serious concerns for biodiversity conservation. The best approach to avoid these impacts is to locate renewable energy projects on degraded lands such as former mine sites or on existing rooftops.

Wind power captures the mechanical energy of wind via large arrays of windmills (wind-powered blades that drive a turbine, which is used to generate electricity). Wind power is a clean, non-carbon-emitting source of power. Its main limitation seems to be the lack of places where the wind is strong and reliable enough to make operation economical. Wind farm proposals often run into local opposition based on aesthetics ("not in my back yard") and opposition from bird lovers and biologists who are concerned about bats and migratory birds, especially large raptors like golden eagles and red-tailed hawks, being killed by the spinning blades.

Hydroelectric energy captures the mechanical energy of falling water via dams and turbines to generate electricity. Hydroelectric power supplies about 10 percent of America's electricity today. The percentage of hydropower in California is higher than the national average, 15 percent. Hydropower is clean in the sense that it emits no carbon and does not contribute to global warming. The unfortunate side of hydropower is that damming rivers dramatically alters the ecology of the river. The Pacific salmon crisis, with 11 species of salmonids on the federal endangered species list and others sure to join it, is largely a result of hydroelectric dams. The same is true of the Colorado River, where three of the original 8 native species of fish are extinct and two are endangered as a result of hydroelectric dams. Before the dams were built, the Colorado River system was a seasonal, muddy, warm-water system. The dams have transformed the river into a cold, clear, low-nutrient system. The Colorado before the dams supported 8 native species of fish and virtually no nonnative fish species. Currently the Colorado supports about 20 species of nonnative fish and reduced populations of the 5 remaining native species.

Ocean wave power and tidal power are largely ideas in the development stage. Both are essentially inexhaustible supplies of energy, if the technical challenges to tapping them can be overcome. Wave power is captured by buoys anchored to the seafloor offshore. Wave power has the classic problem of the difficulty of harnessing a very dilute energy source. The cost of harvesting it makes it uneconomical. Tidal power is generally captured in estuaries, using dams that allow the tide to raise the water level and then run the outflow through turbines to create electricity. Tidal power works well when you have a really good site (e.g., the Rance River on the French side of the English Channel), but not elsewhere. Tidal power dams like Rance have environmental problems similar to river dams.

Alternative forms of liquid fuel for powering vehicles (biofuels) are now being developed. Ethanol is an energy-rich liquid that can (theoretically) be produced from various plant products (sugarcane, corn, wood, agricultural waste, fruits). Biofuels are relatively clean-burning, renewable sources of conveniently transportable energy. They are carbon-emitting energy sources but are cleaner than coal. The technology is still being perfected, but the fact that most cars in Brazil run on an 85/15 blend of ethanol and gasoline is an indication that these renewable sources of energy may be a part of the transportation future.

Technical and social questions regarding biofuels include, what plants will be the sources of energy? The easiest source to process, and thus the first to come onto the market, was sugarcane. One problem with using sugarcane to produce fuel is that it takes prime agricultural land to grow sugarcane, land that could be used to feed people. Will we one day face the choice between driving or feeding people? It takes energy to run the tractors and make the fertilizer to grow corn or sugarcane. Is the energy output more than the input? With sugarcane there is probably a net gain in energy. With corn, if you count the energy required to produce the fertilizer, then there is a net overall loss of usable energy. Without federal subsidies to farmers in the United States and ethanol import taxes, corn-based biofuels may not turn out to be profitable in the United States where farming costs are high. The other important issue for sustainability is that growing biofuels competes with food production, contributing to higher global food prices.

For about 100 years people have tried to produce a biofuel that targets the cellulose in plant cells rather than the glucose. If "cellulosic" biofuels became practical, then entirely new sources of fuel would be available, using wood waste, paper pulp, and other current "waste products" to supply energy needs. Unfortunately, it is technically difficult.

In summary, all of the various forms of energy available to power human activities have advantages and disadvantages. How to evaluate these trade-offs is a complex, often technical, problem. Since the discussion must take place in the political arena, which can limit the depth and quality of the discussion, completely rational energy policy is seldom achieved. These policies, however, do influence how the state and country address global environmental issues that cannot be solved by one country alone.

GLOBAL ENVIRONMENTAL CHALLENGES

Climate Change

The most pressing global environmental problem facing humans today is human-induced (anthropogenic) climate change. Atmospheric and climatic change can be natural phenomena. The ancient atmosphere of the Earth before the advent of green plants contained very little oxygen. The evolution and rise to global dominance of photosynthetic plants completely changed the global atmosphere by emitting oxygen and raising the concentration of oxygen in the atmosphere to 20 percent. This global atmospheric shift was one of the major turning points in the evolutionary history of the Earth, transforming the air in a way that eliminated many organisms while it made the planet hospitable to others. The global climate has a long and complex history of dramatic changes, with cold glacial cycles alternating with warm interglacials. The North American continent has at times hosted tropical forests, been buried under sheets of ice nearly a mile thick, and been a desert so dry it supported virtually no plants or animals. However, the anthropogenic causes of modern climate change are acting on a much faster time scale than natural climate-changing events in the past.

The greenhouse effect is a complex insulation event. Gasses in the atmosphere, especially carbon dioxide, methane, and nitrous oxide, trap heat coming from Earth's surface. More specifically, carbon molecules in the atmosphere absorb and reradiate heat escaping Earth's surface and headed for space. By continually reradiating heat, carbon molecules in the atmosphere regulate the temperature ranges on the surface of the planet. As the concentration of carbon in the atmosphere increases, this greenhouse effect increases. Lowering concentrations of these gasses would allow more of the heat to escape out to space. High concentrations mean more heat is trapped. This trapped heat raises global temperatures, changing precipitation regimes and the timing of the seasons.

Since the beginning of the Industrial Revolution human production of carbon dioxide has increased dramatically. By looking at ancient ice cores and examining air trapped in the ice, scientists have been able to demonstrate multiple patterns of chemical change in the atmosphere over the last 60,000 years. One of the clearest and most important is the increase in the concentration of carbon dioxide in the atmosphere. This increase has been produced largely by removing carbon-rich compounds (fossil fuels) from long-term storage in the ground and burning

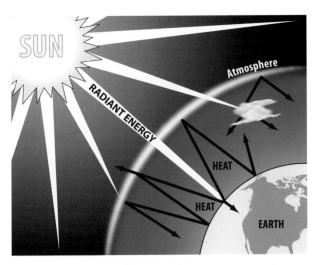

The greenhouse effect. The atmosphere protects organisms from solar radiation, and it insulates the planet from heat loss. Courtesy of the State of Washington Department of Energy

them, releasing CO_2 at a faster than natural rate. Climate scientists and common sense indicate that we need to dramatically reduce our greenhouse gas emissions to avoid catastrophically altering the global climate.

Global warming is underway and its impacts are being felt. Effects of global warming include

· Sea level rise
· Shrinking glaciers
· Changes in the range and distribution of plants and animals
· Lengthening of growing seasons
· Thawing of permafrost
· More extreme weather events

The questions that remain are, how quickly will the temperature rise and how high will the temperature go? Thus far, the news has not been good. Temperatures have risen faster than scientists had predicted. This is in part because there are climate processes acting to accelerate global warming and in part because greenhouse gas emissions have increased faster in the past five years than expected.

While there are efforts in California and elsewhere to limit emissions

California's Future Climate

- Temperatures will increase by an average of 0.5 to 1.0 degrees C by 2025, with less warming in coastal regions and more inland— up to 2.0 degrees—and greater summer than winter increases in temperature, especially in inland areas. One degree might not seem like a lot, but think how your body feels when your temperature goes up one degree!
- Precipitation patterns will shift. Storms will shift northwards, reducing winter precipitation. Winter storms will be more severe while summer drought and heat waves will be more frequent, longer, and more intense—heat wave days are projected to increase by 20 to 30 days per year in the Central Valley.
- Snowfall will be reduced and snowpack will decrease by as much as 25 percent by 2050.
- Summer soil moisture will decrease, further aggravating atmospheric warming.
- Drying of the US Southwest will reduce water available to California; the probability that Lake Mead will go dry by 2025 is 50 percent.
- Sea level will rise steadily, causing salination of soils and greater storm surges; warmer and more acidic ocean water will alter marine ecosystems and fog patterns.

Adapted from T. Paine, I. Fung, S. Wheeler, J. London, D. Roland-Holst, and S. Handy. *What Will California Look Like in 2025: Future Structure of California*. UC Agriculture and Natural Resources white paper.

of CO_2 and other greenhouse gases, much more must be done to slow the growth of these global warming agents in the next two decades. The required changes include altering the sources of energy, from carbon-emitting to non-carbon-emitting sources, as well as changing patterns of activity and consumption.

The United States is currently the largest producer of greenhouse gases per capita. While China is the largest emitter overall, citizens of highly developed, urbanized countries have a far greater per capita impact on the atmosphere than people in less-developed countries. China and India, with about half of the world's population, currently emit far smaller amounts of greenhouse gases per person than the United States or the industrialized countries of western Europe, but they are on a trajectory to overtake us in this regard. This is an alarm-

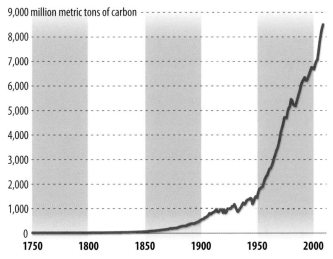

Carbon dioxide emissions from human industry have increased
dramatically since 1850 and have increased exponentially since
1950. Data from the Oak Ridge National Laboratory. Used with
permission from the National Energy Education Development
Project, www.need.org

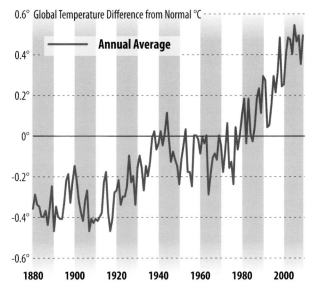

This NASA data shows steadily increasing global temperature
(as temperature change) since 1880, with no reversal on the
horizon. Used with permission from the National Energy
Education Development Project, www.need.org

ing prospect, since the multiplication of the huge numbers of people in less-developed countries by the high consumption rates of the most-developed countries is a recipe for climate disaster if technology or usage patterns do not change. To meet its energy demands, China currently depends largely on burning coal. China has the largest reserves of coal in the world, and China already uses more coal than the United States, the European Union, and Japan combined. Every two weeks another coal-fired power plant large enough to serve all of the households in Dallas or San Diego opens in China.

Clearly more-developed countries need to be cooperating with rapidly developing countries, helping them find technological ways to avoid burning coal, and working together to dodge the climate change bullet. However, increased emissions from giants like China are not a foregone conclusion. Efforts are underway to help developing economies go directly to cleaner energy generation. The combination of new technologies, regulations to drive reduction of emissions, and changes in consumption and behavior will all be necessary to achieve the very ambitious reduction goals necessary to confront this dangerous global threat.

Climate Change in California

Warmer temperatures will fundamentally change the distribution of vegetation and animal populations in California, as well as affect agriculture and the integrity of shoreline construction and tidal ecosystems. Though sea levels will rise globally, off the coast of California the sea level rise could be less than the global average, as changes in winds and hence ocean currents may move some of the water offshore. Warmer and more acidic oceans will alter marine ecosystems. Coastal fog will respond to changes in ocean and land temperatures, which will affect terrestrial ecosystems dependent on it, but for now the direction of these changes is hard to predict.

While it is clear that temperatures in California will rise, changes in rainfall across the state are harder to predict. Precipitation patterns will shift, as will the seasonality, frequency, and intensity of rainfall. One thing is certain: we will no longer be able to rely upon the Sierra snowpack to provide water-holding capacity, as snowpacks are not expected to survive the increasing warmth of the twenty-first century. In fact, the expected decrease in snowpack could be as large as 25 percent by 2050.

As a consequence of early snowmelt in the spring, soils will dry earlier and require irrigation earlier. Heat wave days are projected to increase by 20 to 30 days per year in the Central Valley, and using water for heat protection may not be possible. This will have consequences for both California's ecosystems and its agriculture. Changes to the fire regime are expected, with an increase in catastrophic fires.

Many parts of the state already feel water stressed, but with climate change and land-use changes, there will be a dramatic decline in the availability of freshwater. Already, Lake Mead has a water deficit of 1 million acre-feet per year, and some scientists have estimated that there is a 50 percent chance that Lake Mead will be seasonally dry by 2025. Much of California relies on river water. Expected changes in the frequency and severity of weather will affect the amount and character of the water runoff from California's rivers. With these precipitation changes, there will be changes in the timing and intensity of streamflow. More intense rainfall in winter could lead to increased flooding and landslides, less infiltration into soils, and streams that could carry greater sediment loads.

The impacts of climate change are numerous. A 2008 UC Berkeley study found that the economic damage to the state due to global temperature increases—including water resources, energy, tourism, recreation, real estate, agriculture, forests, fisheries, transportation, and public health—could have an annual price tag of between $7.3 and $46 billion, and that $2.5 trillion of real estate assets would be at risk from extreme weather events, sea level rise, and wildfires.

Global warming's projected impacts in California include the following:

- *Sea level rise, coastal flooding, and coastal erosion*: As sea level rises, erosion along California's coastline and saltwater intrusion into the delta and levee systems will increase, threatening wildlife and drinking water.

- *Higher risk of fires*: Climate change makes forests more vulnerable to fires by increasing temperatures and making forests and brush drier. Today's fire season in the western United States already lasts for 78 days. The frequency and size of forest fires is likely to increase, perhaps severalfold, by the end of the century.

- *Damage to agriculture*: By reducing precipitation, raising temperatures, causing flooding, and increasing the risk of pest infestations and other calamities, global warming poses a threat to the

Flames of the Simi Valley fire ravage a Southern California mountainside. US Air Force photo by Senior Master Sgt. Dennis W. Goff

California agricultural industry, which generated $39 billion in revenue in 2007.

- *Increased demand for electricity*: Higher temperatures and more heat waves will drive up demand for cooling in the summertime.
- *Public health impacts*: As temperatures rise, the number of days of extreme heat events will increase, causing increases in the risk of injury or death from dehydration, heatstroke, heart attack, and respiratory problems.

- *Impacts on low-income and minority communities*: Global warming's impacts are likely to disproportionately affect low-income and minority communities in California, who have the least ability to resist and adapt to the impacts of higher temperatures, heat waves, floods, and other extreme weather events.

- *Habitat modification, destruction, and loss of ecosystems*: Climate change will adversely affect plant and wildlife habitat and the ability of the state's varied ecosystems to provide clean water supplies, wildlife, fish, timber, and other goods and services important for human well-being. These impacts are already occurring: the lower edges of forests in the Sierra Nevada have been retreating upslope over the past 60 years. In Yosemite National Park, certain small mammal taxa are now found at higher elevations compared with earlier in the century. Butterflies in the Central Valley have been arriving earlier in the spring over the past four decades.

- *Water shortage*: The Sierra snowpack, which provides up to 65 percent of California's water supply, will be reduced by at least 25 percent by 2050. In addition, the sea level rise could inundate the Sacramento-San Joaquin Delta with salt water, threatening the water supply for 25 million Californians and millions of acres of farmland.

Californians will be challenged to develop adaptations to these changes, find innovative solutions to the problems that are already becoming manifest, and create a new model for business and culture. Part of that adaptation will be reducing our reliance on carbon-producing energy sources and beginning the transition to lower-carbon-emitting forms of energy. In this respect, California has been a national leader. In 2006, the state legislature set a goal to reduce carbon emissions to 80 percent below 1990 levels by the year 2050. This will take dramatic actions in every sector of society and, predictably, the law has been under attack since its passage.

We need to make changes collectively and as individuals in our own homes in order to stave off rising temperatures and to improve our resilience to expected change. Protecting our natural resources, such as forests, watersheds, and natural areas, is an essential step in ensuring that we can continue to rely on the goods and services nature provides society and that species will have a chance to persist. Many changes in energy, agriculture, and environmental policy are needed to prevent future climate-related disasters. Californians are in a good position to

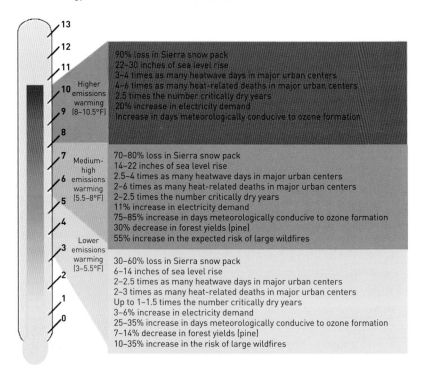

90% loss in Sierra snow pack
22–30 inches of sea level rise
3–4 times as many heatwave days in major urban centers
4–6 times as many heat-related deaths in major urban centers
2.5 times the number critically dry years
20% increase in electricity demand
Increase in days meteorologically conducive to ozone formation

Higher emissions warming (8–10.5°F)

70–80% loss in Sierra snow pack
14–22 inches of sea level rise
2.5–4 times as many heatwave days in major urban centers
2–6 times as many heat-related deaths in major urban centers
2–2.5 times the number critically dry years
11% increase in electricity demand
75–85% increase in days meteorologically conducive to ozone formation
30% decrease in forest yields (pine)
55% increase in the expected risk of large wildfires

Medium-high emissions warming (5.5–8°F)

30–60% loss in Sierra snow pack
6–14 inches of sea level rise
2–2.5 times as many heatwave days in major urban centers
2–3 times as many heat-related deaths in major urban centers
Up to 1–1.5 times the number critically dry years
3–6% increase in electricity demand
25–35% increase in days meteorologically conducive to ozone formation
7–14% decrease in forest yields (pine)
10–35% increase in the risk of large wildfires

Lower emissions warming (3–5.5°F)

Projected global warming impacts for California for 2070–2099, as compared with 1961–1990. Compare individual lines across colors to see what may happen with a range of projected scenarios. Courtesy of the California Department of Energy, reflecting the understanding in 2006 about potential impacts

make these changes. We already lead the nation in energy efficiency, and as early adopters of new technologies and ways of thinking, we can continue to take a leadership role in climate change adaptation.

Most Americans, including most Californians, use far more energy than we really need and can start to reduce consumption with relatively small changes to our lives. As the world's wealthiest nation and the largest emitter of greenhouses gasses per capita, the United States must take a leadership role in reducing greenhouse gas emissions and modeling a less consumptive lifestyle.

Ozone Depletion

Like oxygen (O_2), ozone is a molecule consisting only of oxygen atoms, but with three instead of two oxygen atoms (O_3). At ground level,

Take Action: Climate Change

SIMPLE IDEAS THAT MAKE A DIFFERENCE

Change a light. Replacing one incandescent light bulb with a compact fluorescent or LED lightbulb will save 150 pounds of carbon dioxide a year.*

Drive less. Walk, bike, carpool, or take mass transit more often. You'll save 1 pound of carbon dioxide for every mile you don't drive.

Recycle more. You can save 2,400 pounds of carbon dioxide per year by recycling just half of your household waste.

Check your tires. Keeping your tires inflated properly can improve gas mileage by more than 3 percent. Every gallon of gasoline saved keeps 20 pounds of carbon dioxide out of the atmosphere.

Use less hot water. It takes a lot of energy to heat water. Use less hot water by installing a low-flow showerhead (350 pounds of carbon dioxide saved per year) and washing your clothes in cold or warm water (500 pounds saved per year).

Avoid products with a lot of packaging. You can save 1,200 pounds of carbon dioxide if you cut down your garbage by 10 percent.

Adjust your thermostat. By moving your thermostat down just 2 degrees in winter and up 2 degrees in summer, you can save 2,000 pounds of carbon dioxide a year.

Plant a tree. A single tree will absorb 1 ton of carbon dioxide over its lifetime.

Turn off electronic devices. Simply turning off your television, DVD player, stereo, and computer when you're not using them will save you thousands of pounds of carbon dioxide a year.

Teleconference, vacation locally, and plan trips to reduce plane travel. Airplanes emit far more greenhouse gasses per passenger than car travel (even in a Hummer!) or train travel.

Eat food grown locally. Better yet, grow it yourself! Much of the food sold in supermarkets has been driven and flown thousands of miles. Learn what is in season and locally grown and save the gas guzzlers, such as tropical fruits like bananas, for special treats.

Advocate for renewable energy. Electricity generation produces 40 percent of carbon emissions from the United States.

Offset emissions. Support projects that restore and protect the ocean, forests, and wildlands.

*Note: Compact fluorescent bulbs contain mercury and must be disposed of as hazardous waste or, even better, recycled. However, because of their efficiency, their use reduces mercury contamination in the end by saving energy and decreasing demand on power plants, which produce mercury.

Adapted from Wecansolveit.org.

ozone is a pollutant that is most commonly produced by automobiles. Ozone also exists in small quantities high in the stratosphere, where it provides a vital function: it protects the surface of the planet from ultraviolet radiation. In the 1920s Thomas Midgley, a chemist, was working on creating a substitute for the dangerous gasses then used as refrigerants. He created a new class of synthetic molecules called chlorofluorocarbons (CFCs). CFCs had many advantages over the previously used chemicals and were quickly adopted for all kinds of industrial and household applications, most notably as refrigerants. Half a century later, it was found that CFCs had the unfortunate property of rising through the atmosphere to the upper layers of the stratosphere, where they are broken down by light to form chlorine atoms. In the stratosphere, chlorine reacts chemically with ozone, with the effect of destroying the ozone. Essentially, CFCs were found to be destroying the ozone layer. CFCs are also wonderful heat sponges. When in the troposphere, they are roughly 10,000 times more efficient as greenhouse gasses than carbon dioxide!

The good news is that CFC production and use have been banned since 1990 by signatories to the Montreal Protocol, and this global response has been effective at dramatically reducing CFC use and impact. Other compounds, including those with bromine, have been found to have the same effect of destroying ozone in the stratosphere, and current efforts focus on ODCs—ozone-depleting chemicals. The worldwide reaction to solving this problem may be the first example of a global political response to an environmental threat. It is an example that can give us courage and confidence in confronting the even larger problem of climate change.

Dead Zones, Fertilizers, and Manure Management

Dead zones are low-oxygen areas in the world's oceans and lakes. Oceanographers first began noting dead zones in the 1970s. Dead zones are caused by a process called eutrophication in which excess water-borne nutrients stimulate excessive plant growth, eventually depleting oxygen from the water. As of 2004, 146 dead zones in the world's oceans, where marine life could not be supported by the depleted oxygen levels, were identified. Some of these dead zones are small, but the largest dead zone covers about 70,000 square kilometers. Currently one of the most notorious dead zones is a 22,000-square-kilometer region in the Gulf of Mexico where the Mississippi River discharges into the

Gulf. The Mississippi collects water and agricultural runoff from the breadbasket of the world, the American Midwest, and delivers it to Gulf waters. Because of the high concentration of fertilizer use in this region, combined with animal waste from dairies and stockyards, the waters of the Mississippi are unnaturally high in nitrogen and phosphorus. The high nutrient load of the runoff from this vast drainage basin has devastated the regionally important shrimp fishery of the Gulf.

Dead zones can be reversed. The Black Sea used to have the largest dead zone in the world, but it disappeared between 1991 and 2001 when the collapse of the Soviet Union caused a dramatic reduction in fertilizer use.

Manure management will be an increasingly important problem on spaceship Earth. In addition to poisoning rivers with nutrients, cattle, pigs, and their excrement have a role in global warming. The normal method of composting animal waste creates methane gas, the same kind of gas used for electricity generation and heating. Methane is a potent greenhouse gas, over 20 times more efficient at trapping and reradiating heat to Earth's surface than carbon dioxide. Clearly the day has arrived when we can no longer afford to regard our atmosphere as a global dumping ground for methane, ozone, carbon dioxide, and other gasses.

Agricultural Issues

California is the nation's agricultural powerhouse. California farms produce nearly half the vegetables, fruit, and nuts grown in the United States, and a number of California crops—such as almonds, artichokes, olives, walnuts, and figs—are commercially produced nowhere else in the country. California is also the nation's largest dairy producer and supplies vast amounts of other farm products, including greenhouse and nursery products and cattle. Simply put, California is the leading agricultural producer in the United States in terms of cash farm receipts.

Of the state's 100 million acres, 25.4 million acres (25.4 percent) were dedicated to some form of agriculture in 2008. As vast as that amount sounds, the number of acres in some kind of farm-related activity has been falling in recent years, and California farms are on average quite a bit smaller than the national average: 312 acres for California farms, down from 314 in 2007 and versus 418 nationwide. The Mediterranean climate, freshwater resources, and soils found in

California allow for higher intensity of production compared with other parts of the country.

Like so many concerns in California, agricultural land issues and pressures reflect the complexity of the state as a whole. Population growth, land use, immigration, worker safety, water wars, nonpoint source water pollution, carbon credits, and many other disparate issues find their nexus in California agriculture.

One of the most pressing concerns for California farms is the development and conversion of farmland for urban uses. As the state's population has expanded and land prices have risen, pressure has grown to convert existing farmland into housing developments and other commercial uses.

A 2010 news release from the USDA Natural Resources Conservation Service states, "California has converted 2.1 million acres to urban uses between 1982 and 2007. At the same time, losses were experienced in cropland (900,000 acres), rangeland (1,600,000 acres), and forestland (500,000 acres). . . . The loss of prime farmland, those soils best suited to produce food with the fewest inputs and the least erosion, is particularly troubling and California ranks fourth nationwide in losing such soils between 1982 and 2007. However, between 2002 and 2007 the loss of prime farmland in California stabilized and even experienced a minute increase" (www.ca.nrcs.usda.gov/news/releases/2010/nri_5-4-10.html).

Since many cities in California are located adjacent to prime cropland, urban expansion, particularly exurban development, directly reduces the farmland base. Throughout the Central Valley, about 30,000 acres are converted annually from farmland to urban uses, and California could lose nearly 5 million acres of agricultural land if these lands continue to be converted to urban uses at this rate.

Water Use

Conflicts between residential water needs, environmental water needs, and agricultural water needs have been evident in California for decades. Estimates vary, but all indicate that agriculture uses a substantial amount—more than 50 percent and as much as 90 percent by some estimates—of the state's freshwater.

Delivery of that water is one of the most interesting parts of the California agriculture water story. Much of the farm and ranch land is located in the drier, southern half of the state. Most of the water falls in the north. A high percentage of the water used in Southern California comes from Northern California through a remarkable system of aqueducts and dams. This water delivery system has allowed farms to flourish in areas that would not be able to support commercial agriculture if the farms had to rely solely on local water sources. This system is financially supported by the federal and state governments and results in water subsidies that primarily benefit the largest industrial growers.

Water use by agriculture can trigger ecological concerns. For example, in many parts of coastal California, agricultural water needs during the summer are met by diverting stream water and tapping groundwater resources, which has led to documented decreases in stream flow during the dry season. This has consequences for salmon—including sudden drops in water level, higher water temperatures, and changes in the invertebrate prey base—that imperil their ability to reproduce. In dry years, excessive pumping from wells and springs can collapse aquifers or cause saltwater intrusion. In addition, ground and surface water can be contaminated by surface runoff of fertilizers and pesticides, polluting the water. Construction and maintenance of buffer zones of native vegetation next to water sources can help to mitigate this problem.

Sustainable Agriculture

How agriculture is practiced can make a big difference in its impact. Practices common to large-scale agrobusiness can take a toll on both the land and the people working it, including loss of topsoil, depletion of soil nutrients, groundwater contamination, the loss of small and medium-size family farms, and poor conditions for farm laborers.

To address these issues, sustainable farming systems strive to promote environmental health, economic profitability, and social and economic equity through stewardship of both natural and human resources. In sustainable agriculture, a diversity of crops and livestock are grown and are selected for their suitability to the site. Cultivation techniques are chosen for their ability to conserve and enhance the soil, as well as protect water resources and wildlife habitat. Natural pest management and other farming methods that minimize synthetic inputs are preferred. Animals may be integrated into the cultivation regime, and animal and other wastes may be utilized on-site. Humane treatment of animals is a core value. In addition, sustainable agriculture seeks to enhance the economic viability of small and medium-sized family farms and their communities and ensure worker safety.

Agriculture and Carbon Sequestration

Climate change in California is likely to have significant impacts for agriculture, including a less reliable water supply and a shift in where certain crops can be grown. For example, according to research done at UC Davis, some areas, such as Yolo County, will become too hot over the next 50 years to grow crops that many farmers rely on, such as tomatoes and cucumbers. California agriculture, however, can also be part of the solution by curbing emissions from tractors, reducing or capturing methane produced at dairy and cattle operations, and using sustainable farming techniques.

Carbon sequestration has been suggested for providing income and incentives for keeping land in agricultural production. The EPA lists four practices that can increase carbon storage in agriculture:

- Conservation or riparian buffers for maintaining and restoring vegetation strips along streams and adjacent to croplands
- Conservation tillage, in which a portion of the crop residue remains on the soil after planting, including no till, ridge till, minimum till, and mulch till
- Modifications to grazing regimes or rotational grazing
- Biofuel substitution: substitution of crops or trees grown for biomass rather than food production purposes

According to the USDA Economic Research Service (ERS), if practices like these and others (such as the use of winter cover crops) are adopted, there is the potential to increase carbon storage significantly; somewhere between 29 and 208 million additional metric tons of carbon could be stored each year in US soils. And the ERS notes that these numbers do not include the impact of converting less productive farm and range lands to forests or wetlands, ecological communities that have the potential to sequester carbon.

Air Quality

There are several types of air pollutants of interest to naturalists in California, including smog, particulate matter, sulfur dioxide, carbon monoxide, and carbon dioxide.

Smog in western states is mostly ozone, formed from nitrogen oxides (NO_x) and volatile organic compounds (VOCs) in the presence of sunlight. NO_x comes from combustion sources such as vehicles and power plants and from soil fertilization. VOCs come from such sources as evaporating fuel, vegetation, and consumer products. Ozone is worst on warm, stagnant days. Although originally confined to urban basins such as Los Angeles, ozone is now distributed regionally and is transported between continents. For example, rural areas in far northern California receive some ozone from plumes that travel across the ocean from Asia and make landfall. Ozone causes difficulty in breathing, worsens asthma, and over long periods, reduces lung volume. It also damages plants by reducing photosynthesis, growth, and root development. Many plants exhibit a bronze speckling on the upper leaf surface when exposed to ozone.

Particulate matter can consist of many chemical constituents that come from diverse sources, including wood burning, diesel engine emissions, and road and agricultural dust. Soot in smoke is a fine particle that may be carcinogenic and degrades visibility. Fine particles have been linked to premature death, particularly in vulnerable populations of the old, young, and unhealthy, primarily through worsening cardiovascular symptoms. In general, particulate matter is not damaging to vegetation, though when it contains nitrogen, it may serve as a fertilizer (even leading to harmful nitrogen saturation of ecosystems) when it deposits on vegetation. Exceptions are cement dust, which is alkaline and corrosive, and materials like heavy metals (lead, copper, mercury) which when present can be harmful to grazing animals and consumers of milk and meat. Most particulate matter is in the form of fine particles, including sulfate particles that come from coal-fired power plants.

Sulfur dioxide (SO_2) comes from burning fuels, such as in coal-fired power plants, which contain sulfur. SO_2 is very irritating to the airways, may trigger asthma attacks, and when oxidized to sulfuric acid, contributes to acid precipitation. Acid precipitation may acidify lakes, particularly in granite landscapes such as the Sierra Nevada where natural pH buffering is weak. Oxidation to sulfate particles is a principal cause of visibility degradation in areas where coal is burned for power or industrial processes. This is more of a problem in the east, though visibility in the Grand Canyon is impacted by sulfate particles.

Carbon monoxide is a by-product of incomplete combustion, whether in automobile engines or from campfires or other biomass burning. It may accumulate, for example, in valleys with little air movement, in caves, and in enclosed tents or automobiles. It causes headache and chest pains and can lead to rapid death in humans but surprisingly is not harmful to plants.

Carbon dioxide (CO_2) is also considered an air pollutant. It comes from combustion, in California mostly from vehicles, as well as from many natural processes, including animal respiration.

Warmer temperatures due to climate change will lead to worse ozone air pollution in many places, because more VOCs are emitted at warmer temperatures from plants and evaporating fuels, and because the reactions that form smog increase with temperature. Many of these changes will also increase the risk of wildfire and extend the fire season in California, thereby temporarily but significantly increasing particulate matter and ozone concentrations in communities downwind of the fires.

Solid Waste

In nature, there is no such thing as waste. A tree dies and as it decomposes, it becomes food for fungi, a home for insects and birds, and later, a seed log for new trees. In human society, however, people treat materials as if they can "go away," and we excel at producing waste. The average American generates approximately 30 pounds of trash per week. That's about 1,600 pounds of trash a year for every person in the country. But what happens to that trash? How much of it could have been recycled, reused, or composted? And where did it come from in the first place?

Every item you buy has something called "embodied energy." Embodied energy is the energy that was used to get the product from its source to the consumer: to extract the resources the product is made from (wood from logged trees, plastic from refined petroleum, etc.); to manufacture, package, and advertise the product; to ship it from the manufacturer to the store and then to the home; and finally to collect it for recycling or landfilling. For every product in your house, a certain number of gallons of gas and water were used to create, transport, and dispose of it. When we fail to use something to its fullest potential, we are wasting not only the materials comprising the product but the resources that went into creating it.

Typically, when items are thrown away, they go first to a transfer station or materials recovery facility where they are sorted and recyclable items are removed from the waste stream. The rest is trucked to a landfill. A landfill is a gigantic hole that is lined with clay or plastic

Students work to maintain a compost bin. Photo used by permission © Regents of the University of California

to prevent leakage into the soil and groundwater. Problems associated with landfills are numerous: landfill space is becoming more scarce, and many have been closed because of groundwater contamination. Building new ones is getting harder: few people want a landfill located near their house, and increasingly, the land is wanted for other purposes such as housing and open space. For these reasons, many cities now truck their garbage far away at great expense. The City of San Francisco hauls all of its trash over 50 miles to the Altamont Landfill in Livermore, CA, and Los Angeles and other Southern California cities are actively considering long rail hauling of their garbage for disposal in the Mojave Desert.

Materials in landfills are covered daily with soil to shield them from rain, wind, sun, and air. The result is that many things in a landfill take decades, if not hundreds or even thousands of years, to decompose. A plastic bag may take between 500 and 1,000 years to completely break down. As the materials do degrade, landfills emit a powerful greenhouse gas: methane. Although many landfills now are set up to recover some of this methane gas and use it for productive purposes, every ton of methane that escapes into the atmosphere has over 20 times the greenhouse impact as one ton of carbon dioxide. Food waste,

Material Waste and Material Cycles

How would you reimagine the solid waste problem from a nutrient cycles perspective? We are removing materials (minerals, wood, metal, oil) from the planet's reservoirs at an accelerated rate, using some portion of them and then mixing them together for long-term storage in a landfill. Along the way, during removal, manufacturing, use, and disposal, parts of the materials (pollutants) are discharged into the air and water to be reabsorbed into the system at the natural rate. What cannot be readily reabsorbed is left to accumulate in the atmosphere or taken up in excess by living organisms, contaminating and sometimes killing them.

yard debris, and other organics are the biggest generators of methane, amplifying the importance of composting. Some states have actually banned organic materials from their landfills.

Due to diminishing landfill space and concerns about conservation of resources, California has instituted laws to reduce waste and encourage recycling, and recycling rates in California have improved dramatically in recent decades. But despite these improvements, Californians still throw away about a third of their bottles and cans and recycle less than half of the paper they use.

Does it really matter? Yes. Reuse and recycling are not just about conserving resources. These actions also directly reduce carbon emissions and help in the fight against global climate change. The EPA states, "Harvesting, extracting, and processing the raw materials used to manufacture new products is an energy-intensive activity. Reducing or nearly eliminating the need for these processes, therefore, achieves huge savings in energy. Recycling aluminum cans, for example, saves 95 percent of the energy required to make the same amount of aluminum from its virgin source, bauxite. The amount of energy saved differs by material, but almost all recycling processes achieve significant energy savings compared to production using virgin materials" (http://epa.gov/region4/recycle/faqs.htm).

Right now, there are masses of garbage, mostly plastic, swirling around the world's oceans. The largest garbage mass is in the Pacific. It is nicknamed the Great Pacific Garbage Patch. Due to difficulties in measuring it, its exact extent is not known, but it is likely as large as the state of Texas and probably much larger; in some places, it extends 10 feet below the surface. The plastic breaks down into tiny pieces that make it hard to study or clean up but easy for sea life to mistake for food. Scientists say that 80 percent of the garbage is from land sources—packaging and plastic bags left on beaches, blown from a highway to a storm drain or littered near a creek. It is astonishing to consider, but this mess has a greater mass than all of the plankton available in the northern Pacific Ocean and is now a permanent and very damaging part of the aquatic food chain. For these and other reasons, many communities and even some countries like Ireland have banned plastic bags.

Fortunately, there are ways to ameliorate this situation and prevent others like it: The four R's—reduce, reuse, recycle, and rot (compost). The four R's are just a way of seeing products as a part of the natural material cycle and recognizing that there is no "away." These practices apply to more than just paper, bottles, cans, and banana peels. Computers, cell phones and other electronic devices, tires, and construction and demolition debris can all be recycled. We can draw inspiration from the cities of Oakland and San Francisco, both of which have set the exciting and ambitious goal of generating *zero waste* by 2020. They join cities and counties all over California and the world in passing resolutions to achieve this goal.

Here are some tips for reducing your trash footprint:

- Buy less. Buy only what you really need and intend to use or keep.
- Buy products with little or no packaging. Refuse a bag if you don't need one.
- Try items that can be reused: cloth bags for shopping, cloth napkins for meals, dish towels for the kitchen, and reusable cups for that cup of coffee on the run.
- Buy toys, clothes, and furniture that are gently used. Garage sales are fabulous for this.
- Donate used electronics or recycle them. *Note*: Electronics usually contain hazardous materials and are important to dispose of properly!
- Choose durable items that will last. Avoid items designed to be used only once.
- Buy or build a compost bin. Composting is recycling at your home. There are no transportation costs, and you get a useful product for your garden!

Product Stewardship

Consumers and governments are increasingly looking to manufacturers to be part of the solid waste solution through an approach called product stewardship, or extended product responsibility. The EPA states, "In most cases, manufacturers have the greatest ability, and therefore the greatest responsibility, to reduce the environmental impacts of their products. Companies accepting the challenge recognize that product stewardship represents an opportunity. By rethinking their products, their relationships with the supply chain and the customer, manufacturers are increasing their productivity, reducing costs, fostering product and market innovation, and providing customers with more value at less environmental impact. Using nontoxic substances, designing for reuse and recyclability, and creating 'take back' programs are just a few of the many ways companies become better environmental stewards."

Excerpted from US Environmental Protection Agency, http://www.epa.gov/osw/conserve/tools/stewardship/basic.htm.

- Buy recycled products. Without a market for recycled paper or reclaimed lumber, the recycling system comes to a grinding halt.
- For a complete list of household items that can be conveniently recycled in California, as well as information about recycling of electronics and hazardous waste, visit the website of CalRecycle at http://www.calrecycle.ca.gov.

Population

All of the problems mentioned above are, in one way or another, outgrowths of the size of the human population and the amount of resources we each consume. Human population grew slowly for most of the 200,000 years that *Homo sapiens* has existed as a species, probably hovering for most of that time at about 5 million people. The invention of agriculture about 11,000 years ago led to the first major spike in human numbers, as well as population centers, career specialization, and rapid cultural and technological advances. The following 9,000 years saw human population expand from around 5 million to about 200 million at the time of Christ. Another millennium and a half brought another increase in human numbers, to an estimated 500 million in 1650. Human population reached 1 billion in 1830, stood at 2 billion in 1930, and reached 3 billion by 1960. We reached the fourth billion 14 years later (1974), 5 billion by 1987, and 6 billion in 1999, and we are now over 7 billion as of October 2011.

Predictions about the future provide a mixed report. The United Nations notes that while the world population growth rate has fallen to 1.2 per cent, "nonetheless, world population will continue to increase substantially during the twenty-first century. United Nations projections (medium fertility scenario) indicate that world population will nearly stabilize at just above 10 billion persons after 2200. However, the twenty-first century is expected to be one of comparatively slower population growth than the previous century, and be characterized by declining fertility and the ageing of populations" (http://www.un.org/esa/population/publications/sixbillion/sixbilpart1.pdf).

The population of California is approximately 38 million and is expected to increase in size by more than 22 percent to 46,720,307 by 2025. The increase will be driven by a combination of both births and immigration.

Most of the state's population is concentrated in coastal counties. However, the areas with most rapid growth are projected to be in inland counties. Populations of inland counties could show a 45 percent increase in the next 20 years compared with an increase of 17 percent in coastal counties. However, 60 percent of the population will still be in coastal counties through 2040, and with dramatic rises in inland summer temperatures due to climate change, these areas may be less likely to be able to support large numbers of people and the current agricultural economy.

The age distribution of the population will shift dramatically. In particular, the proportion of seniors age 60 and older in the population will increase from 14 percent of the population in 2008 to 24 percent of the population in 2030, and the proportion of those 20 years old and younger will decrease from 30 percent in 2008 to 27 percent of the total population in 2030. The ethnic makeup of California is also expected to change between 2008 and 2025. The Hispanic population is expected to grow and will constitute a majority by 2040. Asian populations are also expected to grow. By 2025, 30 percent of the state's population will be foreign born. As the state changes ecologically and culturally, it will be increasingly important to find common cause with all Californians in our approach to preserving our intimate link with the environment.

The wonderful and terrifying thing about living on Earth in the twenty-first century is that we have powerful tools that make it abundantly clear that we live on one planet, with nowhere else to go. Virtually everyone has now seen images of the Earth from space, showing a blue sphere rotating in a huge, black void. We are rapidly reaching the limits of human population and resource use that the planet can support. We are creating global environmental dangers that no previous generation has seen or been challenged to solve. We also have unprecedented technological tools to perceive, communicate about, and potentially overcome these problems that no previous generation has possessed. A classic Chinese curse is to wish that one's enemy "live during interesting times." The connotation is that tranquil, ordinary, peaceful times are less "interesting" than times of turmoil and upheaval. The next 100 years promise to be a most interesting time.

Explore!

**VISIT A POWER PLANT AND FIND OUT
WHERE YOUR POWER COMES FROM**

Call your local power company and ask where your power comes from. Your power is likely to come from multiple sources, so find out if any of the power plants are local and if you can go see them.

**VISIT YOUR LOCAL LANDFILL OR TRANSFER STATION
AND FIND OUT WHERE YOUR TRASH GOES**

The location can usually be found in your phone book. Be sure to ask where the materials go if they leave the site. If it's a landfill, see if you can find out how old it is and how full it is.

Both power plants and landfills are large operations and may require permission to visit. However, the operator of the site may have a public information officer who can help you.

VISIT A LEED CERTIFIED BUILDING OR TAKE A GREEN HOME TOUR

You can find a list of projects certified by the Leadership in Energy and Environmental Design (LEED) at the US Green Building Council's website, www.usgbc.org, under Project Profiles. The new California Academy of Sciences in San Francisco is LEED certified and even has a living roof. Green home tours in Northern California can be found at http://www.builditgreen.org/green-home-tours.

CALCULATE YOUR CARBON FOOTPRINT

Go to the websites below and calculate your carbon footprint, then identify three things you can do to reduce it.

htt http://www.carbonfootprint.com/calculator1.html

http://www.epa.gov/climatechange/emissions/ind_calculator.html

DO A DUMPSTER DIVE!

How does your household garbage stack up? Write down everything you think you would find in your garbage can over the course of a week. Be specific and try to assign percentages, such as paper 10 percent, plastic 20 percent. Then actually go through your garbage the day before it's picked up and sort it by material. (Use gloves and goggles.) Then ask yourself, how much of this could have been recycled? How much composted? Why did I buy this product in the first place? Did I use it fully or even need it? How many of these items were disposable and in use for less than one day? One hour? Could I have bought something similar that could have been reused, recycled, or composted? In the following week, see what you can do to cut the waste stream by 50 percent. Then see if you can maintain the lower production of waste.

MAKE YOUR OWN WORM BIN!

You can easily make your own worm bin and start composting kitchen scraps for future use in your garden. Every bucket of kitchen waste that gets composted is a bucket that isn't transported to and buried in a landfill!

Directions can be found at

http://www.gardensimply.com/howto/wormbin.shtml

http://whatcom.wsu.edu/ag/compost/Easywormbin.htm

http://www.stopwaste.org/home/index.asp?page=445#plastic

LEARN ABOUT YOUR FOOD

The carbon impact of food is not restricted to the land on which it is grown. Growing food sustainably may sequester carbon, but processing it and shipping it emits carbon. Do some research on your food. Go to your kitchen and make a list of the countries your food items come from. For packaged foods, look for small print near the ingredients list for "Product of X." The international origin of many unlikely foods—crackers, cereal, canned goods—may surprise you.

Interpretation, Collaboration, and Citizen Science

Translating the language of nature into human meaning is the way naturalists share their sense of wonder at the natural world with others. Communicating knowledge is a key step in any scientific endeavor, and for naturalists this often takes the form of interpreting nature for others. Sharing is what motivates many naturalists to want to learn more.

Taking people for a hike, bringing a snake into a classroom, or giving a short talk at a visitor center are some of the ways naturalists share their knowledge of and passion for nature. Naturalists are also called upon to answer questions about the natural world in public settings. Interpreting nature for the public and communicating with experts and diverse groups about natural history and the environment are important skills for naturalists to develop.

Naturalists also possess knowledge that's useful to planners and policy makers. Learning to communicate with decision makers and collaborate with a diverse suite of interest groups ensures that nature conservation and ecological knowledge are considered in the land-use planning process. In addition, naturalists possess skills that can be applied to the study of nature as part of citizen science projects. By interpreting and participating in science, we advance our own understanding and encourage others to form a lifelong appreciation for nature.

INTERPRETATION: WHY, WHAT, AND HOW

People who do interpretation often are highly motivated to connect with others and to protect the natural world. Encouraging enjoyment of na-

A group of adults and children play a game to learn about a vernal pool in Sonoma County. Photo courtesy of Greg Damron, www.wildvinestudios.com

ture, improving their own and others' health and well-being, and building community are among the motives for interpreting nature. Besides helping people enjoy and learn about nature, interpretation allows organizations to express and meet their goals. For example, the National Park Service trains rangers, with the idea that they will help people care *about* National Parks so people will care *for* National Parks. In Yosemite, for instance, interpreters present programs on bears to help the public become aware of the animals' needs and behaviors. One goal of these programs is making sure that people store their food properly so bears stay wild.

Interpreting nature goes beyond communicating scientific content. The larger goal is to convey a general theme or issue by sharing information in a meaningful and pleasant way that is relevant to the audience. The core objective in interpretation is always connecting the audience to meaning, rather than just dispensing information. So interpretation should be about forming connections rather than presenting facts. The best naturalists lead people to the brink of discovery and then get out of their way and let them immerse themselves in their own experiences. Truly engaging people by facilitating an experience they consider worthwhile leads them to want to experience more.

Audubon Canyon Ranch, a nature preserve just north of San Francisco, set up bleachers where people can sit comfortably and watch herons and egrets nesting. The bleachers offer people an opportunity to quietly observe bird behavior. To deepen observers' understanding, trained interpreters are stationed at this overlook to answer questions. By sitting quietly and answering questions as needed, the interpreters allow people to cultivate their own experience. The hope is that people will connect with the birds, not just "learn" about them. This approach is designed to revolve around the visitors' experience rather than information, and it may provide a meaningful experience that can foster longer-lasting understanding. This style of interpretation, where interpreters make themselves available to visitors instead of doing formal programs, is called informal interpretation. Other forms of informal interpretation include roving on trails and talking with visitors at popular overlooks. This is in contrast to more formal talks and walks, discussed in more detail below.

Interpretation and the presentation of scientific information is related to teaching, and some teachers are great interpreters. A good example is Professor Ken Norris from UC Santa Cruz, who created a program in which college students travel around California on a bus with their professors, stopping to observe the natural world and ask questions. Norris rarely lectured or told his students "how it is." He preferred to set up projects that required his students to have their own experiences, develop their own questions, and seek their own answers.

Norris's students kept naturalist journals, and he loved to read their musings aloud to other students. He assigned students to spend four hours sitting alone in one place, just observing. Another of his "assignments" was to have students choose a plant, any plant, and spend an entire day watching it and thinking about that plant as they walked. They might ask, where does that plant grow? In the sun, or in the shade? On rocks, or in deep rich soil along a creek? Norris used to say to his students, "The object is the authority." In other words, make time to experience a bird, plant, or rock before hearing what an expert has to say about it.

Of course, personal experience needs to be balanced with reading and communicating about organisms and their environment. Reading and writing can be powerful tools for social transmission of knowledge, allowing us to learn from the experiences of people from other cultures or other times. Important experiences can be had from people who have interacted with extinct species, seen forests that no longer exist, or climbed Mt. St. Helens when it was 9,677 feet high.

In order to enrich our experience of nature, we need to keep in mind three important things. First, multitasking can be self-defeating. For example, listening to music on the trail can block out the sound of an eagle protecting its nest. Second, all knowledge is socially constructed. Much of what we learn is by direct transmission from others. We interpret, refine, validate, and reinforce our experiences by describing them to other people, and by reexamining them in writing. Third, everything is learned by connecting it to something we already know. It's by making connections with prior knowledge that we fit new learning into our scheme of the world. Each of us holds a mental map of the world in his or her brain. As we grow in experience, our mental maps become more nuanced, detailed, complex, and refined. It then becomes easier for us to put new information into context, to gain understanding, by making additions to our mental maps of the world.

Naturalists typically don't have captive audiences. Their groups often are on vacation or free time, want to be entertained and have fun, and may not have strong motivation to "learn." Participants can and will leave, physically or mentally, if they are not engaged. To keep people engaged, interpretive presentations need to be relevant, meaningful, and enjoyable. People learn best when they're comfortable. Humor, used well, can help make an audience comfortable and also engaged. Another challenge interpreters face is that questions asked and issues discussed can come from many different disciplines. So, it's important to remember that interpreters can offer a pleasant, informative, and meaningful experience without knowing all the answers. It's fine to simply note that those are not details you're familiar with, and perhaps suggest another source of information for follow-up.

Ask any group of seasoned interpreters how they create presentations, and while their wording will vary, they'll usually express a core list of approaches:

- *Get to know the place or thing the program will focus on—the "resource"*: Hike, read, talk with others, and follow one's passion and the organization's mission in deciding what to interpret. An interpreter's enthusiasm and understanding are infectious.

- *Learn about the audience*: Will schoolchildren attend? Retired people? International visitors? Some combination? What interests them? What do they need or expect? Adapting a program to an audience leads to success.

- *Explore meanings of the topic, especially universal ones*: A desert might represent a deadly wasteland, a complex web of life, or a source of mineral wealth. These larger themes help people connect to the value of nature and unique places.

- *Develop a theme—a main idea—that takes into account the topic, the audience, and the meanings*: The theme of the program provides justification for why the audience should care about the resources and surroundings.

- *Choose techniques that make the theme come alive*: Engaging all five senses and using props, quotes, stories, activities, direct observations, and other techniques help people connect with the topic and theme.

- *Organize the program around the theme*: Choose secondary ideas to support the main idea, and identify potential transitions to move from one idea to the next.

- *Practice the presentation, and over time it will improve*: After each run-through, explore what worked and what didn't, and continue improving the experience to keep it fresh.

Interpretation can take many forms, both formal and informal, and can include nature walks, visitors' desk duty, campfire talks, school trips, and historical reenactments. The interpretive talk and the naturalist walk are two of the more common experiences where naturalists serve as interpreters.

An Interpretive Talk

An interpretive talk—a prepared presentation usually lasting 10 to 20 minutes—can be given in or near an interpretive center, at a campfire, or in a similar venue. Interpretive talks require thorough planning, practice, and feedback from colleagues and audiences. Enjoy the preparation! We learn by teaching, and preparing a talk is like preparing for an engaging class. Plan what to say, and how to say it. What theme will capture the audience's interest? What interpretive techniques will make it come alive? Also, going to other interpreters' programs can help you identify what works and what doesn't and can inspire new ideas.

Let's walk through an example of one way to prepare an interpretive talk, based on the process mentioned above. A naturalist at a state park

A naturalist informs class participants about wetland plants. Photo by Kerry Heise

might choose to do a talk on giant sequoias, the world's most massive trees. She first spends time walking among and observing the giants, and she listens to park visitors to hear what intrigues them and what questions they have. She does library and online research and talks with colleagues to get a broader picture of sequoias' history and ecology.

The naturalist then reviews the park's or organization's mission and thinks about what the trees have meant to people through time: a source of wonder and mystery, a symbol of survival, the target of get-rich-quick lumber schemes, and more. Sequoias' size and survival ability fascinate her and the visitors, so she develops a theme based on this: Sequoias survive long odds to become some of the biggest and oldest beings on Earth.

How can the naturalist help an audience connect with this idea? She might bring tiny sequoia seeds—the size of a Quaker oat flake—to illustrate how hard it is for a sequoia to survive its first year. She could talk about how many hundreds of gallons of water sequoias "drink" every day during the warm months to survive, and how drought makes this difficult. She might show pictures or point out fire scars to help people imagine how sequoias' thick bark protects them from fire.

The naturalist then organizes a talk around the selected theme and related ideas. She plans ways to adapt it for different audiences. For adults, she might address how climate change could hamper sequoias' survival. For children, she might add a game that shows how sequoias depend on insects, squirrels, and fire to spread their seeds. Then after practicing the program with a few friends or colleagues, she is ready to try it on the public and continue to adapt, depending on their responses.

In presenting a talk, naturalists use interpretive techniques to build connections. Some techniques give people an intellectual "aha!" while others affect the way they feel. A balance of both reaches the widest audience and can provide lasting impressions. For example, stories and analogies invite people to connect what's being interpreted to their own experiences and prior knowledge. People love to touch, smell, and look at props and engage all of their senses, and this helps them remember their experience. For example, for a talk about mammals, bringing a few skulls, letting people look at and touch them, and linking them to the theme can make a talk memorable. If the talk has a historical theme, enlargements of photos will give people a connection far more powerful than words. To explain how some volcanic eruptions are powered by gas contained within magma, shaking and shooting a bottle of pop to demonstrate the idea will make it concrete. Humor can help set a relaxed tone, so use it whenever appropriate and not offensive.

Another technique to play with in preparing an interpretive talk is "forecasting": set an audience up with the talk's big ideas at the beginning. A talk lasting 10 or 20 minutes should contain one big idea, or theme. This big idea should be supported by a number of smaller ideas (subthemes) presented throughout your talk that relate back to the original big idea. When you circle back and reemphasize the big idea behind various subthemes, the audience hears it multiple times and has a series of opportunities to grasp it. That ensures that they have an important message or better understanding of an important theme to take home with them.

As they do in other situations, some people at interpretive programs will pay more attention to nonverbal cues than to words. If a naturalist is enthusiastic, interested, and passionate, that message will come across loud and clear. An interpreter worried about getting the facts straight or about impressing people, or one who is bored with giving the same talk day after day, will send a very different signal. So let your passion for what you are presenting come through–let your light shine. It is the beacon that will tell people "this stuff is so cool—check it out!"

A Naturalist Walk

Naturalist walks are like naturalist talks in terms of preparation. They often have designated topics, such as birds, banana slugs, or global change, and they usually have themes. Interpreters must know their topics, their audiences, and their routes really well. Preparing for an outing requires a few other logistics, but don't worry! You have the best props and stage hands in the world—nature!

In thinking through the walk, plan stops, techniques, and transitions. For example, one stop might be a good place to explore feeding behavior by using binoculars to watch birds eating ripe berries, and another might provide an opportunity to examine tracks of bears and coyotes. These stops might shift with the day or the group. Transitions help the group move between stops. For example, questions lead people to look closely or think about a new idea as they walk from one place to the next. It's also important to encourage the group to be silent through parts of the walk so everyone can focus on the natural sounds and subtle interactions happening around them.

In guiding a hike, it's useful to have a few "elevator speeches"— minute-long talks about something commonly seen along a trail. These provide an opportunity to generalize a specific observation, make meaning of an experience, or connect facts to big ideas. For instance, a question about an Indian paintbrush flower might allow an interpreter to tie that flower to the broader idea of pollination, weaving in the fact that hummingbirds are attracted to the color red and that red Indian paintbrushes are pollinated by hummingbirds.

On the day of the walk, arrive early and get to know the audience. This can help in tailoring the walk to the group. At the start time, welcome people, introduce yourself, and perhaps mention reasons you love the particular place you are walking. Give a brief description of the program, so that the audience knows what's coming.

It's important to keep safety and comfort in mind. Thirst, heat, and cold are conditions you must keep tabs on because they will sap attention as effectively as a boring lecture. If people are physically uncomfortable, they won't be able to take in the experience. Part of a standard introduction might be to remind everyone to carry water and layers of clothing they can add or subtract, then allow them time to arrange their gear. Let the group know where the restrooms are and how long it will be until the next bathroom stop.

In addition, make the audience aware of safety concerns that might

Pacific tree frog *(Pseudacris regilla)* under close examination. Photo by Linda Barnhart, Pepperwood Preserve

crop up. Safety first! For example, poison oak is so common in California that it should be written into the naturalists' job description that on each hike they show the plant to people and explain how to recognize it. If asked, people will often say they know poison oak, but it's wise to assume no one has ever seen the plant before, especially in the late fall and winter when it doesn't have leaves.

Rattlesnakes and ticks are other common hazards that naturalists should address in California. Learning how to recognize and deal with rattlesnakes protects both people and snakes. Good rules of thumb include watching where you put your hands, feet, and rear and giving snakes a wide berth rather than trying to kill them. Be sure to let the group know guidelines for an area, such as staying on the trail, acceptable noise level, and whether it's appropriate to pick flowers.

During the walk, regularly take the pulse of the group. Doing this can be challenging at first, but it's worth the effort. Are they done with this flower? Have they spent enough time walking? Are they tired and in need of water or shade? Watch people's body language. Are they making eye contact? Are they ignoring the program or wandering away physically or mentally? Are they falling behind as the group ascends a hill? Are they fidgeting? Asking people how they feel is legitimate, and they will usually respond if asked.

On a walk, let the world be the guide. If the group comes across a snake or a beetle in the path, stop and observe it. Let people experience it and then talk about it. Sharing an experience and talking about it will be more meaningful to the group than knowledge alone. When the group is observing an object, excellent naturalists keep the focus on the object, rather than on themselves.

On guided walks people often ask, what's the name of that thing (bird, bug, flower, etc.)? Naming gives the impression that a thing is known, when it may really allow participants to *not* observe closely! Instead of answering and moving on, try turning the naming question into a question that requires observation and encourages people to look more closely. When asked the name of a flower, a naturalist might respond with, what do you notice about that flower? or, are all the petals the same? If the question is about a bird, consider asking, how many colors can you see on the bird? or suggesting, let's just listen for a few minutes so we can all hear this bird's song. Extending the observation allows more people to be drawn into the experience and to make it their own.

Well-trained spokespeople in the media often avoid answering questions or talk around them. In contrast, naturalists usually serve best when they answer questions directly. Sometimes this means cultivating the ability to say "I don't know." The natural world is bigger, more diverse, and more complex than any one person can comprehend. "I don't know" doesn't mean "end of story, let's move on." It can mean "we're all beginners here, so what questions can we ask?" It might mean "this is a new experience, isn't that wonderful?" Or it could mean "I'm not the only authority on this walk; perhaps someone else can add something here." Offer ways that people can discover an answer. Invite them to enjoy the idea that nature is a mystery. Or use the question to draw connections between what they're observing and the big ideas in the program.

Saying "I don't know" can also be followed with a suggestion on how to follow up and find out. Taking a questioner's name and email address, finding the answer to the question, and sending it reconnects the questioner to the experience and often leaves a lasting impression. Typically, interpreters who lead walks repeatedly in one place are asked a finite set of questions over and over. These questions inform them of the audience's interests. Jotting down questions and then learning the answers deepens knowledge and experience for both you and your audience.

COLLABORATION

Beyond interpretation, naturalists use many other approaches for communicating ecological information. They talk with decision makers about policies, organize action groups, and get help creating and implementing restoration projects. While technical solutions are essential for solving ecological problems, perhaps the most important skills for restoring landscapes are interpersonal ones.

Collaboration in the Community

Collaborating with other community members can be a powerful tool for ecological change. Speaking to neighbors or city councils, organizing field trips, getting information from resource agency personnel, or making decisions as part of a watershed group are all facets of becoming an active steward and building effective community relationships. Working with an existing group or forming a new group to work on an environmental issue of concern is often the most effective way to achieve a workable solution. The following tips can guide successful communication at a formal or informal meeting.

Speaking at Public Forums

- Arrive before the meeting starts and sign up to speak, if necessary.
- Prepare your comments ahead of time, making sure they fit into the time limit.
- Be specific about your reasons for supporting or opposing proposals or actions.
- Try to be calm while still being passionate.
- Stay positive! Talk about the desired outcome, rather than assigning blame.
- Be willing to listen to opposing points of view and to find common interests with an unenthusiastic audience.
- Stay for the relevant part of the meeting rather than leaving after you make a statement. Listen to others and be available for discussion.

Informing the Community about a Project

To encourage others in the community to learn about or participate in a worthwhile project, or to start one of their own, consider these ideas:

- Invite the public to tour your project.
- Write an article about your project for a local newsletter or newspaper, or start a blog about it.
- Give out contact information or brochures offering assistance with similar projects.
- Provide information on a website.
- Use social media to inform people about new developments and encourage participation in events.

Running Effective Meetings

Watershed groups, planning committees, and resource councils are effective forums for working with a variety of stakeholders to meet common goals. When done well, meetings can be efficient places to share ideas and get business done. The following tips are for running productive meetings:

- Draw up and communicate a realistic agenda, and then stick to it.
- Determine ahead of time how decisions will be made.
- Learn whether a formal structure (such as Robert's Rules of Order) will be required or desired for meeting discussions.
- Rotate the leader/facilitator role among regular participants in an ongoing project.
- Assign a timekeeper and a note taker.
- End meetings on time. This is very important, to encourage ongoing participation.

Facilitating Thoughtful Discussion

When feelings about an issue are intense, effective group discussion is critical. It's important that people can talk about difficult topics in a productive way. Part of this includes trying to understand what different parties may really want out of the processes. Equally important is creating an environment of mutual respect and purpose, and suggesting methods for correcting the situation if these are missing. This necessarily includes listening deeply to others' stories and having people commit to moving toward creative solutions.

Here are some ideas for creating a safe environment for discussion:

· Ensure that only one person speaks at a time.
· Focus on ideas or issues, not personalities.
· Listen actively to all points of view.
· Seek win-win solutions.

Collaborative Conservation

Besides talking with the public at large, naturalists also may participate in focused communication on behalf of the land. Collaborative conservation brings together diverse groups and people who work together, trying to develop solutions that address the needs and perspectives of everyone involved. It can be an important first step in planning for a natural resource project or policy, especially one involving a wide range of opinions and strong feelings. Stakeholders in these projects might include land management agencies, neighbors, commercial users (timber, livestock, agriculture), recreational users (hiking, fishing, hunting), local or state conservation groups, real estate developers, and downtown business owners. Boards, councils, or other decision-making bodies should be represented as well. Unless all the stakeholders are involved from the beginning, an otherwise excellent initiative can fail.

Collaborative conservation often requires public participation and frequently falls into one of two kinds of efforts: community based and policy based. A community-based project involves people who share the same place or are part of the same community, or a group of people who share a desire to address specific policies or interests. A local watershed group might involve members who live in the watershed but also members who recreate but don't live there. A policy-based project, on the other hand, might involve government agencies or officials working to develop a regional plan or local ordinance.

There is some evidence that community-based efforts work best when they're led by local participants and when the process is open and includes and accommodates everyone's perspectives. This includes government representatives. Groups focused on smaller areas are more likely to succeed. Those involved can relate to the landscape in question, and regular participation from people spread across a large geographic area is not required.

The Quincy Library Group in Northern California is an illustrative example of a good faith effort that faced challenges we can learn from. An approximately 30-person steering committee developed a plan for 2.5 million acres of public forestland. Though laudable for the group's attempt to try to work cooperatively and include multiple stakeholders, in the end, the process faced many challenges, in part because of the many interests in this large and relatively populated area. Confusion, failure, and even damage can result when individuals are held accountable, or hold themselves accountable, for large and diverse interest groups. Such larger-scale conservation projects are better addressed through a network of local efforts.

No matter the format, making the objectives clear and agreeing on goals are important first steps for any group process. The goals should be specific, and they should be identified individually even if multiple goals overlap. Also, getting everyone on the same page about what information is available is critical. One way to do this is to collect and evaluate existing information and share it with the group. This will increase their understanding of the problem and possible solutions and provide opportunities for people to test their hypotheses. And it's a good way to empower the group early on.

Presenting preliminary ideas to different interest or expert groups at various times during the planning process for feedback can also be an effective way to involve stakeholders. In the case of emotional issues that may polarize a community, this approach can keep opposing interest groups from derailing the process. Collaborative conservation plays an important role in later stages of discussion, too: the coalitions that can arise are often in a good position to respond to future disagreements or policy disputes, perhaps preventing future crises from arising. In summary, successful collaborative conservation efforts can increase community resilience to challenging environmental issues.

CITIZEN SCIENCE

Citizen science is an exciting and growing method of collecting scientific data in which the general public participates in scientific studies ranging in scale from local stream monitoring to annual bird counts

Group of citizen scientists collecting field data. Photo by Deborah Stanger Edelman

spanning the globe. These studies take advantage of having tens to thousands of observers in the field contributing important data. For example, bird-watchers have become essential for studying changes in bird abundance and distribution by collecting data during the National Audubon Society's annual Christmas Bird Count. Many anglers are experts in identifying stream insects and contribute to projects monitoring invertebrate populations and other indicators of water quality. These projects allow scientists to gain a greater understanding of how, for example, water quality may change across a watershed, or how a warming climate may affect bird populations.

Members of the public participate in citizen science for many different reasons—it's fun to participate in scientific research, it uses observations people are already making in nature, it helps society better understand nature, and it provides a growing body of scientific data.

Besides aiding scientific studies, citizen scientists learn key scientific concepts and a lot about the ecosystems they study. They experience the excitement of doing scientific research, which fosters their continued interest. Participants often become experts at identifying organisms or measuring environmental factors, such as air quality, and they can document ongoing changes in local plant and animal populations. Citizen scientists also may become more active in making positive changes in their communities because of the experience they gain in carrying out research.

Volunteer monitoring programs engage people with a wide range of experience and knowledge, from people with little scientific training to naturalists with greater local knowledge than some academics. Projects may be "contributory," in which participants follow protocols developed by scientists; "collaborative," in which participants inform and improve research design and disseminate findings; or "co-created," in which the public helps generate research questions, analyze data, and distribute results.

The range of opportunities for citizen scientists is growing, and new online communication tools and even cell phones are being used to help collect data. Many projects need input and would welcome the participation of California naturalists. The UC California Naturalist Program has an online citizen science project portal that offers an exciting selection of projects to explore (visit http://ucanr.edu/sites/UCCNP/California_PPSR/).

Explore!

VISIT A NATURE CENTER

Most nature centers have well-established interpretive programs that can provide examples of success. Nothing beats seeing experts at work for inspiration.

VISIT A HISTORIC INTERPRETIVE SITE

These sites often have well-developed living history programs that can offer innovative ways to present programs.

CITIZEN SCIENCE

Become a citizen scientist to learn more about research and nature. You can select from a wide range of projects on the UC California Naturalist web site http://ucanr.edu/sites/UCCNP/California_PPSR/ or create your own at CitSci.org.

Glossary

ABIOTIC Physical rather than biological; not derived from living organisms.

ACCRETIONARY WEDGE Sediments and oceanic lithosphere scraped off the top of a subducting oceanic crustal plate and onto the less dense, nonsubducting plate at a convergent plate boundary.

ACID PRECIPITATION Rain or any other form of precipitation that is unusually acidic, mostly caused by human emissions of sulfur and nitrogen compounds which react in the atmosphere to produce acids.

ADAPTATION The process whereby an organism becomes better suited to its habitat, or a characteristic which is especially important for an organism's survival.

ALCOHOL A colorless, volatile, flammable liquid synthesized or obtained by fermentation of sugars and starches and widely used, either pure or denatured.

ALLUVIAL Describing sediment which is or has been carried by water. See also colluvial.

ALLUVIAL FAN A geological feature created when a fast-moving confined stream with a high suspended load suddenly widens out, slows down, and drops a portion of its sediment, creating a broad fan of alluvial deposit.

ALLUVIAL VALLEY A valley along a stream or former stream where most of the upper layers of the soil have been deposited by alluvial processes.

ALTERNATE LEAVES An arrangement of leaves (or buds) on a stem in which one leaf arises from a node, creating the appearance of leaves alternating on the stem. See also opposite and whorled leaves.

AMNIOTIC EGG A water-tight, fluid-filled egg in which the developing embryo is protected by a series of membranes and often a hard or leathery shell which resists desiccation.

AMPHIBIANS Ectothermic animals that metamorphose from a juvenile water-breathing form to an adult air-breathing form.

ANADROMOUS Describing fish that spend most of their lives in ocean habitats but migrate to freshwater for breeding.

ANIMAL UNIT MONTHS (AUM) Common measure of livestock stocking rates, calculated from the amount of forage required for one mature cow to maintain its weight for one month.

ANNUAL A plant that lives for only one growing season. See also perennial.

ANOXIC Having dangerously low levels of oxygen.

ANTENNA One of the jointed, movable sensory appendages occurring in pairs on the heads of insects and most other arthropods.

ANTHROPOGENIC Relating to or resulting from the influence of human beings on nature.

AQUATIC Living predominantly in water.

AQUIFER A layer of rock, gravel, or soil with high permeability allowing it to hold an underground body of water.

ARTHROPOD An invertebrate animal with bilateral (left-right) symmetry, a hard exoskeleton, jointed legs, a segmented body, and many pairs of limbs. Arthropods include insects, spiders, centipedes, shrimp, and crayfish.

ASPECT The direction that a hill or mountain slope faces.

ATMOSPHERE The gaseous envelope surrounding the Earth; the air.

ATOM The smallest component of an element having the chemical properties of the element.

AUTOCHTHONOUS Describing anything that originates in or is native to the area in which it is found.

AUTOTROPH An organism capable of generating its own food source; generally plants that produce food through photosynthesis.

BEDLOAD Larger, macroscopic particles of rock and mineral carried by a stream or other body of water. See also suspended load.

BEDROCK Solid rock underneath loose material such as soil, sand, clay, or gravel.

BEHAVIOR The actions or reactions of organisms in response to external or internal stimuli.

BILATERAL SYMMETRY A basic body plan in which the left and right sides of the organism are approximate mirror images of each other when the body is divided along the midline.

BINOMIAL NOMENCLATURE The system of two-part Latin names used to give each species a unique name consisting of a combination of a genus and a species name.

BIODIVERSITY The number and variety of organisms within a given ecosystem.

BIOFUEL Fuel produced from renewable resources, especially plant biomass, vegetable oils, and treated municipal and industrial wastes.

BIOGEOCHEMICAL CYCLES The movement of matter through Earth's systems in which a chemical or molecule moves through both biotic and abiotic stages, such as the water cycle, the carbon cycle, and the nitrogen cycle.

BIOGEOGRAPHY The study of the distribution of biodiversity over space and time. It aims to reveal where organisms live, and at what abundance.

BIOMASS The mass of living biological organisms in a given area or ecosystem at a given time.

BIOREGION A region defined by characteristics of its natural environment, such as flora, fauna, climate, habitat type, and topography.

BIOSPHERE The total portion of the Earth in which life exists, taken as the combination of all global ecoregions.

BIOTA The total of all organisms within a given ecosystem at a given time.

BIOTIC Biological; derived from living organisms.

BODY PLAN The blueprint for the way the body of an organism is laid out.

BRACT A leaf in a flower cluster or a leaf base of a flower, usually differing somewhat from an ordinary leaf in size, form, or texture. It is often much reduced but occasionally large and showy, sometimes petallike, highly colored, and very conspicuous.

BROADLEAF HARDWOOD A tree with wide, flat leaves, as contrasted to needles, that is usually deciduous, with examples including oak, cottonwood, and alder. The wood is denser and hence harder than the wood of most conifers.

BRUSH Shrubs; an area composed of woody plants less than 15 feet tall. See also chaparral.

BUD A growing point enclosed by closely overlaid rudimentary leaves.

BULB An underground vertical shoot that has modified leaves (or thickened leaf bases) that are used as food storage organs by a dormant plant.

BUOYANCY The upward force that a fluid exerts on an object that is less dense than the liquid itself.

CAMOUFLAGE Protective coloring or another feature that conceals an animal and enables it to blend into its surroundings.

CARBON EMISSIONS The release of carbon into the atmosphere over a specified area and period of time.

CARBON SEQUESTRATION The process of removing carbon from the atmosphere and depositing it in a reservoir. Carbon sequestration naturally occurs during photosynthesis.

CARNIVORE An animal that feeds primarily on the meat of other animals rather than plant sources.

CARTILAGINOUS Having a skeleton consisting mainly of cartilage, a type of dense connective tissue composed of specialized cells called chondrocytes.

CASCADE RANGE Mountain range in the Sierra-Cascade system running north-south from British Columbia, Canada, all the way through Washington and Oregon and into California.

CELLULOSE A stringy, fibrous substance that forms the main material in the cell walls of plants.

CENTIPEDE Any of numerous predacious, chiefly nocturnal arthropods constituting the class Chilopoda, having an elongated, flattened body composed of 15 to 173 segments, each with a pair of legs, the first pair being modified into poison fangs.

CENTRAL VALLEY The extremely wide and long valley in the center of California bordered by the Coast Ranges to the west and the Sierra Nevada to the east. Sometimes called the Great Valley.

CEPHALOTHORAX The anterior section of arachnids and many crustaceans, consisting of the fused head and thorax.

CHANNELIZATION Any activity that moves, straightens, shortens, cuts off, diverts, or fills a stream channel, whether natural or previously altered.

CHAPARRAL A plant community common to California and other Mediterranean climate regions characterized by very dense growths of evergreen, drought-resistant shrubs and small trees such as scrub oak, chamise, and ceanothus.

CHELICERAE The first pair of usually pincerlike appendages of spiders and other arachnids.

CHEMICAL ENERGY Energy liberated by a chemical reaction or absorbed in the formation of a chemical compound.

CHEMOSYNTHESIS The synthesis of organic compounds by energy derived from chemical reactions, typically in the absence of sunlight.

CHITIN A tough, protective, semitransparent substance, primarily a nitrogen-containing polysaccharide, forming the principal component of arthropod exoskeletons and the cell walls of certain fungi.

CHLOROFLUOROCARBONS Compounds consisting of chlorine, fluorine, and carbon atoms that are degraded by the sun's radiation in the stratosphere and destroy stratospheric ozone.

CHRYSALIS The pupa of certain kinds of insects, especially of moths and butterflies, that is inactive and enclosed in a firm case or cocoon from which the adult eventually emerges.

CIRQUE A shallow horizontal depression formed by glacial action, often holding a small lake.

CISMONTANE CALIFORNIA Land to the west of the Sierra-Cascade mountains.

CLEAR-CUTTING The felling and removal of all trees from a given tract of forest.

CLIMATE The combination of all weather factors, such as temperature, humidity, and precipitation, over a long period of time.

CLOACA The common cavity into which the intestinal, urinary, and generative canals open in birds, reptiles, amphibians, many fishes, and certain mammals.

CLOACAL SCENT GLAND A secretory organ of the cloaca that has been implicated in the scent-marking behavior of some reptiles, amphibians, and monotremes.

CLONE A plant or other organism that has been reproduced asexually to produce a genetically identical offspring.

CO_2 (CARBON DIOXIDE) A chemical compound composed of two oxygen atoms bonded to a single carbon atom. It is a gas at standard temperature and pressure and exists in Earth's atmosphere in this state.

COAL-FIRED POWER Energy produced by the heat from burning coal which is used to generate electricity.

COAST RANGES The group of mostly contiguous mountain ranges more or less directly inland from the Pacific Coast, running north-south from extreme Northern California to Ventura County in the south and making up the western border of the Central Valley.

COCOON The silky envelope spun by the larvae of many insects, such as silk-worms, serving as a covering while they are in the pupal stage.

COLLABORATIVE CONSERVATION A deliberate and inclusive process of two or more people, groups, or entities coming together to work out issues related to sustaining and improving natural resources and human communities.

COLLUVIAL Describing sediment which was moved by gravitational processes rather than water. See also alluvial.

COMMUNITY Populations of different plant and animal species occupying the same geographical area.

COMPLETE METAMORPHOSIS Insect development in which egg, larval, pupal, and adult stages occur, each differing greatly in morphology.

COMPOST A mixture of various decaying organic substances, such as dead leaves or manure, used for fertilizing soil.

COMPOUND LEAF A leaf that has a fully subdivided blade, each leaflet of the blade separated along a main or secondary vein.

CONFINED STREAM A stream with steep canyon walls or other obstructions marking its banks and preventing lateral changes to its morphology.

CONIFER A plant bearing cones, including pine, fir, and spruce.

CONNECTIVITY A measure of the extent to which plants and animals can move among habitat patches. Landscape features such as corridors, green-belts, and ecological networks provide potential means for achieving habitat connectivity.

CONSERVATION The protection, preservation, management, or restoration of natural environments and the ecological communities that inhabit them. Conservation is generally held to include the management of human use of natural resources for current public benefit and sustainable social and economic utilization.

CONSERVATION EASEMENT OR COVENANT A deeded transfer of partial interest in real property to a private or public institution to conserve land or its resources for future generations. Conservation easements can result in tax benefits for landowners and are binding on all future owners of the property.

CONSUMER A heterotrophic organism that derives energy from other organisms or organic matter.

CONVERGENT PLATE BOUNDARY A tectonic boundary where two plates are moving toward each other.

CORE The dense innermost portion of the Earth composed mostly of iron, nickel, and other metals.

CORE HABITAT Habitat that is far enough away from other habitat types to avoid their influences. See also edge habitat.

CREPUSCULAR Describing animals that are primarily active during twilight, that is, at dawn and at dusk.

CROPLAND Land which is managed by humans for intensive agriculture.

CRUST The outermost portion of the Earth comprising the continental surfaces as well as ocean floors and varying in depth from 5 to 70 kilometers (3 to 40 miles).

CRUSTACEAN Any of various predominantly aquatic arthropods of the class Crustacea, including lobsters, crabs, shrimps, and barnacles, characteristically having a segmented body, a chitinous exoskeleton, and paired, jointed limbs.

CUMULATIVE EFFECT The combined toxic effects of pollution or other environmental impacts that build in organisms or an ecosystem over time.

DAM An artificial blockage along a stream created with the purpose of impounding water.

DEAD ZONE A low-oxygen area in the ocean due to an excess of nutrients, typically from chemical fertilizer runoff, and resulting in a large reduction in aquatic life. (The vast middle portions of the oceans which naturally have little life are not considered dead zones.) The term can also be applied to the identical phenomenon in large lakes.

DECIDUOUS Describing a plant that sheds foliage at the end of the growing season.

DECOMPOSER An organism, often a bacterium or fungus, that feeds on and breaks down dead plant or animal matter, thus making organic nutrients available to the ecosystem.

DECOMPOSITION The breakdown of a formerly living entity into simpler materials, minerals, and nutrients that provide sustenance to other organisms.

DELTA The end of a stream where it flows into an ocean or other large standing body of water allowing the stream to deposit its suspended sediment over a widening area.

DENTICLE A toothlike or platelike scale on the outside of a cartilaginous fish, such as a shark or ray.

DEPOSITION ZONE A portion of a stream where large amounts of suspended load sediments are deposited on the banks and/or bed.

DESERT A climate region that receives less than 10 inches of rainfall annually.

DESICCATION The drying out of a living organism through exposure beyond the point where it can survive.

DETRITIVORE An organism that feeds on and breaks down dead plant or animal matter, returning essential nutrients to the ecosystem.

DIAPAUSE A physiological state of dormancy especially in immature insects, with very specific triggering and releasing conditions. It is used as a means to survive predictable, unfavorable environmental conditions, such as temperature extremes, drought, or reduced food availability.

DIURNAL Describing an animal whose behavior is characterized by being active during the day and sleeping at night.

DIVERGENT PLATE BOUNDARY A tectonic boundary where plates split apart or separate from one another and allow molten mantle material to rise up.

DIVERSION Removal of water from a natural stream for human use.

DIVERSION CHANNEL A man-made canal that separates water from a stream and delivers it elsewhere, often for agricultural use.

DOMESTICATED Describing animals that are tamed, especially by generations of breeding, to live in close association with human beings as pets or work animals and that usually have been made dependent so that they lose their ability to live in the wild.

DOMINANCE HIERARCHY A system or set of relationships in animal groups that is based on a hierarchical ranking, usually established and maintained by behavior in aggressive encounters one or a few members hold the highest rank, and the others are submissive to those ranking higher and dominant to those ranking lower.

DORMANT In a state of rest or inactivity; quiescent.

DRAINAGE BASIN The topographic region drained by a river and its tributaries; also called a catchment basin or a watershed.

DYNAMIC EQUILIBRIUM A system in a steady state. In this case it refers to a plant community that is relatively stable.

ECOSYSTEM The combination of all living organisms and natural features of a given geographic area, with emphasis given to their interdependence.

ECOSYSTEM MANAGEMENT The inclusion of biodiversity and ecosystem health into the goals for land and water management at a landscape scale.

ECTOTHERMIC Refers to organisms that control body temperature through external means.

EDGE HABITAT Habitat on or near the boundary between two different habitat types. See also core habitat.

ELECTRICAL ENERGY Energy made available by the flow of electric charge through a conductor.

ELECTROMAGNETIC ENERGY A form of energy that is reflected or emitted from objects in the form of electrical and magnetic waves that can travel through space.

ELECTROMAGNETIC WAVE A wave of energy having a frequency within the electromagnetic spectrum and propagated as a periodic disturbance of the electromagnetic field when an electric charge oscillates or accelerates.

ELIASOME A fleshy, protein-rich "food patch" on some seeds or fruits.

EMBODIED ENERGY The energy that was used to make a product and to get it from its source to the consumer.

ENDEMIC Describing a species (or other well-defined group) that is native only to a single geographical range. See also paleoendemic.

ENDOTHERMIC Describing organisms with the ability to control their body temperatures through internal means such as muscle shivering or fat burning; that is, they keep their body temperatures at roughly constant levels, regardless of the ambient temperature.

EPICORMIC SPROUTING Growth that emerges from dormant buds along the trunk and branches of a tree.

EPIPHYTE A plant that grows above the ground, supported nonparasitically by another plant or object and deriving its nutrients and water from rain, the air, dust, etc.

EROSION The movement of soil and rocks from the surface of one area and their eventual deposition elsewhere by processes such as gravity, water flow, wind, or glacial action.

ESTIVATE To pass the summer in a state of torpor; to be dormant in the hot, dry season.

ESTIVATION Also known as "summer sleep," a state of animal dormancy somewhat similar to hibernation. Animals are known to enter this state to avoid damage from high temperatures and the risk of desiccation.

ESTUARY An aquatic coastal habitat created by a mix of freshwater and marine influences.

ETHANOL A volatile, flammable, colorless liquid best known as the type of alcohol found in alcoholic beverages and in modern thermometers.

EUKARYOTE Any organism having as its fundamental structural unit a cell type that contains specialized organelles in the cytoplasm, a membrane-bound nucleus enclosing genetic material organized into chromosomes, and an elaborate system of division by mitosis or meiosis, characteristic of all life-forms except bacteria, blue-green algae, and other microorganisms.

EUTROPHIC Having an abundance of mineral nutrients, particularly nitrogen and phosphorous, usually due to chemical fertilizer pollution.

EUTROPHICATION A process where water bodies receive excess nutrients that stimulate excessive plant growth, especially of algae.

EVERGREEN Having leaves all year-round. This contrasts with deciduous plants, which completely lose their foliage for part of the year.

EVOLUTION Change in the genetic composition of a population during successive generations, as a result of natural selection acting on the genetic variation among individuals, and resulting in the development of new species.

EXOSKELETON A hard, protective outer body covering of an animal, such as an insect, crustacean, or mollusk. The exoskeletons of insects and crustaceans are largely made of chitin.

EXOTHERMIC Describing an animal whose body temperature is regulated by external factors.

EXOTIC SPECIES Species of organisms introduced into habitats where they are not native.

EXTINCT No longer in existence. It is used to describe species that have ended or died out.

EXTINCTION The state or process of causing a population, species, or taxa to cease to exist.

EXTIRPATED Locally extinct. It is used to describe species (or other taxa) no longer existing in the chosen area of study but still existing elsewhere.

EXTRUSIVE Describing igneous rock that cools and forms aboveground.

FERTILIZER Any of a large number of natural or synthetic materials, including manure and nitrogen, phosphorus, and potassium compounds, spread on or worked into soil to increase its capacity to support plant growth.

FISHERY Harvesting of fish, shellfish, and sea mammals as a commercial enterprise; also the location or season of commercial fishing.

FLOODPLAIN The portion of land surrounding a stream that receives periodic seasonal flooding.

FLOWER The part of a seed plant comprising the reproductive organs and their envelopes if any, especially when such envelopes are more or less conspicuous in form and color.

FOOD WEB A series of organisms related by predator-prey and consumer-resource interactions; the entirety of interrelated food chains in an ecological community.

FORAGE To wander in search of food or provisions; also the food or provisions found by this method.

FORAGING FLOCK Animals that join each other and move together while searching for food.

FORB An herb (a nonwoody plant, annual or perennial) that is not a grass.

FOREST CERTIFICATION Certification verifying that forests are well managed as defined by a particular standard and ensuring that certain wood and paper products come from responsibly managed forests.

FORESTRY The art and science of managing forests, tree plantations, and related natural resources and generally concerned with assisting forests to provide timber as raw material for wood products; wildlife habitat; natural water quality management; recreation; landscape and community protection; employment; aesthetically appealing landscapes; biodiversity management; watershed management; erosion control; and using forests as "sinks" for atmospheric carbon dioxide.

FOSSIL FUEL A hydrocarbon deposit, such as petroleum, coal, or natural gas, derived from living matter of a previous geologic time and used for fuel.

FRUIT The ripened ovary or ovaries of a seed-bearing plant, together with accessory parts, containing the seeds and occurring in a wide variety of forms.

FRY A recently hatched fish which has fully absorbed its yolk sac and can now hunt and consume live food. The fry of live-bearers do not have a yolk sac and therefore need to begin feeding immediately after birth.

GASEOUS Existing in the state of a gas; not solid or liquid.

GEOGRAPHICAL RANGE The overall area within which a given species can be expected to be found.

GEOTHERMAL ENERGY Power extracted from heat stored in the earth. Geothermal energy originates from the original formation of the planet, from radioactive decay of minerals, and from solar energy absorbed at the surface.

GILL The respiratory organ of aquatic animals, such as fish, that breathe oxygen dissolved in water.

GLACIAL ACTION The impacts that the presence and movement of a glacier have on the surrounding geology, including the shaping of the landscape through erosion and deposition of soil, minerals, rocks, and boulders and the compaction of the Earth's crust and mantle under the glacier's weight.

GLACIAL CYCLE Periods characterized by cooler and drier climates over most of the Earth and large land and sea ice masses extending outward from the poles.

GLACIER A large sheet of ice formed in an alpine or other cool area.

GREENHOUSE EFFECT The heating of the surface of a planet or moon due to the presence of an atmosphere containing gases that absorb and emit infrared radiation.

GREENHOUSE GAS Any of the atmospheric gases that contribute to the greenhouse effect by absorbing infrared radiation produced by solar warming of the Earth's surface. They include carbon dioxide (CO_2), methane (CH_4), nitrous oxide (N_2O), and water vapor.

GROUNDWATER Any water found beneath the ground surface, including aquifers, permafrost, and general soil moisture.

GRUB A soft, thick wormlike larva of an insect.

HABITAT The plants, animals, climate, topography, and other natural factors that comprise the place where an organism or population lives.

HABITAT FRAGMENTATION A landscape-scale process involving the breaking up of large expanses of continuous habitat into smaller patches of discontinuous habitat.

HEADWATERS The tributary stream farthest upstream from a river's eventual drainage basin.

HEAVY METALS A broad group of metallic elements that are known to have toxic effects under high concentrations, such as mercury, iron, copper, and lead.

HEMIMETABOLOUS Describing an organism that undergoes incomplete metamorphosis.

HERBACEOUS Describing a plant with little or no woody tissue and which dies down at the end of the growing season to the soil level.

HERBIVORE An animal that eats mostly plants.

HETEROTROPH An organism that must consume other organisms in order to survive.

HIBERNATION A state of inactivity and metabolic depression in animals, characterized by lower body temperature, slower breathing, and lower metabolic rate.

HOLOMETABOLOUS Describing an organism that undergoes complete metamorphosis.

HORTICULTURE The industry and science of plant cultivation.

HYBRIDIZATION Crossbreeding of individuals from genetically different populations or species.

HYDRAULIC MINING A form of mining that employs water to dislodge rock material or move sediment.

HYDROELECTRIC ENERGY Electricity generated by the production of power through use of the gravitational force of falling or flowing water.

HYDROGEN BOND A special type of bond exhibited by molecules showing polarity and containing hydrogen, notably water.

HYDROLOGY The field of study relating to the Earth's water resources, including their movement, changes, and quality.

HYPHAE The strands of long cells that comprise the living bodies of multicellular fungi.

IGNEOUS ROCK A rock type formed by the cooling and solidifying of molten magma. Igneous rocks can be either intrusive or extrusive.

INCOMPLETE METAMORPHOSIS Insect development, as in the grasshopper and cricket, in which the change is gradual and characterized by the absence of a pupal stage. See also complete metamorphosis.

INDIGENOUS Originating in and characteristic of a particular region or country; native.

INSECT An arthropod of the class Insecta that has three pairs of legs, a segmented body divided into three regions (head, thorax, and abdomen), one pair of antennae, and usually wings.

INTERGLACIAL A geological interval of warmer global average temperature that separates glacial periods within an ice age.

INTERNODES The sections of a plant stem between nodes.

INTERTIDAL ZONE The region between the high-tide mark and the low-tide mark.

INTRUSIVE Describing igneous rock that forms and cools underground.

INVASIVE Describing any nonnative (exotic) species whose introduction does or is likely to cause economic or environmental harm or harm to human health.

INVERTEBRATE An animal, such as an insect or mollusk, that lacks a backbone or spinal column.

JET STREAM Narrow, powerful bands of fast-moving wind in upper portions of the Earth's atmosphere on the boundaries between large air masses of differing temperatures.

KINETIC ENERGY The energy which an object possesses due to its motion. It is defined as the work needed to accelerate a body of a given mass from rest to its current velocity.

LADDER FUELS Fuels which provide vertical continuity between strata, thereby allowing fire to carry from surface fuels into the crowns of trees or shrubs with relative ease.

LANDFILL A burial site for the disposal of waste materials, usually lined to prevent leakage of fluids.

LARGE WOODY DEBRIS Fallen trees, logs and stumps, root wads, and piles of branches along the edges of streams, lakes, and bays, often defined as material that is greater than 4 inches in diameter.

LARVA The immature, wingless, feeding stage of an insect that undergoes complete metamorphosis.

LEAF An aboveground plant organ specialized for photosynthesis.

LEAF LITTER Dead plant material, such as leaves, bark, needles, and twigs, that has fallen to the ground.

LEVEE A man-made wall or embankment intended to contain the flow of a river or other body of water and prevent flooding of the surrounding land.

LIANA Any of various long-stemmed, usually woody vines that are rooted in the soil at ground level and use trees, as well as other means of vertical support, to climb up to the canopy in order to get access to well-lit areas of the forest.

LICHEN An organism that is the result of a symbiotic relationship between a fungus and algae and grows in leaflike, crustlike, or branching forms on rocks and trees.

LIFE CYCLE The series of changes in the growth and development of an organism from its beginning as an independent life-form to its mature state in which offspring are produced.

LILIACEOUS Of, relating to, or denoting plants of the lily family (Liliaceae).

LIMITING FACTOR A factor that controls a process, such as organism growth or species population, size, or distribution. The availability of food, predation pressure, and availability of shelter are examples of factors that could be limiting for an organism.

LITHIFICATION The process in which loosely deposited sediments compact under pressure to become hard rock.

LITHOSPHERE The outer solid part of the Earth, including the crust and uppermost mantle.

LITTORAL ZONE The part of a lake, stream, or the ocean that is closest to the shore.

MACROINVERTEBRATE An invertebrate large enough to be seen with the unaided eye.

MAGMA Molten rock beneath the Earth's surface which is usually associated with tectonic faults or other specific hot spot areas. When extruding to the surface, molten rock is known as lava.

MAMMAL Any vertebrate of the class Mammalia, having the body more or less covered with hair, nourishing the young with milk from the mammary glands, and with the exception of the egg-laying monotremes, giving birth to live young.

MANDIBLE One of the pincerlike mouthparts of insects and other arthropods.

MANTLE The portion of the Earth's interior between the core and the crust.

MARSUPIAL Any of various mammals of the order Marsupialia, whose young are undeveloped when born and continue developing outside their mother's body attached to one of her nipples. Most marsupials have longer hind legs than forelimbs, and the females usually have pouches in which they carry their young.

MARSUPIUM The pouch or fold of skin on the abdomen of a female marsupial.

MECHANICAL ENERGY The sum of potential energy and kinetic energy present in the components of a mechanical system.

MEDITERRANEAN CLIMATE The climate of regions found, roughly speaking, between 30 and 40 degrees latitude north and south of the equator, on the western side of continents; a climate having sunny, hot, dry summers and mild, rainy winters.

METAMORPHIC ROCK Rock formed when existing rock is subjected to high heat and pressure transforming it into a new rock type.

METHANE An odorless, colorless, flammable gas that is the major constituent of natural gas and is used as a fuel and as an important source of hydrogen.

MICROBE An organism that is microscopic (usually too small to be seen by the naked human eye).

MICROCLIMATE A small climate zone where climatic factors differ from the surrounding area due to localized influences such as slope, aspect, and elevation.

MICROORGANISM Catchall term for any microscopic life-form, including plankton, algae, bacteria, fungi, protists, and many others.

MIGRATORY Traveling from one place to another at regular times of the year, often over long distances.

MILLIPEDE Any terrestrial arthropod of the class Diplopoda, having a cylindrical body composed of 20 to more than 100 segments, each with two pairs of legs.

MOLECULE A group of two or more atoms linked together by sharing electrons in a chemical bond. Molecules are the fundamental components of chemical compounds and are the smallest parts of compounds that can participate in chemical reactions.

MOLT To periodically shed part or all of a coat or an outer covering, such as feathers, cuticle, or skin, which is then replaced by a new growth.

MONOTREMES The most primitive order of mammals, characterized by certain birdlike and reptilian features, such as hatching young from eggs, and having a single opening for the digestive, urinary, and genital organs, comprising only the platypus and the echidnas of Australia and New Guinea.

MORPHOLOGY The shape of a thing. Plant or animal morphology is the study of common forms and features that can identify a species. Geomorphology and river morphology involve the description of important land or stream features.

MOSS A flowerless plant belonging to the Bryophyta phylum which grows in tufts, sods, or mats in moist areas such as tree trunks, the ground, and rocks.

MUSHROOM The reproductive structure of some fungi, often called a fruiting body and viewed as analogous to the fruit of a plant.

MYCELIUM The mass of hyphae that makes up the growing body of most fungi.

MYCORRHIZAL FUNGI A type of fungi that lives in a mutually beneficial symbiotic relationship with a plant's root system, supporting as well as receiving support from its host.

NATIVE Describing a plant or animal that occurs naturally in a given environment without having been introduced by human activity.

NATURAL GAS A gas consisting primarily of methane that occurs naturally beneath the Earth's surface, often with or near petroleum deposits.

NATURALIST A scientist who studies the natural world and environment in all its forms and relations, with an emphasis on observational rather than experimental methods.

NATURALIZED Describing any nonnative species that has adapted and grows or multiplies as if native.

NECTAR A sugar-rich liquid produced by plants.

NICHE A particular relationship to the various species and climate that allows an individual or species to live within an ecosystem.

NITROGEN OXIDES Binary compounds of oxygen and nitrogen. They are commonly found in vehicle exhaust, cigarette smoke, and smog. When dissolved in the atmosphere, they can lead to acid rain which damages ecosystems.

NOCTURNAL Describing an animal whose behavior is characterized by being active during the night and sleeping during the day.

NODE The place on a plant stem where buds, leaves, and branches originate.

NODULE A swelling such as a root nodule that is formed on plants in the pea family (Fabaceae) housing symbiotic bacteria that fix atmospheric nitrogen for the plant.

NONAMNIOTIC EGG An egg that lacks a covering and must be fertilized externally.

NONNATIVE Describing organisms that are not indigenous to the ecosystem to which they were introduced and that are capable of surviving and reproducing without human intervention.

NONPOINT SOURCE (NPS) POLLUTION Pollution that comes from many disparate sources.

NONRENEWABLE RESOURCE A natural resource that cannot be produced, regrown, regenerated, or reused on a scale which can sustain its consumption rate.

NOXIOUS WEED A plant species that has been designated by state or national agricultural authorities as a plant that is injurious to agricultural and/or horticultural crops and/or humans and livestock.

NUCLEUS The central region of the cell, in which DNA is stored.

NUTRIENT CYCLING The process by which mineral and gas nutrients are moved from the soil, water, or atmosphere to plants and then to animals and microorganisms and eventually back into the soil, water, and atmosphere.

NUTRIENT LOADING The contribution of large amounts nutrients to an ecosystem, usually due to fertilizer or other chemical pollution runoff.

OLD-GROWTH FOREST A forest significantly past the age of maturity of its dominant species. Usually characterized by well-developed structure, many snags, and dead wood on the ground; a late-successional forest type for the area. It sometimes refers to undisturbed or never-harvested areas.

OLIGOTROPHIC Having a marked deficiency of nutrients or other materials needed to sustain life.

OMNIVORE An animal that eats both plant and animal material.

OPPOSITE LEAVES Leaves that arise from a single node in opposing pairs on either side of a stem. See also alternate and whorled leaves.

ORGANELLE A specialized part of a cell having some specific function; a cell organ.

OUTCROSSING The practice of introducing unrelated genetic material into a breeding line to increase genetic diversity.

OUTLET The terminal end of a stream where it flows into the ocean or other large body of water.

OVARY (PLANT) The ovule-bearing lower part of a pistil that ripens into a fruit.

OXBOW LAKE A crescent-shaped lake formed when a meander of a stream is cut off from the main channel.

OXYGEN An element constituting 21 percent of the atmosphere by volume that occurs as a diatomic gas, O_2, combines with most elements, is essential for plant and animal respiration, and is required for nearly all combustion.

OZONE An unstable, poisonous allotrope of oxygen, O_3, that is formed naturally in the ozone layer from atmospheric oxygen by electric discharge or exposure to ultraviolet radiation. It is also produced in the lower atmosphere by the photochemical reaction of certain pollutants.

OZONE LAYER The layer of the upper atmosphere where most atmospheric ozone is concentrated, from about 8 to 30 miles above the Earth's surface.

PALEOENDEMIC An endemic species with a long geological record and which once had a more extensive geological range than currently found.

PARASITE An organism that lives in a symbiotic relationship with another, deriving benefit from its host at some cost to the host.

PARASITIC FUNGI A type of fungi that lives in or on another organism, often weakening or eventually killing its host.

PARENT MATERIAL The underlying material that soil develops from, generally bedrock that has decomposed in place, or material that has been deposited by wind, water, or ice.

PAROTID GLAND An external skin gland on the back, neck, and shoulder of toads and some frogs and salamanders.

PARTICULATE MATTER Material suspended in the air in the form of minute solid particles or liquid droplets, especially when considered as an atmospheric pollutant.

PECTORAL FIN Either of the anterior pair of fins just behind the head of a fish, attached to the pectoral girdle, corresponding to the forelimbs of higher vertebrates.

PENINSULAR RANGES Mountain ranges of the Sierra-Cascade system with a north-south axis and running from Riverside County in Southern California all the way through Baja California, Mexico.

PERENNIAL A plant that lives for more than two years. See also annual.

PERIPHYTON The mixture of algae, bacteria, other microorganisms, and organic detritus that coats underwater surfaces in a stream, lake, or other body of water.

PERMEABILITY The ease with which water moves through a particular soil or rock.

PETAL One of the often brightly colored parts of a flower surrounding the reproductive organs. Petals are attached to the receptacle underneath the carpels and stamens and may be separate or joined at their bases.

PHEROMONE Any chemical substance released by an animal that serves to influence the physiology or behavior of other members of the same species.

PHOTOSYNTHESIS A process by which plants convert carbon dioxide into organic compounds, especially sugars, using the energy from sunlight.

PHYLOGENY The evolutionary development and history of a species or higher taxonomic grouping of organisms.

PHYTOPLANKTON Chlorophyll-containing microorganisms which form the base of the food web in many aquatic ecosystems.

PISTIL The female, ovule-bearing organ of a flower, including the stigma, style, and ovary.

PLACENTAL Describing mammals having a placenta; all mammals except monotremes and marsupials.

PLANT COMMUNITY The plant populations existing in a shared habitat or environment.

PLANT MORPHOLOGY The general term for the study of the morphology (physical form and external structure) of plants.

PLATE A section of the Earth's crust that moves about as a discrete whole, relative to other plates.

PLEISTOCENE The geologic epoch covering the most recent periods of glaciation, from about 2.6 mya to 10,000 years ago when the Holocene epoch is marked as beginning.

POIKILOTHERMIC Describing an animal whose internal temperature varies along with that of the ambient environmental temperature. Most, but not all, ectotherms are poikilothermic.

POLLEN The male sex cells in plants. In flowering plants, pollen is produced in thin filaments in the flower, called stamens.

POLLINATION The fertilization of a seed due to the movement of pollen from male flower parts to female flower parts, often requiring wind or pollinators such as bees or other insects.

POLLINATOR The biotic agent (vector) that moves pollen from the male anthers of a flower to the female stigma of a flower to accomplish fertilization.

POTENTIAL ENERGY Energy stored within a physical system. It is called potential energy because it has the potential to be converted into other forms of energy, such as kinetic energy, and to do work in the process.

PRECIPITATION Condensed water vapor in the atmosphere that falls to Earth's surface, including rain, snow, and hail.

PREDATOR An organism that feeds on other organisms (prey).

PRE-IMAGO An insect in the stage preceding its sexually mature adult stage.

PRESERVATION Keeping in perfect or unaltered condition.

PRIMARY CONSUMER An animal that feeds on plants; an herbivore.

PROKARYOTE Any cellular organism that has no nuclear membrane and no organelles in the cytoplasm except ribosomes and that has its genetic material in the form of single continuous strands forming coils or loops, characteristic of all organisms in the kingdom Monera, such as the bacteria and blue-green algae.

PROTISTS A diverse group of eukaryotic microorganisms that are either unicellular or multicellular without specialized tissues.

PUPA The nonfeeding stage between the larva and adult in the metamorphosis of some insects during which the larva typically undergoes complete transformation within a protective cocoon or hardened case.

PUPATE Among insects, to go into a pupal stage, often wrapped in a cocoon or chrysalis, from which the insect will emerge as a fully formed adult.

RADIOACTIVE DECAY The process in which an unstable atomic nucleus spontaneously loses energy by emitting ionizing particles and radiation.

RAIN SHADOW The area of dry land that lies on the leeward (or downwind) side of a mountain range, thereby receiving much less rainfall.

RAINFOREST A forested area where the annual rainfall is very high (often but not always defined as greater than 160 inches a year), usually characterized by high levels of biodiversity.

REACH A segment of a stream, usually marked by geographic boundaries at the up- and downstream ends.

REPRODUCTION The sexual or asexual process by which organisms generate new individuals of the same kind.

RESERVOIR (WATER) A natural or artificial pond or lake used for the storage and regulation of water.

RESTORATION The process of assisting the recovery of an ecosystem that has been degraded, damaged, or destroyed.

RIPARIAN ZONE The habitat area directly on either side of a stream's banks.

ROCK CYCLE The cycle in which the three classes of rocks—igneous, sedimentary, and metamorphic—transform into one another by geological processes.

RUNOFF The flow of rain or snowmelt over land, typically when the land has become saturated or is impervious.

SALINITY The amount of salt present, especially dissolved salt in a body of water.

SALMONID The family of fish containing salmon, trout, whitefish, and others.

SAN ANDREAS FAULT Significant California earthquake fault running more than 800 miles from the Salton Sea to Cape Mendocino, formed by the relative horizontal movement of the Pacific and North American tectonic plates.

SAPROPHYTIC FUNGI A type of fungi that thrives on dead trees, plants, or other organic matter, thereby contributing to the decomposition process.

SCALE (PLANT PART) A small, thin, usually dry, often appressed plant structure, such as any of the protective leaves that cover a tree bud or the bract that subtends a flower in a sedge spikelet.

SCAT Excrement, especially of an animal.

SCAVENGER A carnivore that feeds on already dead animal tissues, which aids the decomposition process.

SCLEROPHYLLOUS Describing leaves of trees and shrubs that are evergreen, hard, thick, leathery, and usually small.

SEDIMENT Material that is carried in a suspended state by water or glacial action, ranging in size from microscopic particles of silt or clay up to rocks and boulders.

SEDIMENTARY ROCK Rock formed by the deposition of sediment out of its suspension in water or air, followed by a gradual solidification and hardening under pressure.

SEDIMENTATION The deposition of a stream's suspended load sediment over a given area.

SELECTION PRESSURE The effect of selection on the relative frequency of one or more genes within a population.

SEPAL One of the usually separate, green parts that surround and protect the flower bud and extend from the base of a flower after it has opened.

SERPENTINE SOIL A soil type characterized by a high magnesium-calcium ratio and generally low nutrient levels.

SHEETFLOW Water that flows over a large and irregular area, usually with a shallow depth, rather than in a restricted stream bed.

SHRUB Category of woody plant, distinguished from a tree by its multiple stems and lower height, usually less than 5 to 6 meters (15 to 20 feet) tall.

SIERRA NEVADA The significant mountain range of Eastern California running north-south from Plumas County to the area east of Bakersfield and comprising the eastern border of the Central Valley.

SILK Also known as gossamer, a protein fiber spun by spiders. It is often used to make webs or other structures, which function as nets to catch other creatures or as nests or cocoons for protection for their offspring.

SILT A sedimentary material consisting of very fine particles intermediate in size between sand and clay.

SILVICULTURE The art and science of controlling the establishment, growth, composition, health, and quality of forests to meet diverse needs and values of the many landowners, societies, and cultures.

SIMPLE LEAF A leaf that has an undivided blade. See also compound leaf.

SLOPE The steepness or angle of a hillside, usually in degrees.

SLOUGH A type of swamp or shallow lake system, typically formed as or by the backwater of a larger waterway.

SMOG Air pollution containing ozone and other reactive chemical compounds formed by the action of sunlight on nitrogen oxides and hydrocarbons, especially those in automobile exhaust.

SOLAR POWER The result of converting sunlight into electricity.

SNAG A standing, partly or completely dead tree, often missing a top or most of the smaller branches.

SOCIOBIOLOGY The study of the biological bases for animal social behavior.

SOIL A mixture of fine-particle mineral constituents, such as clay, silt, sand, and many trace minerals, along with decomposed organic matter, air, and water.

SOIL DEPOSITION The geological process by which material is added to a landform or landmass.

SPAWN The mass of eggs deposited by fishes, amphibians, mollusks, crustaceans, etc.

SPECIALIST A species that requires a very specific habitat, food source, or other limiting factor in order to survive.

SPECIES A group of related organisms having common characteristics and capable of interbreeding.

SPINNERET Any of various tubular structures from which spiders and certain insect larvae, such as silkworms, secrete the silk threads from which they form webs or cocoons.

SPIRACLE An aperture or orifice through which air or water passes in the act of respiration, such as the blowhole of a whale.

STAMEN The pollen-bearing organ of a flower, consisting of the filament and the anther.

STEM The supporting structure of a plant, serving also to conduct and to store food materials.

STOMATE A pore, found in the leaf and stem epidermis, that is used for gas exchange.

STRATOSPHERE The region of the Earth's atmosphere extending from the tropopause to about 50 kilometers (31 miles) above the Earth's surface. The stratosphere is characterized by the presence of ozone gas (in the ozone layer) and by temperatures which rise slightly with altitude because of the absorption of ultraviolet radiation.

STREAM ORDER Classification system for streams. First-order streams are source streams, and order ranking increases only when two tributaries of the same order join.

SUBDUCTION ZONE A zone in which one crustal plate goes beneath another.

SUBSTRATE (ORGANISMS) The surface on or in which plants, algae, or certain animals, such as barnacles or clams, live or grow. A substrate may serve as a source of food for an organism or simply provide support.

SUBSTRATE (STREAMS) The material that rests at the bottom of a stream.

SUSPENDED LOAD Sediment which is carried in a suspended state in a stream or other body of water.

SYMBIONT One member of a symbiotic relationship.

SYMBIOTIC Describing any relationship in which an organism lives together with another of a different species. Symbiotic relationships can be mutualistic, in which both organisms benefit; parasitic, in which one benefits and the other is harmed; or commensal, in which one benefits and the other is unaffected.

SYRINX The vocal organ of a bird, consisting of thin vibrating muscles at or close to the division of the trachea into the bronchi.

TACTILE Of, pertaining to, endowed with, or affecting the sense of touch.

TAXA Units used in biological classification or taxonomy, such as kingdom, phylum, class, order, family, genus, or species; plural of taxon.

TECTONICS The motions of the Earth's plates and upper mantle.

TEMPERATE Describing the two geographical zones on the Earth's surface between the tropical zone and the Arctic or Antarctic Circle, where seasons are generally pronounced and variable.

TERRESTRIAL Living predominantly or entirely on land.

TETRAPOD Vertebrate animal having four feet, legs, or leglike appendages or descended from four-limbed ancestors.

THERMAL ENERGY A form of energy that manifests itself as an increase in temperature.

THORAX The middle division of the body of an insect, to which the wings and legs are attached. The thorax lies between the head and the abdomen.

THREATENED (SPECIES OR COMMUNITY) Describing any species or community (including animals, plants, fungi, etc.) which are vulnerable to extinction in the near future.

TIDAL FLUX The difference in the water level at high tide and low tide; high-tide level minus low-tide level, typically measured in feet.

TIDAL POWER A form of hydropower that converts the energy of tides into electricity or other useful forms of power.

TOPOGRAPHY The terrain in a given area, including a description of the changes in elevation, aspect, prominent features such as rocks, and in some cases characteristic vegetation and soil types.

TORPOR A (usually short-term) state of decreased physiological activity in an animal, usually characterized by a reduced body temperature and rate of metabolism.

TRANSFORM PLATE BOUNDARY A tectonic boundary where two plates slide horizontally past one another in opposite directions.

TRANSLOCATE Move or transfer from one place to another; cause to change location.

TRANSMONTANE CALIFORNIA Land to the east of the Sierra-Cascade mountains.

TRANSVERSE RANGES The mostly east-west mountain ranges north of the Los Angeles area, sometimes called the Los Angeles Mountains.

TRIBUTARY A stream that flows into a larger stream.

TROPHIC LEVEL Any class of organisms that occupy the same position in a food chain, such as primary consumers, secondary consumers, and tertiary consumers.

TROPICAL Pertaining to, characteristic of, occurring in, or inhabiting the tropics, which are characterized by uniformly warm and wet weather or sometimes alternating wet and dry seasons.

TROPICS The geographical zone of the Earth's surface between the Tropic of Cancer and Tropic of Capricorn, which experiences uniformly warm and wet weather or sometimes alternating wet and dry seasons.

UNDERSTORY An underlying layer of vegetation, especially the plants that grow beneath a forest's canopy.

VERNAL POOL A seasonal body of standing water that typically forms in the spring from melting snow and other runoff, dries out completely in the hotter months of summer, and often refills in the autumn. Vernal pools range from broad, heavily vegetated lowland bodies to smaller, isolated upland bodies with little permanent vegetation. They are free of fish and provide important breeding habitat for many terrestrial or semiaquatic species such as frogs, salamanders, and turtles.

VERTEBRATE An animal that has a spinal column.

VOLATILE ORGANIC COMPOUNDS Compounds that have a high vapor pressure and low water solubility. Many are human-made chemicals from the manufacture of paints, adhesives, petroleum products, fuels, solvents, pharmaceuticals, and refrigerants. They are a common source of contamination because many are toxic and are known or suspected human carcinogens.

VOMERONASAL ORGAN Also called Jacobson's organ, an organ inside the mouth on the palate. It can be found in all vertebrates, but it is enhanced in only a few. It is used to detect pheromones and is responsible for snakes' sense of smell.

WATER CYCLE The continuous process in which the Earth's water changes form from gas to liquid and sometimes solid and is thus moved around the surface and atmosphere of the planet. It is also known as the hydrologic cycle.

WATERSHED The topographic region drained by a river and its tributaries. Also called a drainage basin.

WAVE POWER The transport of energy by ocean surface waves, and the capture of that energy to do useful work—for example, for electricity generation, water desalination, or the pumping of water into reservoirs.

WETLANDS Transitional zones between land and water that are inundated with water periodically.

WHORLED LEAVES A series of leaves arranged in a ring arising from a single node. See also alternate and opposite leaves.

WOODY PLANT A plant having hard lignified tissues or woody parts, especially stems.

The definitions in the glossary were derived from a variety of sources, including government documents (from the US Geological Survey, US Department of Agriculture, Natural Resource Conservation Service, and others), academic course sites, and online dictionaries, such as Wikipedia.

Index